Industrial Upgrading in the Textiles and Clothing Industry

Industrial Upgrading in the Textiles and Clothing Industry

Pakistan and Late Industrialization

Nazia Nazeer
Rajah Rasiah

OXFORD
UNIVERSITY PRESS

OXFORD
UNIVERSITY PRESS

Great Clarendon Street, Oxford, OX2 6DP,
United Kingdom

Oxford University Press is a department of the University of Oxford.
It furthers the University's objective of excellence in research, scholarship,
and education by publishing worldwide. Oxford is a registered trade mark of
Oxford University Press in the UK and in certain other countries.

Published in the United States of America by Oxford University Press
198 Madison Avenue, New York, NY 10016, United States of America

British Library Cataloguing in Publication Data
Data available

Library of Congress Control Number: 2025937729

ISBN 9780198961673

DOI: 10.1093/9780198961697.001.0001

Printed and bound by
CPI Group (UK) Ltd., Croydon, CR0 4YY

The manufacturer's authorised representative in the EU for product safety is
Oxford University Press España S.A., Parque Empresarial San Fernando de Henares,
Avenida de Castilla, 2 – 28830 Madrid (www.oup.es/en or product.safety@oup.com).
OUP España S.A. also acts as importer into Spain of products made by the manufacturer.

To the memory of Joseph Alois Schumpeter who initiated the path of innovation that many have travelled on to discover the new developments in the different industries

Foreword

This book is a timely and essential academic work resulting from extensive primary research. It provides critical insights by exploring the challenges of industrial upgrading within Pakistan's textiles and clothing industry, focusing on firms striving to bridge the gap with the technological frontier. The text highlights an alternative perspective in examining the industry and firms, drawing from development economics and evolutionary economics to apply a technological capability perspective. It develops a taxonomy based on technological, organizational, and managerial capabilities, emphasizing the pivotal role of the industrial policy framework in driving firms towards the industry frontier. Furthermore, the book advocates for an industrial policy framework that emphasizes the broader ecosystem in which firms are situated, highlighting the interconnectedness of businesses, institutions, and supporting structures in driving accelerated industrialization and technological catch-up.

The textile and clothing industry has long been a cornerstone of industrialization, playing a pivotal role not only during the early First Industrial Revolution but also in the modern era, particularly in countries that are undergoing late industrialization. The textile and apparel sector has been the largest employing industry historically, offering strong production linkage effects and serving as a springboard for export-led industrialization. The authors highlight that the sector remains pivotal in Pakistan, significantly contributing to manufacturing output, employment, and exports. However, Pakistan's textile sector struggles to move beyond low- to medium-value-added exports due to slow technological advancements and limited innovation. This book explores these challenges, providing a comprehensive analysis of industrial upgrading in Pakistan's textile and clothing industry by integrating firm performance, technological capability, and the broader ecosystem.

Organized around key themes essential to understanding the trajectory of Pakistan's textile sector, the book begins by examining Pakistan's industrial catch-up strategy within the broader manufacturing landscape. Subsequent chapters explore technological capabilities, firm-level organizational practices, and the role of technology transfer in enhancing performance. Furthermore, it develops an industrial upgrading index that incorporates the embedding ecosystem—policy frameworks, supply chain dynamics, and market access—that shapes industrial transformation.

The book presents an innovative framework for industrial upgrading, linking technological, organizational, and managerial capabilities at the firm level to broader industrial transformation. It highlights the crucial role of manufacturing in economic growth and advocates for innovation-driven strategies to compete globally. This analysis is based on primary research, including a comprehensive survey of 600 textile firms in Pakistan (with over 500 respondents) and expert insights from 50 industry professionals.

By refining the conceptual framework of industrial upgrading and introducing a knowledge accumulation taxonomy, this book provides a robust methodology for assessing the technological, organizational, and managerial capabilities of Pakistan's textile firms. It underscores the need for an integrated industrial policy that fosters technological advancement, enhances firm competitiveness, and supports sustainable economic growth.

This work stands as a vital academic contribution and an invaluable resource for policy-makers, industry leaders, and scholars. By bridging gaps between theory, empirical research, and policy implications, it offers strategic insights for strengthening Pakistan's position in the global textile value chain while addressing pressing challenges in competitiveness and innovation. The book has significant relevance for late developers in Asia and Africa, and other countries.

Arkebe Oqubay (PhD)
British Academy Global Professor, SOAS University of London

Preface

The textile and clothing industry is among the earliest propellants of industrialization. It has also been the largest manufacturing sector by value-added, employment, and exports in Pakistan. Despite being endowed with the finest cotton, slow technological upgrading has left the country largely entrenched in low to medium value-added exports over the period 1947–2020. The most sophisticated textiles and clothing firms in Pakistan are at level 7 of the nine technological capability levels and level 4 of the six organizational and management capability levels in the technology trajectory of the industry. Industrial policy, through the first, second, and third textiles and apparel policies, has been important in the progression of the 21 firms in this study of 503 firms to move from level 4 to level 7 technological capabilities and level 3 to level 4 organizational and management capabilities. Using a profound review of the extant literature and a novel refining of the concept of industrial upgrading, the book highlights the importance of industrial policy to spur industrial upgrading. Building from a novel reformulation of technological, organizational, and management capabilities by taxonomies and trajectory, the book examines the link between technology transfer and technological capabilities, and firm performance with organizational and management capabilities as a mediating variable, and the critical embedding ecosystem's influence on firms' upgrading. In doing so, the book extended the understanding of industrial upgrading in textiles and clothing firms to produce not only a taxonomy by trajectory and horizontal classifications of how firms upgrade in the industry, but also an industrial upgrading index for policy-makers to use as a guide to promote technological progress in the industry.

Drawing on a sample of 600 textile and clothing firms with 503 respondents, and 50 opinions of professionals with expertise on the industry, the book first developed a knowledge accumulation taxonomy to locate Pakistan's textiles and clothing firms in the technological, organizational, and management capabilities trajectory. Second, the book examines the relationship between technology transfer and technological capabilities on firm performance, and the mediating role of organizational and management capabilities on this relationship. Third, the book develops an industrial upgrading index, which takes account of the critical embedding ecosystem that influence industrial upgrading in the textiles and clothing industry.

Given the importance of locating Pakistan's firms in the global technology trajectory of the textiles and clothing industry, lead firms were identified from exporters of high value-added products. This book benefited from the Distinguished Professor of Economics Award Fund (Project number: MO004-2018) awarded to Rajah Rasiah whose focus is on explicating industrial policy through the dynamics of industrial upgrading in the textiles and clothing, electronics, and automotive industries in 2018. In pursuing the study on the textiles and clothing industry, Rajah Rasiah learnt extensively about the dynamics of technology of the different sub-sectors in the industry, and the complementary industries that constitute the textiles and clothing cluster from Lee Ow Kim (former managing director of Penfabric) and Tan Yik Yuay (former managing director of Pen Apparel). Both their firms are lead firms in the textiles and clothing industries respectively. Nazia Nazeer subsequently conducted a survey of 600 textile and clothing firms with 503 respondents in Pakistan in 2017–18 for her doctoral degree to provide the main fodder for locating Pakistan's firms in the industrial trajectory through differentiating by technological capabilities, and organizational and management capabilities. All data were subsequently updated to 2018. Rajah Rasiah visited the entire production floor of two leading firms, that is, Sapphire Textiles and Nishat Chunian, in 2020 to have a direct feel of the most advanced manufacturing operations in Pakistan.

The results reveal that industrial upgrading is a function of the knowledge regime of the industry as firms start at different points and times in the technology trajectory. Large firms in Pakistan are mostly locked in the mid-phase of catch-up, and unable to move to the advanced level, though a handful of them have reached the transition phase at level 7. Of the 503 firms, 31 were at level 7 of technological capabilities among the nine levels in 2018, which comprise 30 large firms and one medium firm. In addition, most firms in Pakistan have hardly networked with other firms in the textiles and clothing cluster, training institutions, and R&D institutions and universities to acquire the knowledge necessary to upgrade. The statistical analysis examining the relationship between technology transfer and technological capabilities on firm performance with the mediating effect of organizational and management capabilities using Smart PLS-SEM method produced some interesting results. The findings show that organizational and management capabilities mediate positively and significantly the relationship between technological capabilities and technology transfer, and firm performance with the former stronger than the latter. The four systemic pillars used to estimate the industrial upgrading index (IUI) had global integration showing the strongest influence followed by network cohesion and science, technology, and innovation (STI) infrastructure and basic infrastructure. Also, management strategies and global production networks show the strongest impact on technological upgrading. Almost all of the 50 experts interviewed emphasized the influence of producer–user relationships in industrial upgrading. The IUI produced a mean score of 2.3 out of a possible 5.0, which indicates that the overall textiles and clothing industry of Pakistan are located in an ecosystem that is generally weak. Amidst the low IUI mean scores and poor infrastructure, as well as macroeconomic conditions facing firms, the textile and apparel policies have helped 21 firms in the sample to achieve considerable industrial upgrading.

Taken together, the evidence shows that the existing developmental initiatives in Pakistan have successfully stimulated industrial upgrading in some firms in the textiles and clothing industry to level 7 of technological capabilities and level 4 of organizational and management capabilities, though the bulk of them, including those that are small, are in simpler activities. The reasons for this are varied but the most crucial appears to be a weak embedding ecosystem system with serious weaknesses in the basic infrastructure, STI infrastructure, integration globally with the key knowledge nodes, markets, and buyers and suppliers, and network cohesion. The findings call for the Pakistan government specifically but developing countries in general to target catch-up from cut, make, and pack operations generally by improving the basic and STI infrastructure support, and strengthening integration of firms in global production and institutional networks, as well as raise network cohesion in the clusters where these firms are located. Finally, the book for the first time offers a path governments and firms can take to stimulate industrial upgrading to the technology frontier in the clothing and textiles industry in particular, and manufacturing in general, and in low- and middle-income countries in particular but also in the world in general.

Rajah Rasiah and Nazia Nazeer

Acknowledgements

We take this opportunity to acknowledge several members without whose support the preparation of this book would not have been possible. Foremost, we would also like to thank Nazia Nazeer's parents, the late Chaudhry Nazeer Ahmed Sindhu and Mrs Saleema Nazeer, and her sisters Dr Shazia and Sadia, as well as Dr Kashif Imran for the encouragement they have given her to collect the firm-level data set from Pakistan, Rajah Rasiah's parents, the late Rasiah Govindasamy and the late Subaletchumi Nadeson for being his greatest role models in life. Rajah Rasiah also wishes to thank his wife, Krishna Kumari K. Raman; daughter, Dayita Priya; and son, Dharmin Kumar, for their support. Special thanks go for the many discussions we had with the late Sanjaya Lall, Paulo Figueiredo, and Gabriela Dutrenit on technological capabilities; Clair Brown and Michael Best on industry dynamics; Bengt Ake Lundvall and Richard Nelson on innovation systems; the late Linsu Kim and Jorge Katz on the governance of technological upgrading; and learning from the works of Adam Smith, Karl Marx, Allyn Young, Joseph Schumpeter, Nathan Rosenberg, Bruce McFarlane, Luigi Pasinetti, Michael Landesmann, John Sender, and Albert Hirschman on the role of technology in economic development; Arkebe Oqubay, Christopher Cramer, Ha-joon Chang, and Eric Reinert on industrial policy; and Kamal Salih and Dwight Perkins on Asian development. Also, we would like to extend my gratitude to Fumitaka Furuoka, Cheong Kee Cheok, Shujaat Mubarik, Rohana Jani, and Goh Kim Leng for their invaluable comments and feedback to Nazeer's Phd thesis. We are also indebted to numerous other individuals and firms that participated in our study. In this regard, we acknowledge the special support given by Faisal Nazeer Sindhu, Abrar Kaim Khani, Waseem Javaid Mir (General Manager, Interasia Textiles), Arif Sial (Technical Director Weaving & Cone Dyeing, Al-Karam Textile Mills), and the managing directors of Sapphire Textiles (Faisalabad) and Nishat Chunian (Lahore), and key officials from TAL, Toray, Everest Textiles, and Recron Malaysia. Rajah Rasiah visited the entire production floor of Sapphire Textiles and Nishat Chunian to benchmark and locate lead firms in Pakistan against the world's lead firms in the industry, such as the Toray Group of Companies and Everest Textiles of Taiwan in the textiles industry, and TAL Apparel Limited (TAL) group of companies of Hong Kong in the clothing industry. Special thanks go to Datuk

Lee Ow Kim (*Penfabric*) and Datuk Tan Yik Huay (*Pen Apparel*) who mentored Rajah Rasiah over the periods 1989–2005 and 1989–2018 respectively on textiles and clothing value chains, the different stages, processes, firm-level innovations, and buyer–supplier relationships in the industry, including on logistics where both their firms are at the technology frontier. We wish to also thank Azam Chaudhry of the Lahore School Economics for organizing the visits for Rajah Rasiah; the management of the Lahore School of Economics (especially Professors Shahid Amjad Chaudhry, Azam Chaudhry, and Naved Hamed) for financing our fieldwork in the month of January 2020, and generous funding from the Distinguished Professor project (MO004-2018), and to Universiti Malaya for approving our project leave to undertake that research. Finally, we wish to thank Hemant Kedia, who in 2020 was the Procurement and Strategy Head of Recron for updating us on recent progress in technology at textiles and clothing firms, including following the proliferation of digitalization and robotization in the textiles and clothing industry, and Kiranjeet Kaur for establishing the link between us.

Rajah Rasiah and Nazia Nazeer

Contents

List of Figures

List of Tables

List of Abbreviations

ACC	Acquisition
ASS	Assimilation
AHP	Analytical Hierarchy Process
APTMA	All Pakistan Textile Mills Association
AVE	Average Variance Extracted
BI	Basic Infrastructure
CFA	Confirmatory Factor Analysis
CR	Consistency Ratio
EPB	Export Promotion Bureau
FDI	Foreign Direct Investment
FTA	Free Trade Agreement
GI	Global Integration
GDP	Gross Domestic Product
GPNs	Global Production Networks
GVCs	Global Value Chains
HR	Human Resources
IPR	Intellectual Property Rights
IJV	International Joint Venture
ILO	International Labour Organization
IMI	Adaptation and Imitation
ITT	International Technology Transfer
IUI	Industrial Upgrading Index
KCA	Karachi Cotton Association
KBV	Knowledge-Based View
KSE	Karachi Stock Exchange
KM	Knowledge Management
MTC	Ministry of Textiles and Clothing
MFA	Multi-Fibre Arrangement
MNCs	Multinational Corporations
MCGI	Multan Cotton Ginning Institute
NTU	National Textiles University
NC	Network Cohesion
OC	Organizational Capabilities
OBM	Original Brand Manufacturer
ODM	Original Design Manufacturer
OEM	Original Equipment Manufacturer
PCGA	Pakistan Cotton Growers Association
PCSI	Pakistan Cotton Standards Institute
PCCC	Pakistan Central Cotton Committee

PCJM	Pairwise Comparison Judgement Matrices
PIFD	Pakistan Institute of Fashion and Design
PITC	Pak-Italy Textile Centre
PLS	Partial Least Square
PSX	Pakistan Stock Exchange
RBV	Resource Based View
R&D	Research and Development
RIS	Research and Information System
ROA	Return on Assets
SECP	Securities and Exchange Commission of Pakistan
SMEDA	Small and Medium Enterprises Development Authority
STI	Science, Technology, and Innovation
STII	Science, Technology, and Innovation Infrastructure
TSMC	Taiwan Semiconductor Manufacturing Corporation
TC	Technological Capabilities
TIP	Textile Institute of Pakistan
T&C	Textiles and Clothing
TNCs	Transnational Corporations
TT	Technology Transfer
TTRI	Taiwan Textile Research Institute
UMC	United Microelectronics Company
UN	United Nations
UNCTAD	United Nations Conference on Trade and Development
UNDP	United Nations Development Programme
UNIDO	United Nations Industrial Development Organization
VTI	Vocational Training Institute

1

Pakistan and Industrial Catch-Up

At the time of independence in 1947, Pakistan enjoyed the human capital to spur rapid growth and structural change. Despite the major wars with India, and subsequently the departure of East Pakistan (Bangladesh, which gained independence in 1971), Pakistan generally enjoyed higher GDP growth rates than India and Bangladesh until the late 1980s. The GDP growth rates of India and Bangladesh gradually only overtook Pakistan's from the 1990s (Amjad & Burki, 2015). The nominal GDP per capita of India, Bangladesh, and Pakistan were US$2411, US$2688, and US$1589 respectively in 2022 (World Bank, 2023). To make matters worse, Pakistan has been experiencing premature deindustrialization after the manufacturing sector's contribution to GDP peaked at a low share of 15.7 per cent in 1994 (Nazeer & Rasiah, 2016), while average annual manufacturing value-added growth fell from 7.6 per cent per annum in 2000–2009 to 3.5 per cent per annum in 2010–2019.[1] When the COVID19 pandemic erupted to send shock waves across the world in 2020, Pakistan was already riddled with high inflation and unemployment. Efforts to absorb the International Monetary Fund's belt tightening conditions were targeted at addressing its worsening balance of payments deficits and soaring external debt service suggests that the fundamental problems gripping the country go beyond the premature deindustrialization facing the country (Rasiah & Nazeer, 2016).

Most neoclassical works on the role of the textile and clothing industry in economic development have used the relative price theoretic to explain production and trade specialization, that is, based on factor endowments (Bhagwati, 1979; Krueger, 1995; cf. Bernstein & Wernstein, 2002). In fact, such arguments make the case that Hong Kong, South Korea, and Taiwan grew initially with specialization in the textile and clothing industry and that these so-called labour-intensive industries gradually contracted in contribution as changing relative prices made such an industry gradually unsustainable. While textiles and clothing were indeed the propellants of

[1] Computed using Pakistan Rupee at constant prices using data from the World Bank (2023).

Industrial Upgrading in the Textiles and Clothing Industry. Nazia Nazeer and Rajah Rasiah, Oxford University Press.
 DOI: 10.1093/9780198961697.003.0001

early expansion into export markets, such an argument misses completely the importance of technological upgrading.

Yet, while Smith (1776) had argued over the division of labour being determined by the size of the market, he had also made the point that the size of the market is also determined by the division of labour (see also Amsden, 1985). It is the differentiating and speciating characteristics of manufacturing that led Young (1928) to call for governments to focus on increasing returns sectors when pursuing economic progress (see also Best, 2001). Whereas structural change subsequently resulted in the export composition of these countries shifting significantly from labour- to capital- and knowledge-intensive industries (Chang, 2003), two major developments ensured that textile and clothing firms from these countries evolved vertically.[2] A combination of rising wages and changes in trade privileges resulted in Hong Kong, South Korea, and Taiwan losing preferential access following the withdrawal of the most favoured nation (MFN) clause by the developed countries, and the retention of such preferential access among some developing countries since the Plaza Accord of 1985 (Rasiah, 1988). The emergence of preferential access for the Least Developed Countries (LDCs), (such as Bangladesh, Cambodia, and Lao PDR) since 2004, resulted in the relocation of Hong Kong, South Korean, and Taiwanese firms abroad (Rasiah, 2012). These firms also upgraded technologically to operate as original equipment manufacturers (OEMs), while handling logistics operations. Some firms, such as TAL in Hong Kong, Toray in Japan, and Everest Textiles in Taiwan have evolved to the technology frontier of the industry to retain significant manufacturing activities at home-sites. These firms have evolved the capacity to innovate extensively (including digital coordination of automated systems) where their ecosystem support is strong (Rasiah, 2019). Whereas most Taiwanese firms focused only on OEM operations with significant investments in R&D, South Korean firms are also heavily into ODM and OBM operations.

The extant literature on technology transfer through FDI recognizes the potential through demonstration effects, direct and indirect spillovers, competition to stimulate innovation, and organizational change to enhance firm and employee productivity by improving human resource skills, operational efficiency, integration into export markets, and customer satisfaction (Hirschman, 1958, 1970; Rasiah, 1995; Rodriguez & Rodriguez, 2005, Guan et al., 2006; Kotabe et al., 2007). However, apart from some exceptions

[2] The use of trade indices, such as the trade balance coefficient, the Grubel-Lloyd index, and the revealed comparative advantage (RCA) masks upgrading from low to high value-added activities. Indeed, this is why electronics exports from Malaysia and Thailand continue to enjoy strong RCA, but only in low- and medium value-added segments (Rasiah and Wong, 2021).

(Hirschman, 1970; Rasiah, 1995), such studies have hardly broached the key aspects of technology from an embodied perspective. Especially neoclassical accounts of the textiles and clothing industry largely miss the role of industrial upgrading[3] as much of their accounts on technology has remained confined to the black box (see Rosenberg, 1982). Hence, whereas significant textile and clothing manufacturing have remained in Japan, Taiwan, and China, where firms have upgraded to specialize in high value-added activities, neoclassical accounts are stuck with arguments that these firms would relocate to labour-surplus sites to appropriate competitiveness from low-cost labour (Itoh & Krueger, 1995).

This book starts with the proposition that the lack of effective innovation policies has undermined Pakistan's capacity to stimulate technological upgrading, which explains the lack of shift from low and medium value-added to high value-added activities among most textiles and clothing firms in the country. While a number of works point to stagnating effects caused by Dutch Disease (Hamna, 2009) and fallacy of composition problems (Nazeer & Rasiah, 2016), a lack of industrial upgrading has restricted the transition to high value-added activities (Rasiah & Nazeer, 2015). Textiles and clothing accounted for 38.2 per cent of Pakistan's exports in 2020 (Comtrade, 2021).

Therefore, this book investigates the role of technological, organizational, and management capabilities in the transformation of textiles and clothing firms from low- and medium-value-added to high value-added activities in Pakistan by focusing on technology transfer and technological, organizational, and management capabilities at the meso and micro levels. While expositions of industrial policy have moved on from its demonstrative effect on differentiation and division of labour (Smith, 1776; Young, 1928), to the broad-based advantages latecomers enjoy (Gerschenkron, 1952; Abramovitz, 1956), and subsequently nation-specific catch up achieved (Johnson, 1982; Amsden, 1989; Wade, 1990; Chang, 2003), this book extends it further to draw on firm-level experiences in great detail to identify the strategies taken on by textiles and clothing firms using a global trajectory of technological, organizational, and management capabilities. National firms are important actors whose growth from processes of technology transfer and technological capability accumulation, and access to external sources of knowledge through specific technological, organizational, and management capability building efforts, are critical for stimulating upgrading in the industry. Technology transfer and technological capability building are important for

[3] Industrial upgrading in this book is characterized by both the extension of industrial activities to include functional activities, as well as the increasing sophistication of the activity vertically (Humprey & Schmitz, 2000).

Pakistan's manufacturing sector as its economy has for several decades been dominated by low value-added activities. An insufficient supply of technical and vocational training and education has limited the capabilities of the bulk of the firms to absorb cutting-edge practices in the industry (Nazeer, 2018).

This introductory chapter consists of seven sections. Following the background and motivation, we problematize the issues gripping the textile and clothing industry in Pakistan. Research questions and objectives of this study are then discussed. The subsequent sections present the key concepts used in the book and the methodology adopted. The final section finishes with the outline of the book.

Problematizing Industrial Upgrading

The driver of upgrading—that is, knowledge—is a public good, which is both non-rivalrous and non-excludable. Hence, because technology is dominated by knowledge, there is a need for governments to intervene when social returns exceed private returns. Also, with the intensification of globalization, individual economies seeking to engender the conditions for rapid economic development enjoy the opportunity to focus on industries that offer them both strategic positioning as well as rapid growth potential. However, technology acquisition has traditionally been the first step firms seek to perform operational activities to spur industrial upgrading (Tallman et al., 2004; Dutreinit, 2007; Hobday & Rush, 2007; Morrison et al., 2008). The acquisition and adaptation of imported technologies and their further development are critical to support industrial upgrading (Lall, 1987; Amsden, 1991; Bell & Pavitt, 1995).

Technology offers the potential to improve individuals' well-being, encourage economic progress, and offer firms and countries the capacity to compete in global markets. However, the kind of technologies used in the catching-up process differs across economic sectors, and hence, requires different skills, and management and organizational capabilities (Teece, 2007). Also, as has been argued by Nelson (2008), the strategies firms use to catch up technologically are often conditioned by industry type, location, and timing.

Marx (1867), Veblen (1915), and Schumpeter (1934, 1942) laid the early foundations of how competition creatively destroys old technologies to enable their replacement with new ones to stimulate economic progress. Young (1928) had articulated lucidly the differentiating and division of labour properties of manufacturing to argue over its capacity to stimulate increasing returns, including its speciation capabilities. While Gerschenkron

(1952) and Abramovitz (1956) explained the latecomer advantages in the catch-up process, Amsden (1989) emphasized 'getting relative prices wrong', and Mazzucato (2013, 2018), Kattel and Mazzucato (2018), Foray (2018), and Schot and Steinmuller (2018) emphasized 'mission-oriented' and 'transformative' industrial policies. What is not adequately addressed in the literature is the need to link the macro and meso to institutions and meso organizations to effect industrial upgrading in firms. With arguably the exception of Rasiah (2019), the extant literature appears to overly focus on firm-level (micro) technological, organizational, and management capability building with little link to the meso and macro intermediary organizations and policy instruments.

While the neoclassical literature lays claim to have identified and proven the role of technology in economic development (see Solow, 1957; Romer, 1994), critics argue that the assumptions used in such approaches renders them inadequate to estimate, as well as explain technological upgrading (Rosenberg, 1976, 1982; Dosi, 1995; Rasiah, 1995).[4] Consequently, this book pursues the direction taken by technological capability experts to provide a meaningful framework for stimulating industrial upgrading (e.g., Dahlman et al., 1987; Lall, 1992) and a profound effort to link such developments against the embedding ecosystem. Also, these studies took on Nelson and Winter's (1982) argument that firms and industries constantly evolve, and hence, are driven at least in the early stages through learning and adaptations of existing technologies to boost competitiveness (see also Ranft & Lord, 2002).

Transferring technologies from the industrialized to the emerging nations has been a major channel through which firms from the latter have caught up (Amsden, 1991; Szulanski, 1996; Gupta & Govindarajan, 2000). However, it is not an easy and costless process as it requires a focus on the science, technology, and innovation (STI) infrastructure; including human capital and eventually R&D, and cultural, social, and political readiness to make that happen (Lall, 1992). Thus, it is vital to look at all complimentary components that are critical to introduce the strategies to stimulate industrial upgrading.

Indeed, technology acquisition and licensing were the critical paths taken by the East Asian economies of Japan, South Korea, and Taiwan, which successfully transformed from poor to rich income economies (Johnson, 1982; Amsden, 1989; Wade, 1990; Reinert, 2007). Indeed, a strong interventionist state backed by sound regulatory procedures was instrumental in South

[4] It also important to revisit Sen's (1983) incisive argument that the market is an excellent servant but a poor master.

Korea and Taiwan becoming developed countries in one generation (Rasiah & Zhang, 2024). Their progress from underdeveloped status to developed status was accomplished at first by organizing the external and internal structures for adapting imported technology. Meanwhile, Japan, South Korea, and Taiwan started as creative imitators of manufacturing processes before forging ahead to become creators of knowledge new to the universe. Among recent latecomers, South Korea and Taiwan have been exceptionally effective in industrial advancement in high-tech industries, such as electronics, automotives, and machinery and equipment, which has been made possible by systematic institutional change directed at strengthening the basic infrastructure, science technology, and innovation (STI) infrastructure, and integration with the global economy with strong connectivity and coordination between individuals, firms, intermediary organizations, and supporting government agencies.

Undoubtedly, developing nations have limited resources to tackle the challenges of innovation (Hoekman, Maskus, & Saggi, 2005). However, developing nations need to strengthen innovation and technological capabilities to accelerate catch-up' (Rasiah, 1995; Fu & Gong, 2011). Neither independent innovations nor FDI-dependent strategies are costless (Lall, 1992). Therefore, the efficient management of technology transfer is crucial for individuals, firms, and organizations to stimulate economic catch up.

Industrial upgrading begins in the course of accumulating technological capabilities to creatively adapt and adopt process and product technologies (Kim, 1997; Kim, 2000). However, the spread and appropriation of embodied knowledge over the world is not homogeneous since technological capabilities are not uniformly distributed (UNCTAD, 2014). Although the conceptualization of technological capabilities has evolved extensively (e.g., Lall, 1992; Kim, 1997; Rasiah, 2003; Figueiredo, 2003; Dutrénit, 2004, 2006), its appropriate use to map industries still requires a profound understanding of the specificities associated with different industries, changes that take place over time, and locational conditions. Thus, to study technological capabilities is particularly important among firms that are pursuing industrial upgrading.

While technological capabilities can be enhanced through technology transfer and internal development, the sequence of functional capabilities changes as firms move from technology-using to innovation-driving production capabilities, and from production capabilities to R&D competence to radically transform industries (Lall, 1992; Rasiah, 2004b). The upward progression of firms in the taxonomies of technological capabilities, such as process and product technologies, and organizational and management capabilities, helps assist firms to upgrade from low to high value-added activities (UNCTAD, 2014).

Organizational and management capabilities are the utmost intangible firm-level resource (Tomer, 1987). Technology transfers in building organizational capabilities, especially in the development of human resources, are critical for the absorption of foreign sources of knowledge, and for the development of new processes and products (Yli-Renko et al., 2001; Tsang et al., 2004). The crucial role of firms' learning capability to develop recipients' knowledge accumulation capability is important, to achieve effective technology transfer (Grant, 1996; Argote & Ingram, 2000). The ability of employees (including their constituent firm-level competencies) and how they are appropriated effectively are fundamental to firm performance. In this regard, economic progress is not an aggregate economic phenomenon that is achieved from innovative activities, with each sector characterized by its particular dynamics that are linked to critical intermediary organizations, such as research universities and training bodies, science parks, and supplier firms (Rasiah, 2019).

Whereas the industrial structure of Pakistan was not too dissimilar from that of South Korea and Taiwan in the 1950s (Hamdani, 2014), massive institutional change has transformed the latter two economies to propel national firms to high value-added activities while Pakistan is languishing in low and middle value-added activities. Textiles and clothing manufacturing, which accounted for around 60 per cent of Pakistan's overall exports and 40 per cent of industrial employment (Pakistan, 2021: 39), and 30 per cent of manufacturing value-added in 2018 (World Bank, 2023).

Unlike South Korea, Taiwan, and China, where the functional diversification of sectors and industries has led to the contribution textiles and clothing to fall in relative significance as the electronics, machinery, and automobile industries grew rapidly, the contribution of textiles and clothing industry to Pakistan's manufactured exports rose from 44 per cent in 2005 to 62 per cent in 2022. High technology exports have grown significantly since the 1970s in South Korea, and since 2000 in China so that textiles and clothing only accounted for 5.4 and 3.7 per cent of overall exports in 2005 and 4.8 and 2.2 per cent of overall exports respectively in China and South Korea in 2013 (Rasiah & Nazeer, 2015). It is the rapid accumulation of technological, organizational, and management capabilities that stimulated such a structural change in China, Taiwan, and South Korea. High-technology exports from Pakistan have largely been absent, though exports of medium technology synthetic textiles have risen marginally.

Also, the textiles and clothing industry in China (including Hong Kong), Japan, South Korea, and Taiwan have shown remarkable industrial upgrading from low to high value-added activities with several firms, such as the TAL, Toray, Everest Textiles, Sunkyong Textiles, and Tai Yuen sharing the leadership of the global value chain leadership with brandholders. The progression of some of these firms to the technology frontier will be examined in detail in this book.

Economic growth does not only involve investment in the production of products and services but is also associated with significant accumulation of knowledge and technology. Globalization has allowed the dispersal of production linkages via global production networks (GPNs), which gives latecomer firms an opening for learning and catching up with first mover firms by inserting directly in such chains as original equipment manufacturers (OEM) (Rasiah, 2009). However, firms in most developing economies are trapped in low-technology activities and, hence, are incapable of competing internationally in high value-added activities (Rasiah & Yap, 2015b). From its highest manufacturing growth in the 1950s and 1960s, Pakistan's manufacturing grew slowly and unevenly until 2006 (Rasiah & Nazeer, 2015). Consequently, not only has Pakistan undergone little industrial structural change, its leading manufactured export, that is, cotton and cotton-based products, has also experienced little aggregate upgrading into high value-added activities (Rasiah & Nazeer, 2016). Indeed, Pakistan's exports of cotton fibres and fabric are still largely exported to downstream producers abroad, including to Bangladesh (Rasiah & Nazeer, 2016). Hence, despite enjoying one of the best cotton raw material and a highly educated diaspora abroad, the lack of technological upgrading has left Pakistan as primarily an exporter of cotton and low value-added clothing and textiles, though a handful of firms have shown some progress that with the right policies, can upgrade to compete with frontier firms abroad.

The need for industrial upgrading in the textile and clothing industry in Pakistan cannot be understated as its economy relies heavily on the industry for generating employment, value-added, and exports. Especially, the cotton-based apparel value chain is the major source of Pakistan's foreign exchange, which is categorized by an integrated production chain from cotton cultivation to ginning, spinning, weaving, knitting, processing, finishing of fabrics, and garment manufacturing (Government of Pakistan, 2018; Pakistan, 2021). While some large firms enjoy the potential to compete in global markets, the bulk of them lack the technological, organizational, and management capabilities to upgrade into high value-added activities. The reasons for their failures are different but are predominantly linked to a weak embedding ecosystem facing the firms, Furthermore, the lack of vocational and technical education has restricted the capacity of the managements and workers to absorb best practices in the industry (Rasiah & Nazeer, 2015).

The lack of industrial upgrading at the firm-level in Pakistan is both a consequence of a lack of technology transfer from abroad, as well as in-house technological, organizational, and management capability building (Rasiah & Nazeer, 2015). Hence, the motivation of this book is to undertake a rigorous analysis of the textile and clothing sector of Pakistan, which has stagnated owing to low industrial upgrading. In addressing this, the book seeks to disentangle technological, and organizational and management capabilities to examine the factors that influence successful technological catch-up. A profound understanding of the relationship between technology transfer and technology capabilities through the mediating effect of organizational and management capability on firm performance will provide policy-relevant insights for promoting industrial upgrading in Pakistan's textile and clothing firms.

Objectives of the Book

This book seeks to identify the drivers of industrial upgrading and firm performance in the textiles and clothing industry through constructing a taxonomy by trajectories to locate Pakistan's textiles and clothing firms in the international technological, and organizational and management capabilities grid, and to formulate an industrial upgrading index to assess the strengthen of the embedding ecosystem to stimulate upgrading. In doing so, the book first investigates the knowledge accumulation sources and levels by taxonomy and trajectory through which firms acquire and develop technological, and organizational and management capabilities. Second, the study investigates empirically the relationship between technology transfer and technological capabilities on firm performance with the mediating effect of organizational and management capabilities on the relationship. Third, the study attempts to determine the critical embedding ecosystem instruments and factors that stimulate industrial upgrading. To achieve these three objectives, the book seeks to undertake the following three exercises:

- To develop a knowledge accumulation taxonomy by trajectories for textiles and clothing firms by including frontier firms from the world to locate Pakistan's firms against the frontier firms.[5]

[5] The knowledge accumulation taxonomy is used in the book to denote the classifications of technological, and organizational and management capabilities by trajectories.

- To evaluate the relationship between technology transfer and technological capabilities, firm performance, and the mediating role of organizational and management capabilities in this relationship.
- To develop an industrial upgrading index that takes account of the embedding ecosystem influences on industrial upgrading in the textiles and clothing industry of Pakistan.

Key Concepts

While the general meaning of the concepts related to technology and capabilities are largely captured by several works, their boundaries differ. Consequently, this section presents the most important concepts examined in this book to help readers comprehend them as they are used.

Technology

The early concept of technology as information or skills posits that technologies can be reused and reproduced simply (Arrow, 1962). However, as Tihanyi and Roath (2002) note, technology can include information that is not easily reproducible and transferable, while Pavitt (1984) argued that technology can be differentiated between a particular application and tacitness that is often uncodified, which carries cumulative elements associated with it. Consequently, as Penrose (1959) had argued, technology includes firms' 'intangible assets' or 'firm-specific' assets, which forms the basis of a firm's competitiveness (see also Dunning, 2001).[6] In other words, among other things, technology includes tacit knowledge, secrets, or knowledge known by particular organizations, which are firm-specific (Polanyi, 1967).

Robock and Calkins (1980) formulated technological taxonomies by splitting product designs, production practices, and managerial functions. Simon (1991) classified technologies into two categories: (1) technologies directly related to harvesting and production of national commodities (for instance, agriculture and textiles products) and (2) technologies that are linked to military items. However, the claim of a lacuna that seemingly existed in the past on the lack of attention devoted to process, product, and managerial technologies raised by Sammarra and Biggerio (2008) is unfounded as Rasiah (1995) among others has treated this issue profoundly in the

[6] In making this point, we wish to note that Schumacher's (1973) notion of appropriate technology is not addressed here as he was referring to what he thought should be what the poor countries would require to address their developmental problems.

past. This covers both explicit and tacit components of embodied knowledge. However, the latter is not captured by mainstream economists using endogenous measurements of technology (cf. Romer, 1986).

Product technology refers to specific technology embodied in products, which are produced using a wide range of knowledge embodied in humans and machinery (Rasiah, 2003). Firms at the bottom of the technological ladder tend to use simple technologies that they have acquired, while they seek access to buyer specs, designs, and patents to participate in the manufacture of products. Once firms have acquired the technology to manufacture, design, and use their own brand name, their classification moves respectively to original equipment manufacturer (OEM), Original Design Manufacturer (ODM), and eventually to Original Brand Manufacturer (OBM). Firms tend to specialize on any one, two or all three of them. Frontier firms generally tend to also own OBMs, but there are exceptions, such as TSMC, which has remained an OEM with no involvement in ODM and OBM activities but invests heavily in R&D activities to shape the logic chips technology frontier (Rasiah and Yap, 2019). Technology transfer agreements generally entail the permission to use technological knowledge from the owner by recipient firms/organizations through the provision of proprietary knowhow, transfer of designs and technology specifications, technical consultations with the owners assisting through the use of new technologies with constant feedbacks on specified product performance, and collaboration in R&D (UNCTAD, 2014).

Process technology refers to the processes through which a specific product is produced (Rasiah, 1995), which involves knowledge that is utilized in the production process to manage inputs using machinery and equipment through production planning and quality management (including inventory, quality control, and inspection) (Rasiah, 1995; UNCTAD, 2014). Many firms also use just-in-time, *kaizen*, total preventive maintenance, and cellular manufacturing in their production systems.

Technology Transfer

The concept of technology transfer is in general used with no consensus on a 'canonical definition' of what the concept means (Bozeman, 2000). According to WIPO (2014: 6–8), technology transfer refers to 'a series of processes of sharing ideas, knowledge, technologies, and skills with other individuals or organizations (such as firms, universities and government agencies) and acquisition from one or more by others of ideas, knowledge, technologies, and skills'.

The United Nations Draft Code of Conduct on Transfer of Technology refers technology transfer to the transfer of the components of technology from one economic agent to another. It includes, plant, machinery, and equipment, production processes, software, manuals, and patents—all of which contain technological knowledge (either codified or uncodified) that is either 'embodied' (such as, in machinery or people) or 'disembodied' (UNCTAD, 2014: 1). Meanwhile, Nahar et al. (2006) defined international technology transfer as a set of processes by which technology suppliers communicate and transmit technology through multiple activities to receivers across national borders.

Technological Capabilities

Rosenberg (1982) defined technological capabilities (TC) as 'a process of accumulating technical knowledge or a process of organizational learning'. Also, TC is the capability to make effective use of technical knowledge and skills not only to improve and develop products and processes but also to improve existing technologies and to generate new technologies and skills in response to competition.

Rasiah (2004b) referred to firm-level technological capabilities as in-house knowledge resource accumulated to make efficient and effective use of technological information and knowledge for the adaptation and assimilation of knowhow targeted at raising firm performance. In doing so, Rasiah (2004b) departed from Lall's (1992) concept of capabilities by excluding investment capability from the concept to focus on just technological capabilities to establish in the process a taxonomy by trajectories. While Schumpeter (1942) had argued that the capital endowments of large firms are essential to support R&D operations, as Rasiah (2019) pointed out, knowledge networks have evolved enormously to enable small and medium firms' endowed with little capital resources to participate in frontier R&D activities by connecting with public labs and research labs at universities, as well as incubators at science parks. Also, Rasiah (1995) argued that differences in scale and scope economies, stages of production in product cycles, technological and industry specificities, and firm-strategies make investment capability a variable inappropriate to be classified among the core components of technological capabilities. For example, in semiconductor manufacturing, chip design requires significantly lower capital investment than chip assembly, but the latter requires less knowledge intensity than the former (Rasiah and Yap, 2019). This framework allows the measurement of the different types of technological capabilitiesm, for example, human resources, process technology, and product technology, which this study uses as a guide for examining technological capabilities in the textile and clothing industry of Pakistan.

The attempt to classify technological, organizational, and management capabilities by trajectories also helps to address shortcomings associated with Lall's (1998), UNCTAD's (2002), and UNIDO's (2002) classification of industries technologies by high, medium, and low as the latter does not address the high-technology industry of electronics, medium technology industry of automotives, and low technology industry of textiles and clothing. Instead, firms in these industries have been decentralized so much that each one of them often lacks R&D and designing when operating in the developing countries, including subsidiaries of transnational corporations. Besides, the proliferation of digitization in all industries through the deployment of robots and centrally controlled and coordinated electronic systems that link producers and buyers operating in distant places have made such distinctions no longer useful (Rasiah, 2019; Rasiah & Yap, 2019).

Technological capability offers firms the capacity to undertake productive tasks, ranging from pre-investment exploration to product and process engineering, manufacturing, and eventually to introduce new technologies as they progress. Technological capabilities can also simply be viewed as firms' capability to identify its technological requirements and to deploy the best combination of technologies to meet that need; to operate, maintain, modify, and improve existing technologies; to promote technological adaptation and finally to generate radical innovations.

Organizational and Management Capabilities

Firms have different ways of achieving their objectives. In this regard, organizations are heterogeneous in nature, and hence take on various organizational and management routines regardless of whether they belong to the same industry or not. Firm-specific organizational and management capabilities that are evolved internally and often with external links are important to facilitate successful solutions to organizational and management problems (Dosi et al., 2001). Consequently, organizational and management capabilities play a critical role in the accumulation and appropriation of technological capabilities and technology transfer to raise firm performance. Such capabilities also capture the strategies and networks firms use to achieve industrial upgrading.

Managerial capability refers to embodied capability in managers or managements to effectively manage their businesses (Rasiah, 1995), including specific managerial skills that firms use to compete by using resources efficiently through support from inventory management, and the use of just-in-time and other inventory and quality control systems that are deployed to implement quality assurance systems, introduction of new practices, such as network management or financial, marketing, and purchasing techniques (UNCTAD, 2014). Managerial knowledge also assists managers to use their tacit capabilities to strategize improvements in the way resources and technologies are deployed to raise the competitiveness of firms.

Data and Methodology

The analysis undertaken in this book relies on primary data collected from firms and quantitative and qualitative methods. As the study focuses on both the micro and macro levels, the methodology is divided into three parts. To address Objectives 1 (Chapter 5) and 2 (Chapter 6), primary data was collected using a stratified random sampling procedure by deploying structured questionnaires that were distributed to textile and clothing firms. These firms are registered under PSX (formerly KSE), SECP, APTMA, and Chamber of Commerce listing, which are the state associations of the registered firms, and located in the three major cities of Karachi, Lahore, and Faisalabad where textile and clothing firms are most concentrated in Pakistan. Chief executive officers, members of top management, middle management, and lower management participated in the survey. The study generated 503 effective responses from the 600 questionnaires distributed. The survey was performed from April 2017 to July 2018.[7] All data was subsequently updated to 2018.

The taxonomy developed for the first methodology used in Chapter 5 is based on trajectories in the textiles and clothing industry to address Objective 1. Structural equation modelling was deployed to address Objective 2 to examine the relationship between technology transfer and technologicalcapabilities, and firm performance, as well as the mediating effects of organizational and management capabilities on this relationship (see Chapter 6).

The third methodology used in this book to develop the industrial upgrading index (IUI) is drawn from the systemic quad advanced by Rasiah (2019) to capture the influence of ecosystem instruments embedding the firms, while the influence of these pillars and instruments were evaluated using the

[7] Nazeer undertook the survey.

decision-making process introduced by Simon (1977) and Analytical Hierarchical Procedure (AHP) that was expounded by Saaty (1990) through the application of an expert sampling technique, using a non-probability sampling approach (see Chapter 7). A total of 50 experts from the textiles and clothing industry, government executives, and academicians associated with the textiles and clothing industry were consulted to give appropriate weights for the dimensions and sub-dimensions by using an AHP comparison questionnaire. A more comprehensive explanation of the methodology used on this is presented in Chapters 4 and 7.

Book Outline

This book is composed of eight chapters. Following Chapter 1, which problematizes the critical issue of industrial upgrading, accompanied by the objectives, key concepts, and methodology used in the book; Chapter 2 discusses in detail textiles and clothing firms and the organizations, and the challenges that face them in Pakistan to provide the context to the study. In doing so, it discusses the characteristics, performance, and global competitiveness of Pakistan's textiles and clothing firms.

Chapter 3 provides a comprehensive review of the extant literature with a focus on technology transfer, technological capabilities, and organizational and management capabilities. The chapter also identifies gaps in the existing literature on industrial upgrading in general, and on the textile and clothing industry in particular. Chapter 4 presents the general research framework and the methodology and data used in the subsequent analytical chapters. The rationale for the selection of the data collection methodology and the sample size is explained in this chapter, including questionnaire distribution, data collection, and data analysis.

Chapters 5, 6, and 7 serve to achieve the objectives of the study through three important exercises. Chapter 5 develops a knowledge accumulation taxonomy by trajectories for textile and clothing firms in Pakistan. In doing so, the world's frontier textiles and clothing manufacturing firms of TAL (Hong Kong), Toray (Japan), and Everest Textiles (Taiwan) were used as the lead firms. Also, only large and medium firms were included in the sample because micro and small firms largely participated informally and did not figure in the records of the textiles and clothing associations of Pakistan.

Using structural equation modelling, Chapter 6 examines the relationship between technology transfer and technological capabilities, and firm performance among textile and clothing firms in Pakistan with organizational and management capabilities as the mediating variable. Chapter 7 develops an industrial upgrading index that takes account of the critical embedding institutions and intermediary organizations that influence technological, organizational, and management capability upgrading in the textile and clothing industry of Pakistan.

Chapter 8 presents the conclusions of the study. It starts with a synthesis of findings, before drawing implications for theory and policy. Also discussed are the likely catch-up paths of firms in Pakistan in particular, and in South Asia in general could take.

2
The Textiles and Clothing Industry of Pakistan

Introduction

Despite being one of the oldest industries to emerge, the textiles and clothing industry has remained a leading export of labour surplus economies. The industry has been recognized as a 'starter' of export-orientated industrialization (Gereffi, 1999). The technological regimes that characterize the textiles and clothing industry have made it suitable for taking the initial steps towards industrialization, especially among underdeveloped countries. Over half of the world's supply of textiles and clothing are produced in the developing nations. With China accounting for almost 40 per cent of world exports, Asia accounted for approximately 55 per cent of the world's textile and clothing exports in 2019 (ILO, 2020, p. 3). Textiles and clothing together have been the pillar of exports from several developing countries located in Asia, Africa, and Latin America (Rasiah, 2004b). Textiles provide the main inputs (woven and knitted fabric) to the clothing sector, and hence, are vertically linked with one another (Rasiah, 1995; Nordas, 2004). However, while linking with global value chains (GVCs) have been important for latecomer textiles and clothing firms, only firms in locations that experience effective learning (which includes considerable adaptations) have enjoyed technological upgrading to participate in high value-added activities.

From a developmental perspective, the textiles and clothing industry have a significant impact on employment in less developed countries, ranging from 35 per cent to 90 per cent of total employment in manufacturing (UNIDO, 2013). Although associated with low-wage workers, it is also a sector where latest technologies can be adapted even in low-income countries at reasonably low costs. The low capital-intensity of the clothing industry in most LDCs, high volatility in product demand, and low technology turnover shows that the industry can adjust quickly to changes in markets and locations (Nordas, 2004).

Industrial Upgrading in the Textiles and Clothing Industry. Nazia Nazeer and Rajah Rasiah, Oxford University Press.
 DOI: 10.1093/9780198961697.003.0002

The successful experience of some East Asian economies, such as South Korea and Taiwan indicate that progress in the textile and clothing sectors can lead to structural change into other industrial sectors, and hence, can help stimulate rapid growth in value-added. Indeed, Pakistan was among the major textile and clothing exporters in the 1960s and 1970s, but while South Korean and Taiwanese firms upgraded rapidly, as well as experienced structural change into higher value-added industries, Pakistan's economy stagnated technologically (see Chapter 5). Textiles and clothing eventually fell in relative significance compared to the successful industrializers of South Korea and Taiwan as their economies evolved to high value-added industries, such as electronics, machinery, and equipment, and automobiles (Johnson, 1982; Fransman, 1986; Amsden, 1989; Rasiah, Zhang, & Kong, 2013). Heavy government investment into science technology, and innovation (STI) infrastructure, and human capital were accompanied by the use of stringent regulatory mechanisms to discourage the dissipation of rents (such as incentives and grants), unproductively (Rasiah, 2010; Rasiah & Wong, 2021).

Consequently, this chapter discusses the structure, technological capabilities, and market structure, as well as government policies launched to promote the textiles and clothing industry in Pakistan. Also examined in this chapter are the challenges faced by the industry.

Structure of the Textile and Clothing Industry

The output of the textiles and apparel industry usually consist of processing of different fibres and manufacturing of yarns through spinning of natural fibres (such as cotton, wool, flex, silk, jute, and hemp) and man-made fibres, such as polymers from petrochemicals (including polyester, nylon, acrylic), and inorganic materials, from glass, ceramic, or carbon and metals (Gupta, 2007). In Pakistan, both scope and scale and the production chain offer opportunities and challenges for generating innovative and competitive exports (Khan & Afzal, 2016; Wadho & Chaudhry, 2016). As a large-scale industry, Pakistan enjoys large domestic demand for textiles and clothing, which along with India had stimulated the early expansion of the industry, including international exports. Exports re-emerged during and after independence, though the brandholders used for exports remain largely in the developed countries. The organization of textiles and clothing under the national framework of Pakistan emerged following independence in 1947. Cotton has contributed significantly for the textile and clothing industry to dominate Pakistan's exports, foreign exchange earnings, employment, value-added and investment in the country. Even as recently as 2019–2020 the textile sector enjoyed the highest weight of 20.9 in the Quantum Index of Manufacturing (QIM), accounting for almost one-fourth of industrial value-added and nearly 40 per cent of the industrial labour force of the country in 2020. Apart from cyclical and seasonal demand swings, textiles have enjoyed a sustained average share of almost 59 per cent of overall exports from Pakistan (Economic Survey of Pakistan, 2020).

However, a number of challenges has restricted industrial upgrading in the industry so that it has not managed to appropriate significant economic synergies from the availability of high-quality raw cotton and cheap labour, even though it enjoys export access to Canada, Japan, the European Union, the United States, China, and México (Hussain, Figueiredo, & Ferreira, 2009). Pakistan also enjoys strong access to textile machinery from Germany, Japan, China, Switzerland, and Belgium (Mahmood, 2014). Machinery imported into Pakistan from abroad is primarily used in ginning, carding, blowing, rings, drawing, doubling, winding, weaving (power looms), twisting, knitting, texturizing, shuttle-less looms (weaving), mercerizing, bleaching, dyeing, stitching, and printing (Textile Policy, Ministry of Textile Industry, Government of Pakistan 2014–2019). However, the bulk of the firms lack access to the latest machinery and equipment.

Nevertheless, unlike the fast-growing exporters of Bangladesh and Cambodia, Pakistan has the entire value chain of the textiles and clothing industry, from cotton picking to modern fashion styles that are used in finished clothing. The industry is generally classified dually with one as large-scale and well-organized sector, and the other as an impartially unorganized small-scale sector. The large scale sector comprise incorporated textile divisions mostly large spinning mills and some weaving firms using shuttles-less looms. The spinning segment was the first in Pakistan's textiles and clothing value chain, which also includes the manufacture of yarn from fibre. The weaving, knitting, processing, and made-up garments come after that. According to the Textiles Commissioner's Organization (TCO), the spinning sector comprised of 517 textile units, including 40 composite units, 477 spinning units with 13.414 million spindles, 198,801 installed rotors, 11.338 million spindles, and 126,583 rotors engaged in processing with an operational capacity of 84.6 per cent and 63.7 per cent, respectively in 2020 (Government of Pakistan, Finance Division, 2021). Most of the textiles firms are located in Karachi, Lahore, Hyderabad, Faisalabad, and Multan. The weaving segment consists of large, medium, and small firms, and are generally clustered in Kasur, Faisalabad, Multan, and Hafizabad (Memon, 2010).

While the textile firms are characterized by large and medium capital-intensive production, clothing firms in comparison range from small to large establishments, with approximately 80 per cent of them operating informally (US International Trade Commission, 2004). The clothing segment is mainly focused in the production of women's and men's wear (woven and knitted), sportswear, babies wear, T-shirts, pullovers, and hosiery (SMEDA, 2016).

Textiles and Clothing Value Chain

Pakistan's textiles and clothing industry is categorized by a production chain from the cultivation of cotton to ginning, weaving, knitting, processing, and finishing of fabrics, and is also not strongly integrated with logistics and international branding activities and universities where frontier textiles and clothing R&D is carried out, and material and machinery suppliers (Figure 2.1). Most sophisticated textiles and clothing firms in Pakistan have only developed and use original equipment manufacturing (OEM) and original design manufacturing (ODM) capabilities in their exports, though some large and medium-size firms have introduced their brands into the domestic economy.

Technological Intensity of Exports

Following Lall's (2000) measure of competitiveness, it can be said that the manufacturing sector of Pakistan has revealed higher growth in medium industries than the low and high technology industries since 2005 (Figure 2.2), but only because its starting base was small. Furthermore, the medium and high technology industries in the country have remained focused on low-end manufacturing activities for the domestic market, (e.g., the manufacturing of electric fans). Consequently, low technology industries accounted for around 98 per cent of Pakistan's export in manufacturing in 2019. Hence, as is argued later in the book, the measurement used by Lall (2000) is weak technology-wise, the manufacturing sector of Pakistan has not experienced significant industrial structural transformation since independence.

Textiles have been the main contributor to overall exports thereby demonstrating minimal functional upgrading in Pakistan. Exports of high-technology products have been insignificant, though a rise in synthetic textile exports has resulted in some structural change from low- to medium-technology industries.

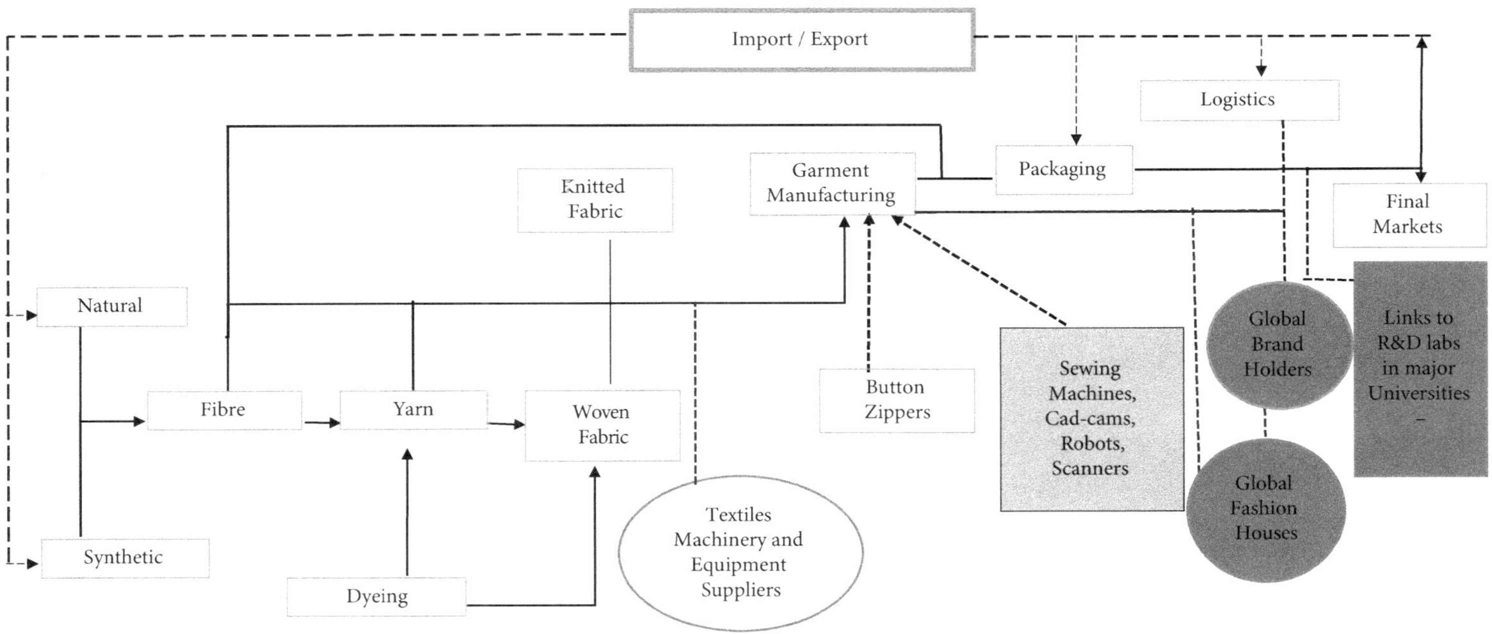

Figure 2.1 Textile and clothing value chain and cluster, 2020

Source: Adapted from Rasiah (2012).

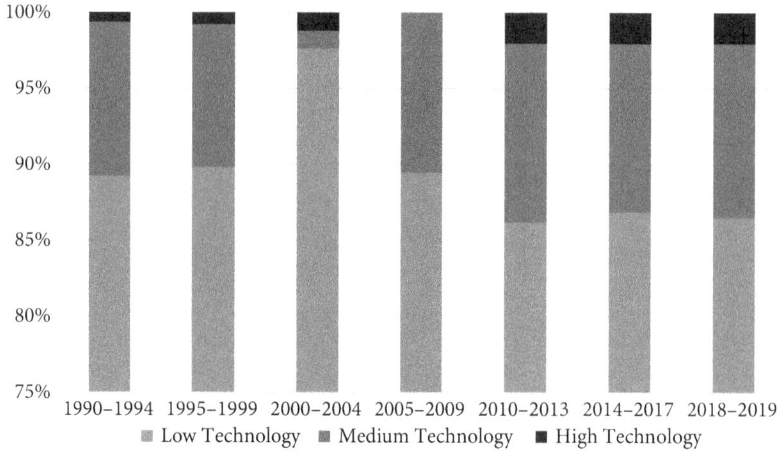

Figure 2.2 Annual average export growth by technological intensity, Pakistan, 1990–2019
Source: Plotted by authors using Comtrade data.

While Malaysia, Philippines, and Thailand may offer lessons for expanding exports, South Korea and Taiwan remain better examples to learn from owing to the successful upgrading of industrial firms in these countries to high value-added frontier operations (Rasiah & Wong, 2021; Rasiah & Zhang, 2024). Also, while it is important to encourage structural change in Pakistan from low- medium- to high-technology industries in general, such a structural change should not just be confined to the textiles and clothing industry. There should also be a transition to high value-added industries, such as machinery, equipment, and chemicals. Within textiles and clothing, efforts must be taken to raise value in cotton fibre, yarn, woven and knitted fabric, and clothing industries. In fact, firms should carry out more R&D, designing, and marketing of Pakistan's own brands in the clothing industry, while linking with complementary sectors, such as dyes, machinery, and logistics. The East Asian industrialized nations, such as Taiwan and Korea, underwent institutional transformation to build their technological capacities towards fostering competitiveness of domestic firms (Amsden, 1989; Yusof & Evenett, 2002). For example, Taiwan and Korea targeted local R&D to develop technology-intensive activities to catch up and leapfrog frontier firms in some industries. Taiwan Semiconductor Manufacturing Corporation (TSMC) and Samsung lead the logic chip and memory chip industries respectively (Rasiah et al., 2015b).

To raise competitiveness of textiles and clothing firms, it is important for firms in Pakistan to be capable of having their own designing capability for product development, and to use automation, robots, and cutting-edge inventory and quality-control techniques, which require rooting in the organized woven clothing sector (Nabi & Hamid, 2013).[1] Such a development can also support upgrading in small and medium-sized firms specializing in niche markets, (e.g., heat-resistant and climate-friendly garments), for branded buyers that use kevlar and denim for bikers, sports uniforms (UK schools), fleece jackets for universities in the United States and baseball and American football uniforms. Furthermore, Pakistan's workforce needs deeper technical and vocational training to absorb best practices in the industry, which is essential to compete effectively with exporters from China, South Korea, and Taiwan.

Significance in Manufacturing

The textiles and clothing industry contributed 44.2 per cent in 2005, 37.1 per cent in 2013, and 29.0 per cent in 2019 of overall exports from Pakistan (Comtrade, 2020). Meanwhile, the share of textiles and clothing in manufacturing value-added in Pakistan rose from 26.1 per cent in 2000–2005 to 30.4 per cent in 2006–2010 before falling to 29.6 per cent in 2016–2019. In contrast, the commensurate shares for Malaysia, Thailand, South Korea, and China fell in trend terms from 3.2, 9.5, 6.7, and 10.8 per cent in 2000–2005 to 2.0, 6.0, 3.0, and 10.0 per cent respectively in 2016–2019 (Figure 2.3). Consequently, Pakistan's dependence on the textiles and clothing industry is far higher than that of Malaysia, Thailand, South Korea, and China.

Textiles and clothing exports from Pakistan grew from USD 5,538.9 million in 1995–2000 to USD 7,070.6 million in 2001–2005, and USD 8,819.1 million in 2006–2010. The growth would have been higher if not for shortages in the supply of gas and electricity. Export growth picked up again in 2011–2015 to USD 10,558.3 million before falling slightly in 2016–2020 to USD 10,269.6 million (Figure 2.4).

Agriculture still dominated Pakistan's economy in 2020 with raw cotton and wool being its major exports. Grey fabric contributed about half of total fabric production in 2020. To develop an integrated high value-added textiles and clothing industry, Pakistan should seek vertical upgrading, and functional upgrading into logistics, designing, R&D, and manufacturing of complementary supportive industries, such as machinery and materials (e.g.,

[1] These firms locally hired designers who can visit Pakistan and look after overseas office. Few mills have invested only in facilities to produce quick samples. In this way they can dispatch samples within a week.

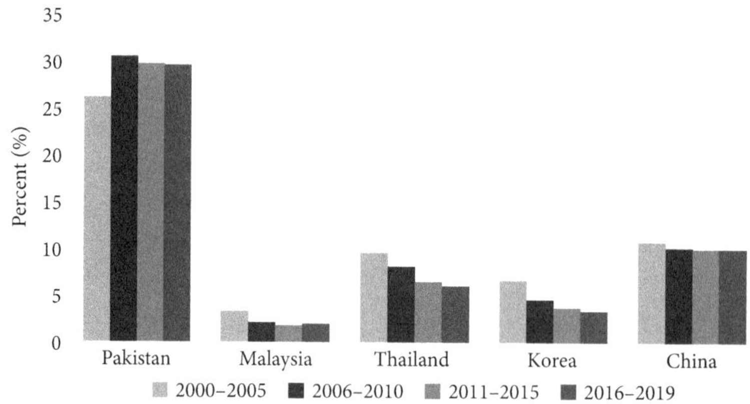

Figure 2.3 Share of textiles and clothing in manufacturing value-added, selected countries, 2000–2019
Source: Authors' calculations from World Bank (2023).

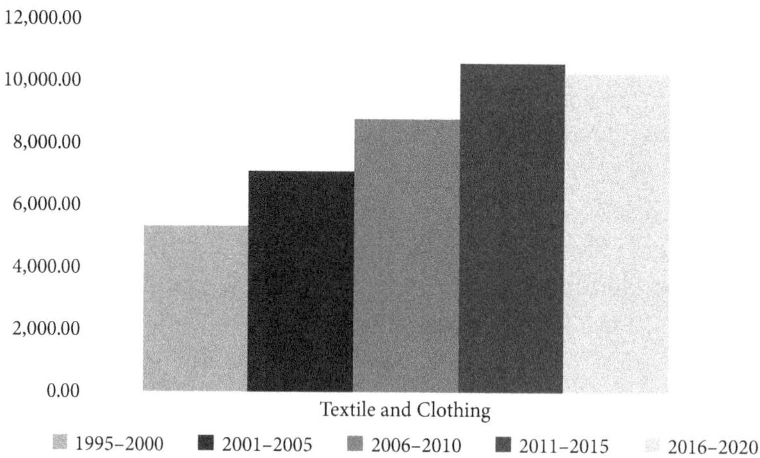

Figure 2.4 Textiles and clothing exports, Pakistan, 1995–2020 (US dollars)
Source: Authors' calculations from Economic Survey of Pakistan (various issues).

resins, air-jet looms, auto-fabric scanners, central-controlled automative processing and assembly, and machinery and equipment to support computer-aided designing (CAD) and computer-aided manufacturing (CAM). This is the approach assumed by lead firms engaged in the frontier level nine technological activities, such as Everest Textiles, Toray, and TAL (see Chapter 5).

Market Access

The global textile and clothing industry has experienced remarkable changes since the beginning of the twentieth century (Rasiah, 2012). Firstly, by the mid-1970s and early 1980s the bulk of production has been relocated from the Western nations to Asia. Secondly, rising competition among exporting and importing nations and the removal of the most favoured nation clause from several countries, and subsequently with the elimination of quota privileges under the Multi-Fibre Arrangement in 2004, drastically changed world trade in textiles and clothing (Rasiah, 2012; ILO, 2014). Only the Least Developed Countries (LDCs) countries, such as Bangladesh, Cambodia, Ethiopia, Kenya, and Uganda began to enjoy special privileges through bilateral and multilateral treaties with the importing countries. Consequently, large numbers of firms relocated production operations from China, Hong Kong, Taiwan, Malaysia, and Singapore to these countries to enjoy the quota privileges allocated to them; so much so that textiles and clothing have become the chief exports of Bangladesh and Cambodia.

The value chain of textiles and clothing firms has undergone considerable transformation, especially in the clothing sector because of constant changes as a consequence of developments in international fashion. Tied to clothing fashion is also fabric design and pattern, which brings with it fabric weaving and knitting, dyeing and finishing, which have all faced frequent changes in demand. Pakistan's clothing industry, particularly ready-made garments using designer brands, have enjoyed little demand in the European Union and the United States because of inadequate marketing strategies and poor publicity (Cororaton & Orden, 2008).

Pakistan is one of the few countries that produces medium- to long-stock staple cotton. The cotton cultivated in Pakistan is of far superior quality than that cultivated in China, and offers better finish when dyed in shine, uniformity, and lustre. Almost 60 per cent of Pakistan's cotton is characterized by the medium to long staple stock, 37 per cent medium staple stock, and 3 per cent long staple stock (Shafiq, 2012). The quality of cotton produced obviously makes Pakistan's textile and apparel sector a potentially world-class performer in cotton-based products, which also explains why cotton jeans and denim cloth are the prime items exported by the weaving clothing industry in the country. The medium staple cotton stock (which is used in denim production) is cultivated in Pakistan.

Pakistan's exports of textiles and clothing to North America, Europe, and Central Asia rose from USD2.6 billion and USD2.7 billion respectively in 2003 to USD3.2 billion and USD5.4 billion respectively in 2015, and USD5.4 billion and USD8.1 billion respectively in 2021 (WITS, 2024). The strategic 'Textile Vision 2005' blueprint of Pakistan ought to be reviewed to focus on industrial upgrading as cotton yarn still constituted 32.8 per cent while clothing accounted for just 8.1 per cent of textiles and clothing exports in 2006 (APTMA, 2014). Although, the government proposed incentives for the expansion of low-cost power looms (Chaudhry & Hamid, 1988), serious power shortages drove milling capacity utilization rates down (APTMA, 2019). Interviews in 2020 confirmed the chronic nature of power outages facing the textiles and clothing industry.[2]

Meanwhile, LDCs, such as Bangladesh and Cambodia managed to cut into Pakistan's traditional clothing markets following the introduction of privileged access offered to these countries since 2004 (Rasiah & Myint, 2013). The relaxation of quotas also stimulated increased exports from China, India, and other East Asian countries.

Intermediary Organizations

Industrial associations and other intermediary organizations exist to solve collective action problems to stimulate economic development. These bodies were launched to support and protect the rights of a specific industry and working individuals in Pakistan. Consequently, several textile associations and related organizations emerged in Pakistan to support textiles and clothing firms to address their needs—from basic infrastructure (such as transport networks and water and power supply), training, import, and export coordination with the customs authorities, as well as trade promotion. A summary of some of the important textile and clothing associations and related organization in Pakistan is shown in Table 2.1.

Textiles and Clothing Policies

Pakistan's Ministry of Textiles and Clothing (MTC) was founded in 2004, which by 2020 had launched the first textile policy (2009–2014), the second textile policy (2015–2019), and the textiles and apparel policy (2020–2025).

[2] Interview conducted by Rajah Rasiah with Sapphire Textiles (Faisalabad) on 11 January, 2020 and Nishat Chunian (Lahore) on 15 January 2020.

Table 2.1 Textile associations and related organizations, Pakistan, 2020

Association/organization	Abbreviation	Role
Ministry of Textiles and Clothing	MTC	Supports the textile and clothing sector advice to firms. Also, builds linkages with textile and cotton importing countries.
All Pakistan Textile Mills Association	APTMA	Supports domestic procurement of cotton, import, income sales tax law, and cotton legislation, customs regulations concerning textiles exports and imports.
Pakistan Securities and Exchange Commission	SECP	Regulates the capital market and insured companies. Has enforcement and investigative powers
Pakistan Central Cotton Committee	PCCC	Carries out mono-crop, multifaceted research on cotton countrywide in many organic zones to support high performance yield and fibre quality.
Pakistan Institute	PCSI	Maintains standards, rating, and quality system during harvesting, handling, and selling of cotton.
Karachi Cotton Association	KCA	Upholds a code of rational and equitable trade practices by implementing rules, regulations and laws It provides useful information about the cotton prices and current world market situation.
Pakistan Cotton Ginners' Association	PCGA	The bridge between textile mills and growers and has links with APTMA, Growers, KCA, and provincial and federal organizations

Continued

Table 2.1 *Continued*

Association/organization	Abbreviation	Role
Small and Medium Enterprise (SME) Development Authority	SMEDA	Supports SMEs in Pakistan by offering marketing and technical advice, short training programmes (low and middle management, business plan, and provides loans and legal services.
Export Promotion Bureau	EPB	The EPB endorses domestic products for global markets with special quota for SMEs (20%) in international trade exhibitions, trade conferences, and trade delegations. Organizes exhibitions to promote clothing industry of Pakistan.
Vocational Training Institute	VTI	Specifically meant for those individuals who do not have enough money for textile and garment stitching training.
Pakistan Readymade Garments	PREGMEA	Provides information
Manufacturers and Exporters Association	MEA	Coordinates international trade fairs and handles visa issuance.
National Textile University	NTU	The prime institute of textile related education. Enjoys a close association with industrialists and industry.
Textile Institute of Pakistan	TIP	Provides professional training and education. The Export Promotion Bureau provides TIP financial support. TIP established its first research centre named as Textile Research & Innovation Centre (TRIC) in 2007 to promote latest materials research.
Pakistan Institute of Fashion and Design	PIFD	Offers inclusive designing education with emphasis on relations between product designers and customers providing imaginative new generation training using highly skilful designers who understand local demands and international markets. Also, prepares students with essential management and marketing instruments to seek endorsement in international markets.

Source: Authors' compilation

First Textile Policy (2009–2014)

The first National textile policy (2009–2014) was not successful as the state released less amount of funding compared to the commitments made. Consequently, several initiatives were not implemented, including the payments for domestic taxes and levies, reimbursement of bills arising from research and development, and textile investment support expenses. Also, the Technology Upgradation Support Fund (TUSF) and incentives to stimulate the purchase of textile-related technology and machinery could not be implemented. Furthermore, the national textile policy was undermined by the inability of the government to ensure continuous supply of electricity and gas to the textile industry. Consequently, almost one million spindles closed down operations because of increasing hours of load shedding.

This policy was also not accompanied by strong upgrading in the machine tool industry, let alone in robotization to support digitalization and digitization. Some exceptions took place as funding was released for the establishment of the Multan Cotton Ginning Institute, which helped raise research on bettering ginning methods. In addition, the infrastructure projects of Faisalabad and Lahore Garment Cities were also started in 2005. However, the development of the Pakistan Textile City and Karachi Garment City projects were affected owing to gas supply problems, litigation, electricity, and water shortages caused by a lack of funds. Also, the MTC collaborated with different organizations worldwide, such as Korea International Cooperation Agency (KOICA), the United Nations (UN), and the International Labour Organization (ILO), to support skills developmental programmes targeted at raising value addition in the industry.

Second Textile Policy (2015–2019)

The Pakistan government launched its second Textile Policy (2015–2019) in February 2015 to raise textiles and clothing exports from USD13 billion in 2014 to USD26 billion in 2019 through primarily investment in technology to enhance fibre mixes to strengthen small and medium enterprises (SMEs) and labour regulations. Its focus was on introducing latest management and vocational training methods for workers, professionals, and supervisors, offering easy financing to firms engaged in fibre and product diversification, improving marketing strategies, stimulating technological upgrading, and promoting the creation of model cotton trading houses of world standard (Pakistan, 2015). Although industry officials have expressed their reservations over the second textile policy owing to continuous shortages in energy supply, composite units utilizing their own captive power plants, and improvements in the supply of electricity did help some firms to take advantage of the incentives offered to boost value-added in the industry.

Overall, the Textiles Policies of 2009–2014 and 2015–2019 focused more on the immediate issues confronting the industry than on reducing the cost of doing business, without addressing the long-term structural problems effectively. Therefore, these policies helped sustain exports, including in industrial upgrading but did not see it spread across the country.

Third Textile and Apparel Policy (2020–2025)

The 2020–2025 Textiles and Apparel policy is more ambitions, which goes beyond tariff rationalization and lowering lead times to address industrial upgrading that includes digitalization, sustainability, and marketing, including the promotion of national brands (MTC, 2020). However, a combination of the COVID19 outbreak in 2020, balance of payments problems, and an exchange rate crisis has thwarted any serious introduction of upgrading initiatives.

Nevertheless, a number of the large companies have accessed incentives to install solar panels to avert power outage problems, and at the time deepening their forays into taking up incentives to participate in designs, and to establish collaboration with foreign universities and international fashion houses.

Challenges Facing Textile and Clothing Manufacturers

A number of challenges that do not relate directly to firm-level operations are faced by Pakistan's textiles and clothing firms. Several of these problems need solutions if Pakistan is to achieve upgrading from low and medium to high value-added activities in the textiles and clothing industry. These issues are picked up in the systemic quad model adapted for the construction of the IUI in Chapter 7.

Labour Covenants

The textiles and clothing industry in Asia have generally shown weak industrial relations histories, particularly in implementing international labour standards and recognizing the important role of unions and collective bargaining (Rasiah, 2012). Pakistan is no exception. Such operations are common the world over where the industrial relations environment appears hostile to subcontracting operations that deal with low skills and below subsistence wages that permit firms to hire and fire workers easily. Although the bilateral and regional free trade agreement (FTA) put pressure on host nations, the countries involved have largely appropriated the benefits for accumulating capital while ignoring the wellbeing of workers in both the textiles and clothing industries (Arnold, 2006; Raj-Reichert, 2015). Undoubtedly, the transient nature of low value-added operations and the cut-throat orientation of contractors do not provide subcontractors sufficient returns to finance human resource development.

Embedding Environment for Technological Upgrading

Technological facilities are comprised of science laboratories, research and development facilities, technology parks, incubators, testing and design centres, evaluation facilities, centres for prototyping and testing services, and bureaus for the creation of new organizations. The science, technology, and innovation (STI) infrastructure is important to stimulate upgrading in firms, but they are seriously inadequate and badly managed in Pakistan. Besides, the lack of standards organizations to support standards maintenance, calibration, and quality control has negatively affected the capacity of firms to export (Wajid & Memon, 2002). The industry requires technically trained workers to get better value from the products manufactured.

Monitoring the quality of the products is the greatest challenge faced by buyers, which has a bearing on the selection of exporters (Hirschleifer, 1971). The existing participants in the export business have largely acquired internet access and strong telemonitoring capabilities. Substantial investment is required for expending information technology coordinates with the big customers. The foremost weakness among manufacturing units in the clothing sector of Pakistan is that they are mainly small and family-owned businesses. Exporters who purchase from small and family firms for export have faced serious problems from international buyers as they are not willing to visit Pakistan due to the political instability in the country. It will be useful for the government to install the essential IT infrastructure at particular locations to assist these firms to overcome such problems.

Customs Issues and Exchange Rates

A critical component of basic infrastructure in the systemic quad model is the customs handling and monetary instruments that impact on firms' operations (Rasiah, 2007, 2019). These instruments not only have a bearing on costs; they are also critical for effective coordination to meet agreed lead times. In addition, duties have been imposed indiscriminately on inputs and machinery imports, which has caused considerable fluctuations in costs. Since duties on such items are low in competing countries (including Bangladesh and Cambodia from preferential access offered by export-processing zones), it is only fair that textile and clothing firms are assured relatively low duties that are internationally comparable. Thus, whenever the Rupee appreciates, its Dutch Disease effects have raised the cost of exports to undermine export demand. While export prices fall when the Rupee depreciates, it raises the price of imported inputs, which then produces a knock-on effect on output prices.

Transport and Freight Costs

Textile firms in Punjab and Khyber Pakhtunkhwa face double freight problems as finishing material and the dyes need to be transported to Punjab from Karachi Bin Qasim port. The final textile and clothing products face again transport costs to have them sent to Karachi Bin Qasim port to be exported worldwide (Ahmed, 2008). Foreign shipping firms prefer to transfer their cargo onto big ships, which is most economic when using large containers. Consequently, small producers are disadvantaged owing to the lack of coordination between them and the shipping companies.

Unfortunately, the non-availability of deep maritime container terminals, and the lack of capacity at accessible terminals, can only be addressed if the government intervenes to support their development. Also, the available vessels are not large enough to carry large-scale quantities in containers to reduce unit costs. Consequently, the high port duties discourage cost-effective shipping lines to carry cargo from Pakistan, thereby unduly causing long lead times (Rana, 2017).

Complementary Ancillary Activities

Pakistan's textile and clothing industry has been facing serious problems of load shedding and gas shortage all over the country since 2010. Consequently, the capacity of textile production in different subsectors has fallen, though some large firms have started their personal energy supply stations, such as grids stations. Some of these firms sell the surplus power generated from their plants. Consequently, the production costs of those firms are considerably low as compared to the ones who still depend on government power supply organizations (such as the Water and Power Development Authority (WAPDA) and Karachi Electric Supply Company (KESC)).[3] Where there are large concentrations of firms, such as in Sindh, their industrial structure is more dynamic

[3] A few, such as Nishat Chunian, have begun capital-intensive but less expensive power production. Also, all large manufacturing firms have their own energy audit completed and have undertaken therapeutic procedure to safeguard power. Textile mills and engineering firms have begun sparing 15 to 20 per cent of power with no special investment only by embracing measures proposed by the energy auditor evaluators.

with firms enjoying technological upgrading since 1990. Therefore, industrial growth in Sindh has supported some level of industrial upgrading (Hamid & Khan, 2015).

The private sector usually prefers turnkey projects such as the construction of sites and assembly of machinery and equipment, which provide an effective after-sale facility with a choice for technological upgrading. Small and medium firms normally import obsolete technology or secondhand machinery with very few of them enjoying the capacity to adapt them to raise efficiency. This is generally because of a lack of support programmes to spread awareness about the latest technologies to improve practices. Consequently, while firms in Japan, China, South Korea, and Taiwan established maintenance and upgrading departments, which enabled them to design and fabricate machinery aimed at enhancing performance (Fransman, 1986; Rasiah, 1995; Rasiah, Kong, & Zhang, 2013), they are weak in Pakistan. It is pertinent that the development of such dissimilar but complementary industries is promoted in Pakistan.

Summary

Despite being its chief manufactured export, the textiles and clothing industry in Pakistan has enjoyed little industrial upgrading, though some firms have reached level seven out of nine technological intensity levels (see Chapter 5). While political instability has harmed countries heavily engaged in clothing manufacturing, such as Sri Lanka, the Philippines, Lebanon, Indonesia, Pakistan, and Myanmar, some firms in Pakistan have managed to evolve into high value-added operations by taking a more expensive path). However, despite being endowed with one of the finest raw materials in cotton and an educated diaspora living abroad, the absence of effective technology policies has left the country primarily as an exporter of cotton and low value-added textiles and clothing, while importing high value-added finished clothing from abroad (Rasiah & Nazeer, 2016).

The lack of sufficient technical and vocational training facilities has limited the capacity of the workforce to absorb best practices in the industry, which is essential to compete with exports from China, South Korea, Taiwan. Also, the industry faces considerable logistics and technological challenges owing to a weak basic infrastructure, the STI infrastructure that embed the firms, and fluctuations in duties and exchange rates that show little signs of stabilization. Consequently, it is important that the government reviews the policy framework for the textiles and clothing industry towards turning this resource-rich fibre, yarn, fabric, and clothing industry from a low and medium value-added industry to a high value-added industry.

It is pertinent that the state emphasizes industrial upgrading in the sector, (including raising incremental and radical innovations through R&D support that shall stimulate firm-level upgrading to OEM, ODM, and OBM activities (see Chapter 8). The next chapter deals with the essential arguments on raising capabilities, while the subsequent chapters offer a profound assessment of where Pakistan's textiles and clothing firms are located in the technology ladder, the importance of technology transfer and technological capabilities in increasing firm performance with organizational and management capabilities as a critical mediating variable, and finally the development of the Industrial Upgrading Index to assist governments to stimulate industrial upgrading.

3
Capabilities, Industrial Upgrading, and Firm Performance

Introduction

Having established the significance of the textiles and clothing industry in Pakistan, and the dismal state of industrial upgrading achieved despite enjoying strong natural endowments, this chapter seeks to examine the fundamental causes of a lack of industrial upgrading experience in the industry by reviewing the extant literature on technological, organizational, and management capabilities. In doing so, it breaks ground from mainstream works that have largely focused on the link between the relative price theoretic, factor endowments, and exports. Instead, while exports are important as a major stimulant, the literature dealing with the central concepts of technology transfer, and technological, organizational, and management capabilities are broached. Furthermore, the chapter focuses on the relationship among these variables, which is driven by the research objectives developed earlier in Chapter 1, and also establishes the grounds for formulating the methodological framework necessary for the analytical chapters.

The industrial policy literature can be traced to Smith (1776), Hamilton (1791), List (1856), and Young (1928). Gerschenkron (1952) then lucidly articulated the latecomer catch-up thesis using a broad-brush approach. Johnson (1982), Amsden (1989), and Wade (1990) subsequently examined the governance role played by Japan, South Korea, and Taiwan respectively in creating the conditions for catch-up by national firms. Whereas Nelson and Winter (1982) focused on institutions and institutional change as the basis for driving technological upgrading, Freeman (1995) emphasized the role of national innovation systems, especially the role of critical intermediary organizations to stimulate industrial transformation. Mazzucato (2018) addressed the mission-oriented entrepreneurial role by governments. While these works offered a policy-relevant emphasis on economic catch up, they did not provide concrete instruments to capture these developments to connect policy with firm-level industrial upgrading.

Industrial Upgrading in the Textiles and Clothing Industry. Nazia Nazeer and Rajah Rasiah, Oxford University Press.
 DOI: 10.1093/9780198961697.003.0003

Kim (1997) offered empirical evidence of how firms creatively transform transferred technologies in firms. Katz (2001) argued over the importance of macro–micro coordination to strengthen industrial policy from being harmed by macroeconomic shocks. Following emphasis by Rosenberg (1976, 1982) and Nelson and Winter (1982) on the importance of examining technologies by looking inside firms, studies by Dahlman et al. (1987), Lall (1992), and Bell and Pavitt (1995) attempted to construct typologies by taxonomies and trajectories to examine catch-up in particular industries, which was taken up later by Figueiredo (2003), Rasiah (2003), and Dutrénit (2006) who produced more detailed taxonomies of technological upgrading in particular industries. However, there have still been problems with these studies as they have not seriously connected those exercises with the promotion of catching up to the technology frontier that could strengthen industrial policy promotion. Hence, this book seeks to undertake a profound analysis, including by constructing a path required to stimulate industrial upgrading in general, and in the textiles and clothing industry in particular, by focusing on the critical variables of technology transfer and technological, and organizational and management capabilities.

The subsequent structure of the chapter is as follows: the next section deals with the relevant literature on technology transfer, while the third and fourth sections review the literature on technological, and organizational and management capabilities. The fourth section develops the theoretical framework for the empirical research undertaken in the subsequent chapters. The chapter also identifies existing gaps in the literature and provides the justification for why it adds novelty to deepening the use and promotion of technological, and organizational and management upgrading.

Technology Transfer

Although there are different opinions on how big the technology gap is between the developed and developing countries, and whether that gap is widening or narrowing, there is common agreement that a serious technological gap exists between these two sets of countries (Lall, 2000). Although it is obvious that the capacity to absorb the latest knowledge is easier if the technological gap between the leaders and learners are small (UNCTAD, 2014), as Rasiah (2009) argued, the wider the gap the greater the potential for learning and transfer. In doing so, Rasiah built on the argument advanced by Hirschman (1958, 1970) that wider gaps offer more potential for catch-up.

Also, as argued by Gerschenkron (1952) and Abramowitz (1956), the follower can quicken the catch-up process by looking at the leader, avoiding mistakes, and taking more effective steps to catch up. Chang (2003) and Reinert (2007), argued that imitation may act as an influential tool to help in designing catch-up strategies and upgrading production capabilities in developing countries, though their works hardly address the adaptive elements involved in learning and innovation (see Kim, 1997). Prahalad (2012) alluded to that by arguing that the better implementation of existing technologies can have a significant impact on recipient nations than the adoption of new technologies. Indeed, by adapting technologies efficiently, firms in the developing nations may be able to upgrade their capabilities to generate better results than their buyers and suppliers. Besides, it is costly for firms in underdeveloped locations to develop technologies by themselves as they are largely located in weak embedding ecosystems that are characterized by poor institutions, and weak access to external sources of knowledge.

Definitions, Specificities, and Composition

Industry-specific technological development that is driven by timing and location is the essential evolutionary focus of firms seeking to upgrade (Rasiah, 2011). Despite the arguments of Gerschenkron (1952), catching up has always been difficult for the developing economies as most of them continue to fall behind the technologically advanced nations. It has long been recognized that learning from adapting imported technologies is a critical source of technological catch up (Amsden, 1989, 1991; Rasiah et al., 2015). Meanwhile, Cohen and Levinthal (1990) and Lall (1992) provided evidence to argue that the adoption and diffusion of technology require well-coordinated and extensive technical efforts with the capacity to absorb. These channels enable technologically backward nations to catch up with the most advanced technologies (Amsden, 1991; Grossman & Helpman, 1994; Romer, 1994). Besides, technology transmission from abroad is arguably the key source for building innovation capabilities among latecomer economies (Amsden, 1991; Rasiah, 1995). Furthermore, as Hoekman et al. (2005) and Fu et al. (2011) have argued, foreign sources of knowledge can transform economies through inter-sectoral spillover.[1]

Knowledge absorption refers to a process through which economic agents access others knowledge through several channels (see table 3.1), which

[1] See Rasiah (1995) for an extensive account of knowledge flows from the semiconductor industry supporting innovation in the machine tools sector in Malaysia.

Table 3.1 Channels of technology transfer

Transfer mode	Strength and Weaknesses
Foreign Direct Investment	Foreign firms bring with them internationally competitive technologies that can offer learning potential for national employees and firms. However, they can also crowd out national firms, and at the same time exhaust available human capital.
International Joint Venture (IJV)	IJVs help recipient firms to protect their long-term production capabilities at low capital risks and with a competitive advantage in external or domestic markets. IJV offers the opportunity to retain domestic materials from the monopoly of overseas firms by offering recipients needed technologies, technological advice, and market and capital access.
Turnkey Projects (TP)	Supplier usually controls all technical decisions and installation of TP. TP offers limited training with narrow opportunities for learning, while raising dependency on suppliers.
Licensing Agreements	Licensor keeps control of dissemination, usage, and intellectual proprietary rights. Licensor might be inefficient in case they do not have distributor agents or representative proposing maintenance services and warranties in host countries. Licensing might provide a relative less-risk, stable income, from royalties and by means of margins and technical fees on components supplied. Licensing is one of the better strategies for firms that do not have adequate financial management resources to generate FDI abroad in numerous countries where they sold their products. Multinationals can use licensing as an internal transfer-pricing method when they license their technologies to their affiliates abroad. Nevertheless, licensing may be more appropriate for less complex technologies.
Subcontracting	Subcontracting reduces the size of work tasks thereby increasing opportunities for 'domestic competitive bidding'. Scarce resources, inadequate management capacity, and absence of work stability of local organizations tied up in subcontracting limits internal technology transfer in national firms.
Knowhow Agreement	Knowhow contracts with TNCs assist firms to support improvements to processes and products, which provide technical information required in the adoption of latest technologies.
Spin-off	Spin-offs present technology transfer from innovation opportunity towards markets. Entrepreneurs emerge as prototyping helps bring innovations to buyers.
Management Contracts and Franchising	Management contracts are the key mode of entry into foreign markets that provide production and personnel management procurement of services and goods, and access to brands. The franchise agreement is a contract involving the franchise and franchiser. The franchiser delivers rights, to utilize brand name, and trademarks, along with the technical support, merchandising, and training.

Source: Adapted from Cusumao & Elenkov (1994).

include repositories, manuals, purchases, licensing, acquisition, and hiring of personnel carrying embodied knowledge (Rasiah, 1995; Gray & Meister, 2004; Gray & Durcikova, 2006). Giuliani (2005) found that the inability to create links with international knowledge sources could lead towards unfavourable effects, such as 'technology lock-in', 'entropic death', and 'cognitive inbreeding'. Thus, while knowledge is important, sources of knowledge can be classified into external and internal. External sources of knowledge may be further divided into domestic, national, and global, subject to wherever the source is found (Crema et al., 2014). In this regard, Malmberg and Maskell (2006) emphasize the importance of organizational needs to associate with outside sources in international networks, which are important to absorb the latest knowledge and information in rapidly changing technologies that is critical for stimulating innovations.

The rapid growth and structural change recorded by the East Asian economies of Japan, South Korea, and Taiwan stemmed initially from the acquisition of knowledge through licensing and acquisitions, and the employment of human capital that had gained experiential and tacit knowledge from studying and working abroad (Johnson, 1982; Edquist & Jacobssen, 1987; Amsden, 1989; Wade, 1990; Amsden & Chu, 2003; Rasiah & Lin, 2005; Saxenian, 2006). Also, the promotion of economic development in Ireland and Singapore has relied extensively on foreign direct investment (Best, 2001). In addition, significant industrial transformation took place in several countries from inter-firm flows of knowledge embodied in personnel (Saxenian, 1994, 2006; Rasiah, 1995; Polidano, 2001; Stiglitz, 2002). Rasiah (1994, 1995), Saxenian (1994, 2006), Best (2001), and Rasiah and Lin (2005) documented the development and movement of human capital, which supported new firm creation in Penang (Malaysia), Silicon Valley and Route 128 (United States, Hsinchu (Taiwan), Incheon (South Korea), Bangalore (India), and Shenzen (China).

Furthermore, as Malik (2002), Cummings and Teng (2003), De Toni et al. (2011), and De Toni et al., (2012) have noted, technology transfer does not only involve a physical movement of components and machinery, but also the skills and knowledge required to utilize them, that is, it constitutes the movement of tangible and intangible assets, which are critical for using and operating technologies. The presence of tacit knowledge is critical to raise such a potential (Rasiah, 1995), which often provides firms with the capacity to adapt transferred technologies. Kim (1999) used the terms technological platform and platform technology by examining newly emerging semiconductor firms, asserting that platform technologies have the potential to give continuous returns to firms when the firms involved seek to produce new products. This is particularly important owing to increasing competition where 'technological platforms' provide opportunities for diversification into innovative markets. In this regard, Dibiaggio and Nasiriyar (2009) and Nasiriyar et al. (2010) provide evidence to show that such firms enjoy greater diversification into new markets that show similar technologies and wider technological pools than otherwise, which is also influenced by networking synergies that generate positive diffusion through technological complementarities.[2] Successful technology transfers are often characterized by crucial roles by transferees or suppliers, recipients, and the modes used to transfer technology (Al-Obaidi, 1993; Lall, 1992).

The modes of technology transfer have also taken different but related routes. For instance, Marshall (1920), Arrow (1962), Rosenberg (1982), Cohen and Levinthal (1990), and Rasiah (1995) called them learning by interacting, doing, using, operating, training, searching, and hiring. In this context, Mansfield (1975) provided insights on modes of technology transfer by identifying four factors influencing the mechanism of technology transfer, viz., industry-specific factors (including structure- and product-specific), region-specific factors (including cultural norms); nation-specific factors (including political factors), and firm-specific factors.

New technologies are often protected at the pre-prototype and prototype stages, making the institutional arrangements around them difficult to dislodge. Consequently, access and control over the diffusion and use of technologies are compulsory to appropriate technological benefits in foreign and domestic markets (Amsden, 1991). Besides, technology transfer is associated with numerous explicit institutional arrangements, which include joint ventures, foreign direct investment, strategic alliances, technical agreements associated with licensing, subcontracting, turnkey projects, and exporting and trade in capital goods. Although multinational corporations have become a major channel to access the latest technologies (Simonin, 2004; UNCTAD, 2014), foreign direct investment is not necessarily the major platform from where developing nations have organized successful catch-up as is the case with Japan, South Korea, and Taiwan (Johnson, 1982; Amsden, 1989; Rasiah & Wong, 2021).

The processes of appropriating gains from latest technologies through institutional and industrial exchanges established from licensing and acquisitions with foreign firms have arguably been the most important channel for national firms to have achieved technology transfer (Amsden, 1991).

[2] Synergy can be expressed as the increase in performance which resulted through effective and efficient interaction of two firms, generating opportunities that would not been available to the firms functioning separately (Seth, 1990).

However, successful learning during catch-up stages also depends heavily on local innovative efforts (Rasiah et al., 2015b), which has often required the deployment of fiscal and monetary policies to insulate national firms from external economic shocks (Rasiah & Zhang, 2024). This raises serious questions on unbridled financial liberalization that is led by markets, which would undermine the link between technology transfer and domestic technological capability building. Consequently, there have been changes in relations between trade liberalization, production, finance, and technology accumulation patterns arising from financial globalization (Chen, 2017). Carlile and Rebentisch (2003) showed evidence on why firms grapple with managing innovative technologies in the face of extraordinary changes in the financial landscape of the world (Stock & Tatikonda, 2000). When corporations are involved, changes in knowledge, innovation, and technological strategies will need the support of shareholders (Carlile & Rebentisch, 2003; Ferdows, 2006), but the managers rather than shareholders are the key players who assess new technologies and methods, absorption, and implementation in which tacit knowledge is critical (Cohen & Levinthal, 1990; Argote, 1999).

From the evolutionary perspective, tapping global sources of knowledge to facilitate technological upgrading is essentially a means through which firms operating in weaker national innovation systems (NIS) can access knowledge—both embodied and disembodied—from superior NISs (Nelson, 1993; Freeman, 1995). Even among small and medium enterprises (SMEs), Mayer and Blaas (2002) showed how technology transfer was achieved through processes of strategic linking with the NIS of technologically advanced nations. The lack of the requisite supporting science, technology, and innovation infrastructure domestically, and their inability to participate in R&D activities drove them to seek knowledge from abroad to expand exports (Morrissey & Almonacid, 2005).

Factors Stimulating Technology Transfer

Any effort to understand the factors that influence technology transfer requires the need to unbundle and look inside the black box (Rosenberg, 1982), to see if the option selected should be to reverse engineer or unpack components of technologies before crossing borders to attract technology transfer contracts through licensing over attracting FDI and joint ventures. Government policies seeking to promote such technology transfer through linkages and collaboration between domestic firms and organizations, and foreign firms and organizations must be carefully crafted. Since the latest technologies are systemic in nature, their adaptation and acquisition (which take place at various stages via certain channels—both direct and indirect) need attention (UNIDO, 2004).

Effective technology transfer also often requires interactions among humans, in-house R&D, and technology acquisition and assimilation from foreign sources (Amsden, 1991). The literature on identifying the factors, and their impact have also contributed to a better understanding of technology transfer programmes. As Attewell (1992) had noted, the lack of knowledge regarding a particular technology and the way it can be used to achieve a firm's objective is the foremost reason why some technology transfer exercises generate sub-optimal outcomes. Tanriverdi and Iacono (1999) expanded the work of Attewell (1992) to include three more important factors, viz., economic (advantages to be gained by the firm), organizational (adjustments to suit organizational processes), and behavioural (capacity to learn technology functions and its impact on work). The concept of stickiness presented by Szulanski (1996) and Venkatesh et al. (2002) highlights the difficulties of transferring knowledge and skills among individuals, firms, and entities. They proposed different constructs, including absorptive capability of recipients, casual ambiguity, problematic relations between suppliers and recipients, understanding of technology use, clients' equipments and the capacity for exchange and use of information, understanding of customers' applications and facilities, and their interactions with regulations and technology.

Knowledge transfer costs include technological and managerial expertise, marketing and R&D support for tangible contract providers, along with the intangible knowledge associated with its application (Teece, 2007), which also includes taxes imposed by host nations on cross-border royalty payments. The number of innovative technologies used by MNC subsidiaries in host nations may also be influenced by the spending power of partners (Bin, 2008).

Technological linkages between research organizations and industry play an important role to positively affect applicability and marketability of research outcomes which are produced by firms that participate in creating knowledge. Lundvall (2010) and Best (2001) emphasize the importance of user-producer relations in knowledge flows. The inter-relationships between producers and buyers often also include the potential identified by employees of firms who then relocate to start their own production to supply their previous employers (Rasiah, 1995; Best, 2001).

A major reason why technology transfer is heavily restricted is because of technical risks associated with testing and enforcement of contractual agreements, which are not only often opaque but are also difficult to operationalize (Guilfoos, 1989). Sometimes this happens because of operators' reluctance to take technical risks that is necessary to achieve effective technology transfer (Guilfoos, 1989). As argued by Sung and Gibson (2005), technology that is more demonstrable, understandable, and explicit is easier to transfer than technology that is complex and embodies considerable tacitness (see also Rasiah, 2019). The embedding environment to stimulate technology transfer has also benefitted from pro-active regulations but one that changes quickly to adapt to the needs of firms catching up. Given that a lot of these regulations vary with industry, location, and timing, it is pertinent that the institutions governing them are flexible enough to change with new information (Nelson & Winter, 1982; Guilfoos, 1989). Such knowledge transfers require that the people involved in the processes are fully aware of the needed capabilities of the latest technology and are actively open to catch the new waves of change. Effective communication arising from geographical and cultural differences is another set of problems recipients must address when seeking technology transfer (Guilfoos, 1989; Sung & Gibson, 2005).

Technology transfer projects vary from simple to complex, from short ones to those involving long gestation periods which can face uncertainties resulting in time and cost overruns. Although technology transfer evaluation models exist, reviews of their performance and successful factors have produced constestable results (e.g., Cooke-Davies, 2002; Bassioni et al., 2004; Toor & Ogunlana, 2008). Furthermore, economic development is a dynamic process in which the successful factors vary with industrial specificity, location, and time (Nelson, 2008; Audretsch et al., 2014). Consequently, the drivers of effective technology transfer in Pakistan will likely differ from those that were successfully transferred in Japan, South Korea, Taiwan, and China.

Nevertheless, there has been some consensus in the extant literature after the 1980s on the factors influencing effective technological transfer. For example, Creighton, Jolly, and Buckles (1985) identified nine factors that explain the transfer of technology, viz., firms' documentation, projects, information sharing, linkages, signals to act, senders' willingness, firms' trust in transactions, receiving and implementing ideas, and incentives. On effective transfer of university-owned technologies to corporations, McMullan and Melnyk (1988), found competencies in marketing research, recognition of useful technologies, searching informative sources, and awareness of knowledge about technology transfer, industrial design, and capabilities of business enterprise as the critical factors.

Cooper (1986) showed that visualization and support of management varies with firms' innovation culture, administration of modern product development, cross-functional teamwork, sharing of mutual interest on latest product development, profoundness of knowledge and knowhow on specific technologies and marketplace, workers' skills and capabilities, identification of goals and landmarks on product development, communication within management processes, and evaluation and re-evaluation of cutting-edge information as critical to complete the commercialization cycle. Meanwhile, when investigating commercialization within an entrepreneurial framework by considering public sector technologies, Radosevich and Smith (1997) proposed two groups as influential, namely, sources of technology and different interactions, which include markets and external firms. Al-Mabrouk and Soar (2009) developed a Delphi-type survey of Arab countries to identify the foremost challenges facing successful transfer of information technologies, and in doing so, presented 10 prime categories for effective transfer of information technologies.

While analysing causal relations among four factors that affect the performance of technology transfer offices through fuzzy cognitive maps, Ustundag et al. (2011) found two internal (R&D budget of university and human resources capacity) and two external factors (economic uncertainty and industry research demand) to influence performance outcomes (licensed income, number of patents awarded, and number of spin-offs). Using structural equation modelling to identify the determinants of technological transfer performance in Libya's petroleum industry, Mohamed et al. (2012) found state support and technological learning capability as the key factors that explain effective technology transfer performance. Jyoti et al. (2010) subsequently used an interpretive structural model (ISM) to examine Indian R&D firms' performance, and in doing so examined the 10 variables of top managements' commitment, clear R&D vision with strategies, R&D project management skills, resource availability, human resource focus and organizational culture, teamwork, constant monitoring of techno markets, market orientation and customer focus, knowledge networks, and performance of domestic R&D organizations. In doing so, they found that 'clear R&D vision and strategies, and performance of national R&D organizations were the most important variables that influenced successful technology transfer'. Meanwhile, Battistella et al. (2012) identified sources, recipients, and intermediaries as the most critical agents among six agents that explain effective technology transfer.

The Sung and Gibson (2005) study of multinationals and subsidiaries showed business and academic standards, knowledge networks and sharing, short- and long-term opinions, research aims and performance appraisal, cost, risk, and transfer process trimming as the critical factors that explain effective technology transfer. In addition, they found four key features for transfer of technology, namely, technological equivocality, communication interactivity, motivation, and distance between recipient and source.

Meanwhile, Malik and Hattasinghe (2013), found human resource as the main factor driving successful technology transfer in their study of 16 MNCs in Thailand. Leischnig et al. (2014) showed evidence of the positive influence of alliance management capabilities, organizational compatibility, and interaction levels in successful inter-firm technology transfer. The Jung et al. (2015) study of Korean public R&D showed that cooperation with developers and marketing capabilities were the foremost factors influential in technology commercialization. In this regard, Newman et al. (2015) found empirical evidence that showed productivity gains in recipient local firms through technology transfer from FDI.

Absorptive Capability

The absorptive capabilities concept (which was developed in the 1980s in the area of organizational learning and knowledge management (Levitt & March, 1988)), examined knowledge accumulated through absorption from external sources, including firms and organizations (Cassiman & Veugelers, 2002; Zahra & George, 2002). The capability of firms to absorb technologies internally is crucial for technology transfer and the development of firms (Cohen & Levinthal, 1990). The ability to absorb cutting-edge knowledge to complement firms' efforts to develop technology is important to raise firms' performance and competitiveness (Burgelman et al., 1996; Kim, 1997, 1999) Absorptive capacity is critical in technology transfer levels, including in modifying or adapting imported technologies or technologies accessed from other domestic firms and organizations (Lall, 1993). In this regard, industrial and firm-level catching-up depends on technological learning, particularly among developing nations to progress from the manufacture of basic goods to designing and development of complex investment products, including in transforming technologies in other industries (Schumpeter, 1934). Firms' absorptive capability also depends on their personnel to enjoy the investment capacity to train their employees (Cohen & Levinthal, 1990; Kim, 1999). However, the processes of evolving technological capabilities are evolutionary in nature rather than one in which complete autonomous intangible assets are relocated through simply a purchase, including through active collaboration and technological learning (Kim, 1997; Stock et al., 2001; Nelson, 2008). Therefore, the firm needs sufficient absorptive capability to identify, adapt, execute, and update modern technologies (Kim, 1997, 1999).

In this context, Rasiah (1995, 2008) investigated Hirschman's (1970) argument that national firms enjoyed high technological spillover potential from foreign firms when the technological distance between them is higher, that is, it presents larger learning and acquisition opportunities. However, as Rasiah's (1995) has argued, the measurement of such a potential should be done from the perspective of national firms as spillover synergies arise from several sources and diffuse through several agents, which is consistent with subsequent evidence on China, South Korea, and Singapore that foreign spillover that are diffused and absorbed by latecomers can drive local and national learning, adaptation, and eventually innovation into their exportable products (Amsden, 1991; Freeman, 1995; Iguchi & Cantwell 2005; Fu, 2011).

Technology Transfer Channels

Cusumao and Elenkov (1994) offered a review of the strengths and weaknesses of the main formal channels of technology transfer (see Figure 3.1). National firms become aware to actively seek to appropriate technology transfer synergies from demonstration effects from the presence of foreign firms. However, while the direct operations of FDI have benefited national firms in some countries, such as Ireland and Singapore, slow upgrading in national firms, such as Malaysia, Philippines, and Thailand suggest that other factors, including institutional governance may be critical to ensure

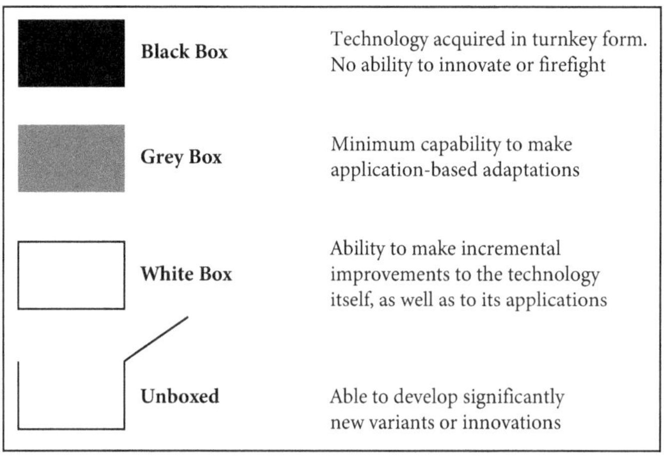

Figure 3.1 Degree of mastery of technologies

Source: Arnold and Thuriaux (1997).

significant transfers (Rasiah, 2020). Also, at host-sites where resources are limited, such as Kenya and Uganda, foreign firms may also crowd out national firms by capturing sales and talented human capital (Rasiah and Gachino, 2005). Owing to problems of transfer associated with attracting foreign firms, some host-governments have assisted their national firms to acquire strategic foreign firms to take direct control of technologies and their markets. The acquisition of Schlumberger by Samsung, and Radio Company of America by United Microelectronic Company are examples (Edquist and Jacobbsen, 1987).

In the clothing industry, Chaudhry and Faran (2016) found three firms seeking to reach the technology frontier in stitching, finishing, and washing jeans. By extending their results the authors also found the same results in the overall manufacturing sector of Pakistan implying that some large firms utilize technologies fairly close to the globe's technology frontier. However, medium and small size firms still rely largely on old technologies, though some new technologies have also spilled over into these firms. Small and micro firms rely on secondhand and obsolete technologies that are often adapted using reverse engineering activities. Rasiah and Nazeer (2016) critically investigated the level of technology in manufacturing firms, including textile and clothing firms in Pakistan using Lall's (1992) approach of measuring technological sophistication in textile and clothing firms, and found that most firms in the sector are far behind from the catch-up stage.

Recognizing the backwardness of most clothing firms in Pakistan, Nazeer (2018) proposed that Pakistan improves the quality and standardization of products through transferring technologies via foreign private investment. Similarly, having examined the existing level of operative competitiveness of textile and apparel manufacturing firms (including the weak and ineffective firm management practices and structure), Kazmi and Takala (2014) proposed technological revival in the industry through proper planning to develop human resource, which is critical to absorb foreign technologies. Alam and Natsuda (2016) concurred with such a proposal calling for urgent financial and technological investment into the industry. In fact, there is consensus that textile and clothing firms in Pakistan that lack the funds for modern technology, while facing high transactions costs, are often exposed to power crisis, high raw material prices, supply chain management issues, lack of FDI, volatile exchange rate fluctuations, weak clustering, and cumbersome customs coordination (e.g., Khan 1998; Hamid & Khan, 2015).

International joint ventures (IJVs) are another channel through which national firms seek technology transfer (Cusumao & Elenkov, 1994). However, successful technology transfer experiences often demonstrate the need for effective management from partners, and proactive engagement of national participants with strong support from host-governments (Amsden, 1989). In this regard, turnkey projects (TP) provide little technology transfer potential because such projects are generally controlled and handled by the foreign supplier.

Product and process licensing agreements have been a major channel of technology transfer that quickened technological catch-up by firms in several countries, including Japan, South Korea, and Taiwan (Edquist & Jacobssen, 1987; Johnson, 1982; Amsden, 1989; Wade, 1990; Cusumao & Elenkov, 1994). While such agreements played a key role in these countries to support technological upgrading, Lall (1987) explained the lack of strict governance by the national approval bodies on the lack of similar catch-up experiences in many developing countries.

Subcontracting has also emerged as a strong channel for technology transfer as it stimulates the insertion of national firms into global value chains, which offer opportunities to appropriate technological learning through pecuniary and technical external economies (Rasiah, 1995; Gereffi et al., 2005). According to UNIDO (2002), globalization has stimulated the differentiation of production activities, which has taken the form of global value chains (GVCs).[3] GVCs have emerged through both the transnationalization of large firms dispersed across the world with headquarters and parent firms enjoying some control, as well as independent subcontract relations between firms specializing in particular segments of the value chain (see Gereffi, 1999). Gereffi et al. (2005) explained the circumstances under which technological upgrading takes place in the value chains. Mathews (2006) adopted this approach to detail how latecomer economies have increased their technological understanding, learning, and build-up of specific capabilities to boost individual nation's industrial growth. Latecomer firms from developing economies in countries, such as Taiwan and South Korea, start as suppliers in such chains by specializing as OEMs subcontractors once they acquire and upgrade technology. Through OEM contracts the 'high-tech content' of exports generates opportunities particularly for developing economies to catch up and transform towards knowledge-rich economies

[3] At least two other related theoretical arguments have emerged since the advent of GVCs. The global production networks (GPNs) and the product fragmentation framework share the spatial spread explained by the architects of GVCs but focus their arguments on control and shifts on neo-Marxist and neoclassical approaches respectively. Whereas the former emphasizes the limited horizontal spread of accumulation across the value chain internationally (Henderson, 1989), the latter discusses how the changing relative factor endowments drives the nature of development across the chain (Ando & Fukunari, 2007). Since the book uses empirical evidence as the basis for the analysis only the spatial spread of the GVC argument is relevant here.

(Rasiah, 1995; Lall, 2000; Lall & Narula, 2004). South Korea and Taiwan effectively made the transition to participate in R&D operations to strengthen their OEM activities (Sturgeon, 2002; Rasiah & Yap, 2015). However, such an upgrading between independent producers is not an easy process, which is why few Malaysian national firms have successfully generated the requisite knowledge and market linkages to upgrade towards ODM operations and OBM in the electronics industry (Rasiah, 1995; Best, 2001; Best & Rasiah, 2003).

Whereas product and process licensing agreements are often specific to the products and processes for use by the recipient, knowhow agreements go beyond to include the opportunity to undertake further research and advancement of that knowledge for commercial purposes (Cusumao & Elenkov, 1994). In this regard, knowhow licences offer licensors, non-exclusive,[4,5] royalty-free,[6,7] and fully paid-up,[8] irrevocable,[9] and perpetual licence.[10] Sometimes knowhow agreements are made jointly with its embodied product and process technologies. The final formal major channel of technology transfer is through management and franchising contracts where licensees utilize either the technology or the brand, or both for an agreed fee, which is common in the hoteling sector.

In addition to formal channels, firms in latecomer countries have also benefitted considerably from informal channels of technology transfer, such as learning from imports of goods (including machinery), and services, manuals of goods purchased, and movement of personnel embodied with experiential and tacit knowledge from one firm or organization to another, and brain circulation (Saxenian, 1994, 2006; Rasiah, 1995; Rasiah et al., 2015). Lead electronics firms, such as Samsung and TSMC, have also benefitted considerably from such technology transfer (Rasiah & Lin, 2005; Saxenian, 2006; Tsai & Cheng, 2006).

More often than not a combination of technology transfer channels operates simultaneously with various intensities of technological diffusion among agents in knowledge networks. The types and nature of knowledge exchange, hence, however difficult they may be, are important in complementing firm-level technological capabilities (UNCTAD, 2014). Also, the contribution and importance of each channel vary with country, timing, and industry.

4 https://www.lawinsider.com/clause/a-non
5 https://www.lawinsider.com/clause/exclusive
6 https://www.lawinsider.com/clause/royalty
7 https://www.lawinsider.com/dictionary/free
8 https://www.lawinsider.com/clause/fully-paid
9 https://www.lawinsider.com/clause/irrevocable
10 https://www.lawinsider.com/clause/perpetual-license

Whereas FDI has been an important source of technology transfer in China, Ireland, Singapore, and Malaysia, licensing and the acquisition of MNC subsidiaries have been the most important source of technology transfer in South Korea, Taiwan, China and Japan (Amsden, 1989; Rasiah, 1995, 2003).

However, despite the voluminous research on international technology transfer reviewed in this section, we could not produce a set of coherent and cogent conclusions on technology transfer that can systematically explain firm performance (see Reddy & Zhao, 1990). In addition, Amsden and Tschang (2003) make a strong case to argue that R&D has been examined in a dodgy way by many scholars without proper differentiation between radical R&D activities and incremental activities. Therefore, the concepts of technology transfer, variables and measures in technology transfer studies are expected to differ between one study to another. Nevertheless, the review in this section offers a rich understanding of the conceptual differences, complexities, composition, and contradictions associated with the concept of technology transfer. All in all, it is clear that technology transfer plays an important role in enhancing recipient firms' overall performance. A major constraint inhibiting technology transfer is the existence of barriers, which vary across nations, industries, and firms (Kumar et al., 2015).

Technological Capabilities

While technology transfer is a major source of technology capability development, the latter also requires learning and accumulation domestically, especially among national firms. Hence, in contrast to the claims that South Korea and Taiwan have developed through importing foreign technology and focusing on capital accumulation, especially human capital) (Amsden, 1989), national firms in these countries have adapted foreign technology but with a strong emphasis on in-house capability development through learning and R&D (Kim, 1997; Rasiah & Lin, 2005). This section examines the critical arguments on technological capabilities.

Origin, Role, and Significance

Veblen (1915), Gerschenkron (1952), and Abramowitz (1956) presented technological catch-up accounts using a macro broad-brush approach by drawing on Marx (1867) and Schumpeter's (1942) view on capitalist accumulation and integration. Rosenberg (1976, 1982) provided arguably the earliest articulation of theory for studying technological capabilities with subsequent translation of it empirically by others to capture and explain the drivers of technological upgrading.[11] Subsequent micro-level studies dealt mostly with firms to investigate technological capabilities (Lall, 1992; Bell & Pavitt, 1995). Technological capabilities refer to a combination of both explicit and tacit capabilities, with the latter a function of competencies embodied in humans, machinery and equipment, production organization, inventory control systems, and products that are difficult to observe and estimate (Teece, 2007). Technological capabilities can also be viewed from the perspective of tangible and intangible resources (Penrose, 1959). Hence, this book refers to technological capabilities as knowledge and skills firms require to acquire, utilize, adapt, and develop to generate innovations while developing technologies through both inserting in internal and external networks (Lall, 1992).

Lall (1987, 1992) made an important contribution to the development of technological taxonomies by trajectories to trace learning and innovation sources, arranging these processes with their role in the development of technological capabilities. Consequently, several studies began to look inside the 'black box' to examine firms from the non-innovating stage, without, for instance, understanding deeply the telephone or computer equipment they utilize each day in their operations. Only in the subsequent stages do firms evolve functional capabilities to move from technology-using to technology-creating capabilities in production. The shift from mere production capabilities to innovation capabilities creates the momentum for conscious firm-level strategies to upgrade technological capabilities (Dahlman et al., 1987; Lall, 1992). Technological capabilities from production-based stages to innovation driven and within that from adaptive incremental innovations to radical innovations that is driven by R&D calls for the use of taxonomies and trajectories, which allows the measurement of industry-specific embodied technological capabilities (Rasiah, 2009).

Important firm-specific technological capability assets include firms' skills in production, and marketing, services, R&D, and engineering (Teece, 2007). However, the most extensively researched technological variables are drawn from firms' selection of technological capabilities that are crucial for their successful operations and upgrading through taxonomy and trajectories (Rasiah, 2009). Pavitt (1984) had outlined from his empirical observations a taxonomy by sectoral patterns of innovation, arguing that it can be within large firms in some industries (electronics and chemicals), within a symbiosis of small and large firms (metal and machinery industry), or suppliers in

[11] Rosenberg (1982) took the first serious step to unbundle the black box of technology to examine its critical components, and the relationships those components have with other variables.

other industries (e.g., textiles), though these observations have been contested by others who researched subsequent transitions in these industries.[12] In this regard, Lall (1992) had illustrated three technological capability components: (a) physical capital, (b) human capital, and (c) technological effort. Physical capital is characterized as a 'basic' capability, based on the assumption that no industry can exist without a certain mass of productive infrastructure (e.g., equipment, railroads, and motorway networks).

In addition to education, human capital is developed through training, as well as learning-by-doing, which increases the capacity to effectively exploit the potential embodied in physical assets (Lucas, 1988). Lall (1987) also established a framework to differentiate between functions and levels of capabilities in two phases. He emphasized the significance of differentiating capabilities within certain technological functions, such as process and product engineering, and execution of projects (see Table 3.2). Ultimately, without steady national technological efforts (with the role of productive enterprises in improving technologies), skilled labour and material infrastructures may be wrongly exploited (see also Lall, 1992).

Technological capability building is indeed the key towards the successful accumulation and use of technologies, along with the ability to adapt, develop, as well as produce firm-level technologies (Lall, 1987, 1992; Bell & Pavitt, 1995; Westphal et al., 1999). In accordance with these considerations, Table 3.3 shows the functions of 'project preparation' level, which consist of a

Table 3.2 Technological capabilities in manufacturing

Project preparation	Process engineering	Product engineering
Identification of suitable project	Debugging new plant	Assimilation of product design
Feasibility studies	Balancing facilities to remove bottlenecks	Adaptation of product to local market
Specification of scale of production	Equipment improvement	Improvement in product design
Negotiation for technology transfer	Process improvement	New product introduction by own development
Site preparation	Formal development of new processes	Basic research

Source: Adapted from Lall (1987).

[12] For example, Rasiah (2009) argued that the semiconductor industry has evolved to become largely fabless as the Taiwanese firms, such as United Microelectronics Company and Taiwan Semiconductor Manufacturing Company) have begun specializing on wafer fabrication since the 1980s. Consequently, the innovation structures have changed.

series of phases within specific projects, that leads to their classification into various functions by diversity and complexity of capability levels. Lall (1992) had sketched these capabilities by focusing on functional classifications as key columns in his framework, transforming them into six divisions, and in doing so, arguing that capability 'levels' are of foremost importance that are differentiated by rows that diagonally cut into each other by functions. All rows are organized by intensity of complexity, moving from simple and basic through intermediate to advanced). These classifications remain connected with activities (such as duplicative and creative innovations demonstrating a shift from lower to higher intensity of innovation capability levels (Haymi & Ruttan, 1971)). Finally, the levels within the industry are differentiated by correlating the functions by specific stages. Out of the two functions and six categories Lall (1992) examined, three are noted in Table 3.3.

Bell and Pavitt (1995) refined the basic production capability dimension, including incorporating slightly with modifications by re-arranging some capability functions among users who are owner-operators, for taking decisions and holding control over important aspects of investment projects. However, their framework retained the differences in investment

Table 3.3 Matrix of technological capabilities

Degrees of Complexity	Simple	Investment Projection Preparation	Production Process Engineering	R&D Product Engineering
Basic	Routine	Pre feasibility and feasibility studies, Site selection, Scheduling of investment, Search for technology source.	Debugging, Balancing, Quality Control Preventive maintenance, Assimilation of process technology, Equipment Stretching	Assimilation of product design, Minor adaptation to market needs, Product Quality improvement
Intermediate	Adaptive Duplicative (Search Based)	Negotiation of contracts through bargaining, Information systems	Process adaptation and cost saving, Licensing new technology	Licensing and assimilating new imported product technology
Advanced		Innovative but risky	In-house process innovation, Basic research	In-house product Innovation, Basic research

Source: Adapted and summarized from Lall (1992).

and production stages within the project cycle. Owing to reasons explained earlier, investment capabilities were dropped altogether from the technological capabilities' typology in this book. Also, excluded from Bell and Pavitt (1995) are the product-centred category within production, and linkages and capital goods supply in supporting activities.

Bell (2006) subsequently advanced a framework for analysing technological levels by attempting to differentiate operating (including routine) and innovative capabilities from investment capability with the latter as a critical variable for executing the former two. However, using firm-level knowledge through internships over six months each, undertaken at the firms, Monolithic Memories Incorporated in 1986 and Advanced Micro Devices in 1990, Rasiah (1995, 2009) argued that such a framework did not realistically capture developments on the factory floor of modern firms. Unlike in small old-fashioned firms entrenched in bazaar cultures, consistent with Schumpeter's (1934) argument on the early entrepreneurs, McClelland (1961) observed that entrepreneurs start innovating as they move from routine operations to incremental changes in their operations. In other words, the element of incremental innovations is inherently entrepreneurial, and hence, should not be viewed as a second phase stage within the metamorphosis of firms, though as argued again by Schumpeter (1939, 1942), R&D capabilities must be differentiated from simpler innovation activities to frontier innovation activities (see also Amsden & Tschang, 2003). It is for these reasons, Schumpeter (1942) glorified the large firm as it enjoyed the capital mass to support participation in R&D activities. Similarly, Rasiah (2009, 2019) also dismissed the need to classify investment capabilities as a component of technological capability, by arguing that small and less financially endowed firms that use offensive strategies built around rapid technology accumulation and strong integration in knowledge networks, have often leapfrogged capital-rich incumbents in particular industries.

Hamid and Khan (2015) adapted the industrial sophistication index that was pioneered by Lall and Narula (2004) to explore Pakistan's industrial structure by considering the Pakistan Standard Industrial Classifications from the Census of Manufacturing Industries. Their research identified several reasons for the weak industrial performance of Pakistan: viz., (a) a drop in industrial sophistication over time; (b) no positive movement in levels of sophistication; (c) specialization largely in level 1 technological sophistication activities constituting almost 50 per cent of the total value-addition of country's manufacturing industries. However, they do not provide convincing evidence about the factors that contribute towards technological upgrading in the industry. Indeed, there are serious shortcomings that act as barriers to catch up in the textiles and clothing industry in

Pakistan, which is why this book sets about to address the problems confronting the industry and the solutions essential to stimulate upgrading in the industry.

Taxonomies and Trajectories

As mentioned earlier in this section, Rosenberg (1976, 1982) had taken on from Marx (1954) and Schumpeter (1934, 1942) to examine deeper the categories, processes, and phases, of technological change from looking inside the black box. Rosenberg (1982) argued that the building of technological capabilities is the route to accumulate technology related knowledge critical for stimulating productive operations, including innovations. In this regard, Desai (1984) differentiated between four kinds of capabilities, viz., capabilities in purchasing technologies, plant function or operations, replica, development, and innovation. Biggs et al. (1988) argued that access to knowledge and learning mechanisms is necessary to obtain knowledge about the latest production and investment capabilities. In this regard, Lee et al. (2007) presented a model using three levels of technology development, viz., (a) low level to assimilate and enhance mature technologies, (b) intermediate level to assimilate and enhance latest technologies, and (c) high level to generate upcoming new technologies. Baranson and Roark (1985) separated operational, duplicative, and innovative capabilities. Katz (2001) identified factors affecting capabilities of developing nations at the national level to develop their technological capabilities through technology transfer, viz., to support capabilities that are external to firms as these factors consist of resources and endowments from abroad that are affected by public policies over time. In addition to affecting firm-level capabilities, such channels of transfer are also conditioned by recipient firms size, specialization, type of production organization, product standardization level, type of ownership, employee training methods, and participation in in-house research and development.

Extending further the concept of technological capabilities, Bell (1987) differentiated technological flows into Flow A, Flow B, and Flow C groups. Flow A contains capital goods, that is supported by managerial and technological support; Flow B contains skills and knowhow associated with functions and maintenance of recently assembled or installed production technologies; and Flow C contains knowledge and capabilities to implement technical change. The framework of Bell 'shows that Flow A progresses to enhance production capabilities, while Flow B contributes to technological capability from the basic, and then to routine levels, while Flow C facilitates firms to develop dynamic technical and organizational changes'. Wei (1995) incorporated Bell's (1987) technological knowledge flow with the functional categories introduced by Lall (1992). However, he underlined that there is no evidence that all technology flows generate technological capabilities, and that to enhance domestic capabilities, linkages with domestic suppliers coupled with other groups that exist in the same economy are important, which is why Rasiah (2004a) reconfigured these classifications as innovations in firms that largely vary in intensity and scale between what has been differentiated by routine and production functions, and dynamic technical (including R&D operations) and organizational functions once they are internalized in industrial firms.[13]

While estimating capabilities this methodology was adapted and refined by Figueiredo (2003) in the steel industry of Brazil, Dutrinet (2006) in a large Mexican industrial group, and Rasiah (2004a) in the electronics industry of Malaysia and Thailand to relate firm-level technological capabilities (micro) with the institutional and systemic capabilities (macro). Therefore, the contributions of Rosenberg (1982), Lall (1992), and Rasiah (1995, 2003), Figueiredo (2003), and Dutrinet (2006), are critical to investigate the development of technological capabilities in firms among the emerging nations. While neoclassical economists focus on technical change and its effects on economic growth using the production function model, these set of studies offer the opportunity to look inside the black box of technology to examine its actual link with industrial upgrading and economic performance.

Meanwhile, Kim (2000) and Lall (1992) asserted that industrial structural change from low to high value-added activities requires a rapid build-up of technological capabilities to support process and product innovations. During the start-up phase, new latecomer entrants generally lack basic technological capability (Figueiredo, 2003). It is only during the growth phase latecomer firms acquire and assimilate knowledge to develop their technological capabilities (Torres & Jasso, 2017). Bell and Pavitt (1995) note that these embodied capabilities relate to their resources, which are desirable to create and manage technological change. Figueiredo (2003) examined the impact of learning processes on technological capability building in firms that deploy firm-level strategies as rigorous screening of technological capabilities allows firms to understand and master technologies. In this context, Arnold and Thuriax (1997) classified four levels or hierarchies of technological capabilities, which in its simplest form is presented in Figure 3.1.

[13] This interpretation is also consistent with Schumpeter's (1934, 1942) articulation of incremental innnovations against radical innovations. Indeed, Schumpeter (1934, 1942) made the deductions by drawing on his immense understanding of firms.

What is clear from the discussion above is that technological catch-up needs not only nation-wide development of supporting capabilities (such as education and skills), but also firm-level capabilities that relate to knowhow, operations, management, and innovation. As discussed by Wei (1995), Kim (1997, 1999), and Lall (1992, 2002), a major motive of technology transfer is to upgrade technological capabilities of firms in recipient countries; therefore, a number of researchers have assessed the relationship between technology transfer and technological capabilities (e.g., Lall, 1993). Further work on this link and into the transformation from duplicative imitation to creative innovation can be viewed from Kim (1997) and Lall (2002).

Successful latecomer nations (such as Japan, Taiwan, and South Korea) stand out due to the interaction between country-level supply of human capital and company-specific technological capabilities to participate in OEM, and ODM activities in Taiwan,[14] and OEM to OBM in South Korea (Kim, 1997; Mathews, 2006). In this regard, Rasiah (2004a) showed strong association between export success and technological capabilities among the East Asian countries. The dynamic participation of the state towards industrial catch-up and export performance could be traced to the work of Johnson (1982), Amsden (1989), and Wade (1990). However, these studies fail to provide a robust empirical link between technological capability building, innovation, and firm performance. Consequently, the industrialized countries of Eastern and Central Europe endowed with high supply of human capital but without significant user-producer driven demand-orientation have lacked firm-level industrial upgrading to stimulate rapid economic growth.

Following Lall's (1992) framework, Figueiredo (2003) used firm-specific technological capabilities to trace learning outcomes. Rasiah (2004a, 2009) expanded the importance of trajectories and taxonomies by considering embodied technologies through related proxies to compare and contrast technological capabilities between firms. In doing so, he dropped investment capabilities for reasons explained earlier in the chapter to focus on technological capabilities embodied in human capital (which also carries competencies), and process and product technologies. Whereas Figueiredo (2003) used the taxonomies developed to trace firms' movement in the catching-up process, Rasiah's (2004a, 2007) works went further to test the impact of technological capabilities on firm performance. Consequently,

[14] Although some Taiwanese firms are in ODM and OBM activities, (such as Acer), most of them are engaged in OEM activities (Rasiah & Wong, 2021).

Rasiah's (2004a, 2007) taxonomy is used but one that is upgraded to absorb Figueiredo's (2013) extensions to examine technological capabilities in the textiles and clothing firms in Pakistan. This framework also views movement in a cumulative way so that some capabilities in the earlier phases remain even when firms move up the three respective trajectories of human resource, process, and product technologies.

Consistent with Schumpeter's (1942) call for shielding firms to stimulate radical innovations, Rasiah's (2007) approach takes account of the need to incentivize firms to upgrade from low to high level of technological capabilities.[15] As grants are recognized as a *sine qua non* for stimulating firm's participation from technological capability levels 5 and 6 activities, a focus on raising knowledge intensities is critical to achieve industrial upgrading as technological capability levels have a positive correlation with firm performance in the textile and garments, food and beverages, electronics, and metal engineering firms in Kenya, Malaysia, Indonesia, Philippines, and Thailand (Rasiah (2004a). While the initial classification of technological levels by functions in this book began with the taxonomies and trajectories shown in Table 3.4, the eventual classification adopted in the book absorbs some features from Figueiredo's (2013) classification before advancing it further to nine levels through interviews with the technical managers of TAL (Hong Kong), Toray (Japan), Everest Textiles (Taiwan), Sapphire Textiles (Pakistan), and Nishat Chunian (Pakistan), and the 50 experts used to develop the industrial upgrading index (see Chapters 4, 5, and 6).

Organizational and Management Capabilities

Organizational and management capabilities share the critical dimensions of both links firms have with other firms and intermediary organizations as well as the internal in-house dynamics of organizational and management capabilities. Consequently, the extant literature of both the inter-firm and firms' embedding linkages with organizational (including the internal firm-level capabilities) are examined.

[15] Schumpeter (1939, 1942) had glorified the large firm because during his time only large firms enjoyed the capital endowments to finance R&D to stimulate radical innovations, which he had argued as essential to initiate new business cycles. Nevertheless, Rasiah (2019) argued that subsequent developments (which includes massive government support to subsidize higher levels of technological upgrading, including the creation of knowledge networks constituting firms' connections with universities, science and technology parks, incubators, venture capitalists, standards organizations, and other critical intermediary organizations) have stimulated small firms' participation in R&D activities.

Table 3.4 Taxonomy by trajectory of technological capabilities in manufacturing

Knowledge depth	HR	Process	Product
Simple activities (1)	On the job and in-house training	Dated machinery with simple inventory control	Assembly or processing of component, CKD, and CBU using foreign technology
Minor improvements (2)	In-house training and performance rewards	Advanced machinery layouts and problem solving	Precision engineering
Major improvements (3)	Extensive focus on training and retraining; staff with training responsibility	Cutting edge inventory control techniques, SPC, TQM, TPM	Cutting edge quality control system (QCC) and equipment manufacturing (OEM) capability
Engineering (4)	Hiring engineers for adaptation activates; separate training department	Process adaptation: layouts, equipment and techniques	Product adaptation
Early R&D (5)	Hiring engineers for product development activities; Separate specialized training activities	Process development layouts, machinery and equipment, materials and processes	Product development capability. Some firms take on original design manufacturing (ODM) capability
Mature (6)	Hiring specialized R&D scientists and engineers wholly engaged wholly engaged in new product research	Process R&D to dives new layouts, machinery and equipment prototypes, materials and processes	New product development capability, with some taking on original brand manufacturing (OBM) capability

Source: Adapted from Lall (1992) and Rasiah (1994 2007).

Linkage Synergies

Institutions and institutional change are essential drivers of learning and innovation (Nelson & Winter, 1982). The processes of innovation do not end at the point of its creation as linkages with external support organizations are imperative in the diffusion and spread of stocks of knowledge, which not only turn out as building blocks for interactive learning that is critical for technological capability building but are also necessary to synergize the continuous creative snowballing of knowledge. Such knowledge flows can emerge through buyer-supplier firms, or movement of human capital endowed with tacit and experiential knowledge, and technical knowhow accessed through manuals and licences, including with multinationals (Rasiah, 1995), and intermediary organizations that support firms' operations, including incubators for scaling up prototypes.

While resources enjoyed by individual firms provide value for potential customers, as well as for networking (Vanhaverbeke & Peeters, 2005), latecomer firms that insert into GVCs can also appropriate economic synergies if they augment stages with more competitive output/service or create new stages, which can assist them to ramp up firm level capabilities for overall national industrial development by establishing strong buyer-supplier links with domestic participants (Mathews, 2006). OEMs create links with other customers; learn particular organizational and management skills to access markets, which offer leveraging advantages (Prahalad & Hamel, 1990). Hence, inter-firm organizational linkages offer a vital knowledge source for latecomer OEMs. Consequently, it is important for latecomer OEMs to cultivate firm-level absorptive capabilities to learn and upgrade through collaboration with experienced OEMs and Original Brand Manufacturers (OBMs) (Cohen & Levinthal, 1990).

In addition, Powell (1998) and Tsai (2001) argue that inter-organizational linkages stimulate learning and innovation from firms located ahead in the technology ladder. In this regard, Rothaermel and Deeds (2004) show evidence of how inter-firm strategic alliances strengthens new process and product development. Cricelli and Grimaldi (2010) used an evaluation procedure to show that complex knowledge flows occur among firms, and in doing so, identified different kinds of knowledge-driven inter-organizational alliances based on strategic, cognitive, and structural features for enhancing knowledge management. Open innovation is increasingly viewed as a springboard for quickening innovations, especially since Chesbrough (2003) proposed that essential resources must not be confined to firms' boundaries (see also Rasiah, 2019). Additionally, inter-organizational linkages are affected by reliability, confidentiality, copyright, tacitness, and trust issues among members (Carrillo et al., 2004). Indeed, an environment built around loyalty and trust is essential to stimulate knowledge sharing among networked firms and organizations (see also Rasiah, 2019).

University–Industry–Government Interactions

In a knowledge-based economy, universities function as important nodes of latest knowledge important for the development of new processes and products (Etzkowitz & Leydesdorff, 2000; Best, 2001; Rasiah, 2019). In this context, government policy and agencies act as catalysts to strengthen connectivity and coordination between universities and firms, including providing scarce R&D funds (Page & Tarp, 2017). While competition has driven technological change that require interactions with critical external knowledge producers, (including universities), it is the responses from firms to not only focus on in-house R&D but also to harness knowledge from the knowledge networks they are connected with to accumulate the capabilities to compete (Bettis & Hitt, 1995). In this regard, universities and public research institutes have emerged as critical pillars of the national innovation system (NIS) to support firm-level upgrading (Nelson, 1993; Freeman, 1995; Lundvall, 2010).

As argued earlier, while size was historically a key factor as it provided the scale and the financial capacity for firms to participate in R&D, scale is now increasingly substituted by R&D collaboration in which firms connect with external resources when they are integrated into knowledge networks (Rasiah, 2019). Also, although large firms are able to attract financial partners to support university–industry collaboration compared to small firms to complement their in-house resources (Tether, 2002), small firms are increasingly able to connect with knowledge networks, which include universities and science parks (including incubators), though often only when governments play a pro-active role in the initial stages by tying incentives and grants to such university–industry linkages and strong sticks are used to discourage the dissipation of rents.[16] Therefore, industry–government–university knowledge networks that are driven by collaborative links, which in Sweden originally emerged as the triple helix but have since evolved into the quadruple helix following the inclusion of civil society as the fourth partner, have increasingly become important to ensure that the R&D funds are society-focused. While firms increase technological capability levels as they move up the technology ladder, such a progression also often involves working with successful academic and research organizations. In addition, governments in such strong national innovation systems complement the research activities at universities and public labs with venture capitalists that actively allocate R&D funds to support entrepreneurs (Etzkowitz, 2003).[17] In doing so, the Swedish, Taiwanese, Singaporean, and United States' governments have also enabled the participation of small firms in such knowledge networks, especially the new start-ups from universities (Best, 2018; Rasiah, 2019, 2020).

[16] See Rasiah and Lin (2005) on government-industry matching grants to stimulate participation in R&D activity in Taiwan.

[17] See Rasiah (2020) for similar roles played by government in Malaysia and Singapore.

Firm-level Organizational and Management Capabilities

Amsden (1989, 1991) had successfully argued that managerial characteristics focused on interactive learning are essential in driving latecomer industrialization as they support firms' efforts to adopt and adapt technologies from developed nations. In doing so, Amsden provided empirical evidence to support Chandler's (1977) argument that the managerial revolution has assisted positive organizational change through innovation in support of industrial development and performance, including the evolution from functional firms to multi-divisional firms. Furthermore, a pool of engineers and technicians endowed with technical knowledge, including both R&D and non-R&D personnel, are critical towards stimulating designing and development of new products and processes. Consequently, Rasiah (2004a) differentiated capabilities by trajectory and taxonomies into human resource, process technology, and product technology capabilities as firms move up from technology using to innovation-driven activities that require adapting, assimilating, and generating knowledge at host-sites as firms evolve to participate in the creation of new stocks of knowledge. In doing so, Rasiah (2007, 2019) introduced the systemic quad to relate firm-level technological capabilities with the embedding systemic pillars to explain how firms and the embedding ecosystem as a whole integrate in dynamic networks to move up the technology ladder to participate in high value-added economic activities (see also Mytelka, 2001; Szulanski, Cappetta, & Jensen, 2004; Van de Ven & Johnson, 2006; Felin & Hesterly, 2007).

There are also extensive works that discuss how managers execute their managerial tasks adequately by utilizing firm-specific knowledge, which is path-dependent, as well as acquired from learning by doing, acquisition of technology from other firms and intermediary organizations, and through in-house R&D (Reed & DeFillippi, 1990; Barney, 1991). In this regard, Teece (2007) found technological and managerial knowledge as crucial in enhancing the competitive performance of firms.

Firm-level management capabilities typically requires well-executed communication and implementation strategies, maintenance of beneficial relations with other firms, organizations, and shareholders, effective allocation of firms' resources, deployment of innovation and entrepreneurial strategies, and inculcation of strong organizational culture, learning characteristics, and the clever appropriation of incentives (Weick, 1979). Although managerial capabilities are embedded in network settings rather than evolved truncatedly within individuals and firms, the development of a comprehensive series of corresponding skills in management teams (such as human and technical skills) requires appropriating competitive advantage in particular markets (Barney, 1991). The accumulation of such management capabilities is a *sine quo non* for achieving, accelerating, and maintaining firm-based competitive advantage.

According to evolutionary theory, knowledge resources in firms are embodied among firms' capabilities, which then impact on their performance (Penrose, 1959; Nelson & Winter, 1982; Nonaka & von Krogh, 2009). Kim (1997) presented an outline to examine the processes of building capabilities in Korean firms, emphasizing strongly the progressive processes of creating knowledge, arguing that firms not only follow thoughtful and constant technology review strategies, but also implement 'management of dynamic learning' or knowledge management as they move from imitative duplication to creative innovation where the intensity of incremental engineering increases over time. Firms can achieve high performance when they acquire distinctive knowledge that is compatible with their knowledge base to raise value-added (Ranft & Lord, 2002). In light of the critical importance of knowledge management, marketing management, and strategic planning they are examined separately among the management capabilities in this book.

Arrow (1962) had noted that learning is the outcome of experience, which can happen only by countless efforts to resolve a problem. Similarly, technical change is often effected by personnel with experience, including production activities, which require problem solving. The level of knowledge employees possess in firms is deemed as a critical strategic factor for firms' survival and expansion in a complex, changing, and competitive environment.

In addition to learning by doing, firms spread adaptability and flexibility through the professional development of their workers (Boxall & Purcell, 2011). Besides, significant efforts to participate in innovation learning often have taken place through management-led learning via empowering employees both horizontally and vertically (Rasiah, 1995; Ellinger et al., 2003). In the evolving framework of firm-level learning, managers increasingly coach, encourage, and facilitate development and training of their workers (Feldman, 2001; Hotek, 2002; Lang & Wittig-Berman, 2000; MacNeil, 2001). Managers also focus on their employees' specialized development to raise their performance (Thornhill & Saunders, 1998; Beattie, 2006). In doing so, successful managers see that the goals of both firms and their employees are congruent to ensure that the development of the latter is in sync with the former.

Hussain et al. (2009) studied textile supply chain management by focusing on minimizing lead times and costs, deploying in the process a strengths, weaknesses, opportunities, and threats (SWOT) analysis of Pakistan's textiles value chain with intersectoral linkages. Their findings indicate that cotton ginning and the manufacture of complementary machines are the weakest components of the textiles cluster in Pakistan. Man-made fibre production, clothing, chemical dye manufacturing, and ICT were identified by them as the next weakest components of the textile industry in Pakistan. Cotton farming, dyeing, weaving, and finishing were classified as strong components, while knitting, printing, and spinning were classified as the strongest components. In addition, they also found that Pakistan's freight charges to export destinations are higher than competing countries (such as Bangladesh, Cambodia, Malaysia, and Thailand), because of its distant geographical location from waterways.

In addition, Wadho and Chaudhry (2016) extensively addressed innovation activities in the textiles and clothing firms of Pakistan, including innovation behaviour, type, degree, and resources deployed in innovation, knowledge spillovers, factors obstructing technological innovation, and return on innovation investment over a period of three years (2013–2015). They concluded that firms were focused on growth and product outcomes when participating in innovative activities, while demonstrating that a lack of funds and the high cost of innovation were crucial factors obstructing innovation in firms. Nevertheless, they also found that the economic significance of innovation appears high, which was estimated through the share of innovative new products introduced.

Knowledge Management

Knowledge is a distinctive asset of firms, which serves as a fundamental resource to drive competiveness (Grant, 1996; Gold et al., 2001). Organizations often fail because of the poor management of knowledge accumulation—both through in-house development and acquisition from external sources. Effective organizational and management practices play a major role in successful technology transfer processes among the developing nations (Goh, 2002). Manufacturing firms with a clear technology transfer agenda have among their business strategies not only plans to hire personnel endowed with the relevant tacit knowledge but also always strengthen the related mechanisms to accumulate and deepen their grasp of the knowledge essential for their self-expansion. In addition, sharing knowledge has an absolute direct relationship with effective transfer of technologies since it serves as a mediator to drive the stronger spread and appropriation of knowledge in firms, viz., embodied in humans, processes, products, organizations, and in the environment. Hence, knowledge management generates the opportunities to enhance the technology transfer related factors, firm performance, and, eventually, to achieve competitive advantage.

Successful knowledge management roles at the firm-level were examined by Gold et al. (2001) using a knowledge infrastructure framework consisting of technologies, culture, structure, knowledge processes of acquisition, adaptation, utilization, and protection, which are crucial organizational capabilities and practices for successful knowledge management. Cole-Gomolski (1999) confirmed that effective knowledge management can raise firm performance by improving firm-level competitiveness and productivity to help dispense information within firms that is targeted at strengthening decision-making processes and procedures, and to raise awareness of competitors' strategies.

Kim (1997) stressed the importance of organizational factors, which are important for the accumulation and utilization of knowledge. A key pillar of his argument is the need not only to follow a technology strategy (which progressively changes firm-level technical capabilities from imitation to innovation), but also to focus on knowledge management. The forces working behind these processes may stem from external movers. Indeed, incumbent firms may seek to abandon their roles owing to unanticipated crises or owing to their inability to compete against new offensive firms that are seeking to leapfrog. Consequently, such falling firms offer opportunities for newly emerging firms to acquire them at low prices (Utterback & Kim, 1985; Tushman & Anderson, 1986). In the semiconductor industry, such buyouts during crises took place in the late 1970s and mid-1980s (Edquist & Jacobsson, 1987), which saw the launching of Samsung Semiconductor, United Microelectronics Company, and Taiwan Semiconductor Manufacturing Corporation as these firms acquired or merged with foreign firms to move up the value chain (Rasiah & Lin, 2005).

Davenport et al. (1998) considered knowledge management as a way to manage firms' knowledge by means of a systematic process in order to gain, organize, maintain, share, use, and spread both explicit and implicit knowledge embodied in workers and management to improve firm performance. In this context, Gold et al. (2001) includes three interconnected processes in knowledge management, viz., (1) knowledge acquisition, (2) knowledge conversion, and (3) knowledge application. Consequently, knowledge management capabilities refer to knowledge management methods and procedures in firms that are used to evolve knowledge in firms (Gold et al., 2001).

Organizational learning is a prerequisite for the successful progression towards higher capabilities within firms (Penrose, 1959; Eishenhardt & Martin, 2000). All organizations are capable of acquiring knowledge. Internal factors in firms influence the build-up of in-house capabilities to utilize knowledge and to support changes in routines that stimulate performance (Levitt & March 1988).

March (1991) documented two primary strategies through which organizations learn, viz., (1) exploitation and (2) exploration. Exploitation focuses on searching for new means of enhancing existing capabilities, which is deployed to increase firm productivity (Jones, 2001). Exploration involves a deep search for new knowledge to improve firms' fundamental competencies (Penrose, 1959; Teece, 2007).

Mowery et al. (1996) constructed a framework for organizations' vicarious learning, arguing that that organizations involved in effective R&D activities stand at a superior place towards learning through acquiring foreign sources of knowledge as compared to organizations that are less involved in R&D activity. Meanwhile, most innovations arise from adapting ideas, which become the reference point for vicarious learning before firms create new ideas (see Kim, 1997). Such creative learning often happens when organizations acquire latest vicarious knowledge by means of observation and using effective imitation and adaptation approaches from different organizations, which has been a major driver of firms in Taiwan and South Korea (Levitt & March, 1988; Kim 1997; Rasiah, 2004a).

Marketing Capabilities

Marketing capability is a powerful driver of a company's competitive advantage, especially in the textiles and clothing value chain (Song et al., 2005). Firms' marketing capabilities refer to the knowledge and skills applied in the development of latest, as well as improved methods of managing businesses, which have been viewed as the utilization of knowledge management, resources, and organizational skills to add value in goods and services to meet competitiveness and receptiveness towards market demands and needs (Day, 2011). The knowledge-based economy includes intangible assets that are knowledge assets, and other factors of production comprising tangible assets, such as land, capital, and workforce. Intangible assets, including through marketing, are considered to play an important role in achieving competitive advantage (Turovets, 2021).

Market experience (especially the embodied knowledge), and processes through which companies develop their knowledge are crucial to understand firm performance internationally (Zahra, 2005).[18] Marketing capabilities support firms' decisions to select entry methods and approaches, such as resource management in international markets (Banerjee & Soberman, 2013). In this regard, market knowledge, experience, and processes through which firms develop knowledge are essential to understand international competitiveness (Zahra, 2005). Marketing capability also constitutes firms' competencies in skills and market knowledge and information required for the successful promotion of latest products and in the development of the supplier–customer relationship to achieve competitiveness.

Marketing capabilities foster the processes required to gain firms' market share in particular products and services, and to appropriate financial gains from that achievement (Merrilees et al., 2011; Ripolles et al., 2011; Nalcacia & Yagci, 2014). Managers' insights on the environment facing their industry when effectively applied will have an impact on firms' market learning and capability building as they can then respond strategically to changes in the external business environment (Weerawardena & O'Cass, 2009). A profound understanding of the embedding environment shall offer managers strategic marketing direction to pilot firms (Rasiah, 2019). In this regard, successful marketing requires firms to have at their disposal market-oriented knowledge. While market knowledge diffusion is significantly correlated with firms' ability to exploit new market opportunities, it also helps with firms' innovation performance (Marinova, 2004). Thus, companies are more likely to encourage investment into market-based innovations right from the start if the development of R&D capabilities is critical for that success. Firms anticipate trade-offs in value creation and appropriation throughout developmental cycles (Mizik & Jacobson, 2003; Tsai & Eisingerich, 2010). In addition, effective marketing can enable firms to use less resources to raise efficiency, while improving customer relationships (Rust et al., 2004). Consistent with the objective of marketing, firms' processes must be continuously arranged according to customers' needs that are expected to change over time (Rust et al., 2004).

In short, firms' marketing capabilities help in the application and promotion of latest knowledge and skills associated with local, national, regional, and global markets (Vorhies & Morgan, 2005). A number of studies show a positive relationship between technological capabilities, marketing capabilities, and firm performance (Song et al., 2008; Zhou & Wu 2010).

[18] For example, organizations product development capabilities support promotion strategies in the long-term to be consecutively better over time (Banerjee & Soberman, 2013).

Strategic Planning

Strategic planning is a formalized process that is targeted at outlining, sensing, and seizing opportunities (Teece, 2007). The rule of success shifts with a constantly changing environment, which includes the emergence of new technologies, changing social values and demographics, unstable economic and political conditions, increasing complexity of rules, rising competition, new approaches to dealing with service and products deliveries, and new methods of operationalizing them. Consequently, there is a need to tailor firm strategies to fit market structures and finally market demand (Day, 2011).

A number of studies use firm-level variables, such as firm size, firm organization, age, capital intensity, and the developmental level to examine their impact on strategic planning (e.g., Armstrong, 1982; Odom & Boxx, 1988). Also, business orientation and decisions are recognized as consequences of effective strategic planning processes (Robinson & Pearce, 1988). As firms develop strategic planning capability, they tend to move towards developing latest functional capabilities and consequently evolve dynamic capabilities, which are complemented by learning and enhancing of skills (Eisenhardt & Martin, 2000). In this context, firms adapt planning processes based on specific situations organizationally (Jennings, 2000; Ocasio & Joseph, 2008; Poister, 2010).

The strategic management of technologies for raising or sustaining business profits needs operative systems and processes that take account of cutting-edge technological resources available in the market, not only to meet day-to-day needs but also needs of the future. Furthermore, strategic management should take account of changes in market and technology, opportunities and threats, complexities of technologies, and markets (Christensen & Fjermestad, 1997). Technological integration into business strategies is a significant feature in business planning. Business strategies require an alignment of firms' activities in a manner that generates and boosts sustainable competitiveness in the market domain (Porter, 1980), which demands a comprehensive understanding of business conditions through a long-run vision and development that is aimed at improving firm-level management capabilities.

Strategic planning can be viewed as a tool to communicate and to regulate its application towards the achievement of particular targets. In this regard, three important elements are generally considered when formulating business strategies related to technology adoption, viz., (1) the market basis to select strategic approaches associated with focus and cost reduction, (2) market direction from the identification of alternative market routes, such as market penetration, market development, product development, diversification, and integration, and (3) technology source, such as acquisition, internal development, and joint development.

Nonetheless, the commitment and the comprehension of strategies by firms' employees are equally important to execute them as designed. Managerial strategies that shape organizational business models are therefore critical in strategic planning. Not only are innovating firms concerned with which and what types of technologies are to be acquired from external sources (Vanhaverbeke & Peeters, 2005), they are also concerned with how to leverage the externally sourced knowledge to create value, including for their customers. Through strategic business models, firms also decide which innovations to be further developed in-house into products and which ones to be licensed out or divested as spin-offs (Vanhaverbeke & Peeters, 2005). Latecomer firms are also concerned with increasing challenges on how to leverage external knowledge, while securing and extending their role within the value system they operate in.

Overall, industrial upgrading targeted at raising firm performance is a function of technology transfer and in-house technological capability development, as well as improvements in organizational and management capabilities. Hence, to upgrade to frontier technologies, firms need to enhance their technological capabilities through technology transfer, as well as in-house development, both of which are significantly enhanced through organizational and management capabilities. While firm-level strategies are important, given the role embedding ecosystems have played in the successful firm and country experiences, government initiatives to introduce effective industrial policies is critical to stimulate firms' movement towards the technology frontier (Rasiah, 2019).

Towards a Theoretical Framework

Three theoretical constructs are used in this book, viz., technological trajectories critical for the progression of firms from entry level to technology frontier, the role of technology transfer and technological capabilities on firm performance with organizational and management capabilities as a critical mediator, and the role of the embedding ecosystem to stimulate firm-level technological upgrading. The broad aspects of these constructs are developed in this chapter, while their specific applications are undertaken in Chapters 5, 6, and 7 respectively.

Firms from developing countries generally take advantage of their latecomer status by importing and adapting technologies from advanced nations to upgrade their technological capabilities (Rasiah, 1995; Kim, 1997). Consequently, several firms networked in value chains have taken advantage of the technical and pecuniary linkages woven in these chains to import, acquire, adapt, and catch up with lead firms in several industries (Amsden, 1989; Mathews, 2006). In many cases, latecomers enter global value chains (GVCs) to establish linkages with international brand producers and potential customers (Gereffi, 1999), which is the initial relationship between latecomers in international markets and their potential buyers in which multinational corporations subcontract out to OEM suppliers the low-end manufacturing stages of the chain that is associated with low production costs. There is a difference though with firms located in LDCs where cut, make, and pack operations involve the least knowledge intensity in clothing value chains (see Rasiah, 2010). Therefore, most large and medium textiles and clothing firms in Pakistan at the stage of integration with GVCs would have already acquired the knowledge to export using OEM capabilities.

While significant automation has proliferated into fabric weaving and knitting, Pakistan's firms engaged in such activities have also acquired a wide range of technologies that range from old to new technologies in textile manufacturing. Indeed, a number of countries, (including Bangladesh and Cambodia) import fabric from Pakistan to manufacture clothing products in the global value chains in which they have been inserted.

Technology Transfer, and Technological, Organizational and Management Capabilities

The next theoretical framework important for this study is the influence of technology transfer and technological capabilities on firm performance with organizational and management capabilities as a critical mediating variable. As has been argued by Teece (2007, 2009), Prahalad (2012), and Kim (1997), that it is critical to strengthen firm-level governance for firms to appropriate the synergies associated with technology transfer, and technological, and organizational and management capabilities to raise firm performance.

Given the specificity of Pakistan's economic structure and the nature of firms and embedding institutions and organizations, as well as of the peculiarity of textiles and clothing firms, the influence of the components that make up the variables of technology transfer, technological capabilities, and organizational and management capabilities on innovation and firm performance should also be examined on their own. Consequently, Chapter 6 deals with these relationships, as well as the important contributors within them to drive both innovation and firm performance.

Embedding Ecosystem

Having examined the literature on the critical drivers of technological capability building and its impact on firm performance, including technology transfer, in-house accumulation, and development of organizational and management capabilities, this section examines the role of the embedding ecosystem that is critical for firm-level upgrading to achieve technological progress. Embracing the two critical aspects of technological capability building in firms through (1) technology transfer, in-house development, and organizational and management capabilities and (2) support from the external embedding ecosystem, a conceptual framework is developed by adapting the systemic quad advanced by Rasiah (2019). In doing so, the approaches by Porter (1990) and Best (2001) are dropped. The former was dropped because it focuses on clusters driven by a dominant industry, does not address inter-firm links associated with dissimilar but complementary industries, and its emphasis is largely on synergizing mature clusters (Rasiah, 2007). The latter takes account of the shortcomings of the Porter (1990) approach but is not built around specific inter-firm links that relate to delivering knowledge inputs essential for firms to upgrade beyond skills formation and inter-firm connections and coordination, and also does not focus on the policy pillars essential to stimulate firm-level upgrading.

The Systemic Quad

The systemic quad envisioned by Rasiah (2019) is useful as a development model for a regionally networked group of economic agents that addresses variations in building systemic support and its influence on knowledge-related activities, including development of technological capabilities, firm productivity, as well as raising wages (see also UNIDO, 2009). The systemic quad is driven by four pillars, viz., (1) basic infrastructure, (2) science, technology, and innovation (STI) infrastructure,[19] (3) network cohesion, and (4) global integration. Although Porter's (1990) diamond and Best's (2001) productivity triad (2001, 2018) have successfully explained the way mature networked regions raise economic synergies, their models lack focus on how underdeveloped regions can be transformed into cohesively integrated clusters for embedded firms to reach the technology frontier.

[19] Rasiah (2019) had originally referred this pillar as high-technology infrastructure, but subsequently changed it to science, technology, and innovation infrastructure.

Also, the systemic quad was adopted as the embedding ecosystem framework because past approaches do not fully absorb the evolutionary arguments of systemic and institutional influences on domestic, regional, and sectoral innovative systems that shape the strategies of individuals, firms, and organizations (Veblen, 1915; Nelson, 1993; Freeman, 1995; Lundvall, 2010; Rasiah, 2011). It is for these reasons, Rasiah (2019) introduced the systemic quad to classify such influences under four embedding pillars that are critical to mould and shape the conduct of individuals, firms, and organizations towards the objective of stimulating innovation activity (including diffusion and appropriation of innovation synergies). In doing so, both formal and informal institutions are given attention with the relative influence of each determined by timing, industry, and locational specificities (Nelson, 2008; Rasiah, 2011).[20] The role of markets and government in providing public goods and utilities to society and individuals are given strong emphasis. Furthermore, trust and loyalty, which constitute social capital, are recognized as critical elements of the glue that brings together socioeconomic agents' (Becatini, 1991; Rasiah, 1994; Rasiah & Lin, 2005) innovation conduct to raise economic performance. Figure 3.2 shows the four critical pillars presented by Rasiah (2019), which form the basis for the development of the industrial upgrading index (IUI) for the textile and clothing industry in Pakistan.

Basic Infrastructure

The first pillar of the systemic quad, that is, basic infrastructure in a vibrant cluster includes the participation of federal, national, and local governments seeking to give macroeconomic and political stability, security, and public utilities, such as transport, information communication technology, water supply, energy supply, healthcare provision, education, and customs coordination. Firms will require these support facilities to perform their operations in the most efficient and organized of ways. The pilot study in Pakistan showed that serious failure in the provision of basic infrastructure has led to the larger firms to internalize such services. For example, Nishat Chunian textiles, located in Lahore, has installed its own power supply using coal owing to frequent disruptions in supply.[21]

However, since Basic Infrastructure is largely a ubiquitous influence among the embedding ecosystem pillars, any upgrading of the basic instruments

[20] In making this point, Rasiah (2011) acknowledged the contributions of the new institutionalists, such as Coase (1937), North (1993), and Williamson (1988) but departs from their assertion that the market defines the relative roles of the other institutions.

[21] Interview conducted in Lahore by Rajah Rasiah on 5 January 2019.

Basic Infrastructure	STI Infrastructure
Provision of water, power, transport, and telecommunications Access to finance Customs coordination Security Health care Basic education	University education and research Human Capital development Standards organizations R&D incentives, grants and centres Intellectual property rights Science and technology parks Venture capital Regulatory functions
Network Cohesion	**Global Integration**
Connectivity and coordination between firms, and suppliers and buyers Connectivity and coordination between firms, and basic infrastructure Connectivity and coordination between firms, and STI infrastructure Connectively and coordination between firms, and intermediary organizations and customers	Integration with input and product markets globally Integration with knowledge nodes globally Human capital suppliers Research universities Integration into GVCs

Figure 3.2 The enabling ecosystem for promoting industrial upgrading

Source: Adapted from Rasiah (2019).

of transport networks, basic education, power, water, telecommunication networks, healthcare provision, access to finance, housing, and customs coordination in the embedding environment should suffice. One can expect serious demand–supply gaps in poor countries (such as Pakistan), and hence, the need for the state to increase their supply across host-sites at least where the textiles and clothing firms are located. At the time of the fieldwork, serious gaps in the provision of basic infrastructure facing textiles and clothing firms in Pakistan existed when compared to where the lead firms of TAL, Toray, and Everest Textiles are located in Hong Kong, Japan, and Taiwan.

Science, Technology and Innovation Infrastructure

The STI infrastructure pillar refers to the ecosystem supporting science, technology, and innovation activities that are critical to provide knowledge-based public goods, which are non-excludable and non-rivalrous. The intermediary organizations that make up the STI infrastructure are institutionally governed to coordinate effectively support for individuals, firms, and organizations' efforts to adapt, creatively imitate, support R&D activity and incubation for scaling up operations, and supply of human capital, and professionals to manage and handle technologies attained through acquisition and licensing. This pillar also addresses the supply of engineers and scientists, standards appraisal mechanisms, higher educational institutes, training programmes, digital infrastructure, and a mechanism for governing intellectual property rights. The STI infrastructure is important to support the continuous development of technological capabilities in firms right to the frontier within the cluster. Lall (2001) considered these facilities critical for developing nations to stimulate upgrading. The responsibility for the development of the embedding STI infrastructure in the initial stages lies with the government because of the inability of private firms to face uncertainties and risks and to protect their knowledge output (Hill, 1990; Rasiah, 2019). Also, such investments tend to enter the public goods domain quickly due to the classical free rider problems and shortcomings in legal systems.

For firms to progress to the highest technological levels in the textiles and clothing industry, the embedding ecosystem should have intermediary organizations to provide support for frontier R&D, training, and knowledge-based activities to support designing activities. Taiwan's Textiles and Clothing department (which was established in 1970) is focused on innovative environment-focused sustainable fashion through curriculum development and collaborative initiatives with industry to train professionals who bring a holistic vision and competitive skills to drive the fashion industry to the frontier. In Taiwan, this college is integrated with the resources of the Department of Textiles and Clothing, the Graduate Institute of Museum Studies, and the master's programme in brand and fashion management to support the global sustainable fashion centre. It has evolved to enjoy an active and robust relationship with partners in academia, government, industry, and research centres in four key research areas of technology and design, business and management, analytics and communication, and culture and heritage to promote innovative and advanced solutions. It has since been incubating designers who are creative and globally connected at constructing a world-class learning environment tied to the industry, and offers networking support for individuals, firms, and organizations (College of Fashion and Textiles, 2022). Everest Textiles is a major beneficiary of such a cohesive embedding ecosystem.

Global Integration

The third pillar of the systemic quad (i.e., global integration), addresses the critical need for dynamic clusters to be globally connected with markets, resources, and value chains. Global production networks or value chains support individuals, firms, and organizations to orientate their action plans and strategic goals to important external sources of knowledge. Such links also offer the opportunity for firms to participate in value chains, markets, access knowledge from foreign personnel and universities, and investment that spread across the world (Gereffi et al., 2005; Pietrobelli & Rabellotti, 2006). Integration into major global markets also provides opportunities to access knowledge from multinationals through foreign direct investment, licensing, and creatively adapting imported equipment and machinery. South Korean, Taiwanese, and Japanese firms benefited enormously from access to external sources of knowledge (Johnson, 1982; Amsden, 1989; Wade, 1990; Edquist & Jacobssen, 1987; Freeman, 1995; Kim, 1997; Saxenian, 2006). Foreign firms usually adapt and relocate technologies at host sites to appropriate relative cost and benefits from such decisions made through a profound focus on the location, ownership, and internalization (Dunning, 2001). In this context, mainly process technologies and HR are greatly transferred into firms located at host sites in developing nations by foreign firms (Rasiah, 1995). However, firms deploying offensive strategies from emerging markets (such as Tai Yuen from China) have relocated in the United States to access both markets, as well as frontier knowledge to develop robots.

Network Cohesion

The fourth pillar of the systemic quad, that is, network cohesion is associated with interdependence and interaction between actors involved in clusters. Nelson and Winter (1982) and Lundvall (2010) discussed the significance of interactions and interdependence between economic actors by emphasizing the producer–user relationship in innovative activities, which Vernon (1966) earlier argued over its significance to explain why key stages related to engineering and R&D remained in developed markets in the 1960s. In this context, Rasiah (2019) argued that coordination and connectivity are essential for continuous and interactive flow of knowledge between actors, intermediary organizations, and government agencies engaged in executing tasks, monitoring, and regulating that are driven by a blend of formal and informal institutions. Intermediary organizations, such as industry-university, government and civil society, which is known as the quadruple helix), coordinating councils and chambers of commerce perform a vital role to enhance coordination and connectivity between these stakeholders to strengthen network cohesion in dynamic clusters. In this regard, the informal institutions of trust and loyalty play a critical role to strengthen the network cohesion pillar (Rasiah & Lin, 2005).

Summary

The extant literature reviewed in this chapter offers several potential propositions that can help locate effectively industrial upgrading in the developing countries in general, and in Pakistan in particular. However, since the focus of this book is on producing an empirically supported and profoundly grounded account of industrial upgrading in the textiles and clothing industry in Pakistan specifically, and to draw policy relevant recommendations in general, this study uses Pakistan's textiles and clothing industry to achieve three objectives. Firstly, the study seeks to go beyond past frameworks tabulating technological capabilities to produce a taxonomy on the basis of technological trajectories, and to include organizational and management capabilities to map firm-level technological, and organizational and management capabilities of firms from the bottom till the frontier of their respective trajectories. In doing so, it seeks to take on the approach used by Rasiah (2004a) that uses templates of the whole trajectory, but applies it specifically to the textiles and clothing industry, which is taken up in Chapter 5. Also, the study seeks to update the use of trajectories—both technological capabilities, and organizational and management capabilities to be contemporaneous. Importantly, this study locates Pakistan's firms in the global textiles and clothing trajectory where the highest levels are still located abroad.

Secondly, the study seeks to examine the impact of technology transfer and technological capabilities on firm performance with organizational and management capabilities as the mediating variable. In doing so, the chapter offers the promise of identifying the key elements of technology that are critical in raising firm performance in the textiles and clothing industry in Pakistan. Also, the statistical exercise differentiates the relative importance of technology transfer, technological capabilities, and organizational and management capabilities in explaining firm performance.

Thirdly, the study seeks to examine the systemic embedding factors external to the textiles and clothing firms, but that are critical for in-house industrial upgrading. The systemic quad is the model used with a wide range of factors drawn to develop the industrial upgrading index, which can help policy-makers to stimulate industrial upgrading in manufacturing firms in general, but in textiles and clothing firms in particular.

4
Methodology and Data

Introduction

Unlike works that treat the formulation of methodology separately, the review undertaken in Chapter 3 has helped the shaping of the methodological framework in this chapter, which is then used to: (1) locate Pakistan's textiles and clothing firms in the technological capability trajectory comprising nine levels and the organizational and management capability trajectory comprising six levels; (2) to capture the influence of technology transfer and technological capabilities on firm performance with organizational and management capabilities as a mediating variable; and (3) to construct the industrial upgrading index (IUI) that the Pakistan government in particular, and governments in general can use to examine the influence of critical embedding institutions and organizations on firm-level industrial upgrading.

This chapter explains the broad methodological approach and the data used for the analysis in the analytical chapters of five, six, and seven. The general methodological framework is defined and described in this chapter whereas the objective-specific methodologies are presented separately in the analytical chapters. This chapter begins with a conceptual framework, which is then followed by the development of a firm level taxonomy to locate Pakistan's textiles and clothing firms in the technological capability, and organizational and management capability trajectories, then to analyse the drivers of firm performance in the textiles and clothing industry of Pakistan, and finally the methodological instruments relevant to examine the embedding ecosystem that is necessary to promote industrial upgrading in textiles and clothing firms.

Conceptual Framework

The central methodological questions used to guide this research are to explain where the textile and clothing firms in Pakistan are: one, located in the technological, and organizational and management capability

Industrial Upgrading in the Textiles and Clothing Industry. Nazia Nazeer and Rajah Rasiah, Oxford University Press.
 DOI: 10.1093/9780198961697.003.0004

trajectories; two, examine the influence of technology transfer and technological capabilities on firm performance, and the mediating effects of organizational and management capabilities in that relationship; and three, to develop a IUI that policy makers can use to promote industrial upgrading in the industry. It follows from the theoretical argument established in chapter three, which assumes that industrial upgrading in Pakistan's textiles and clothing industry will require effective technology transfer, and technological capability building with a strong mediating role from organizational and management capabilities. To examine the link between the latter three variables, the study first seeks to construct technological capability and organizational and management capability trajectories. It then seeks to examine the statistical relationship between technology transfer and technological capabilities, and firm performance with organizational and management capabilities as a mediator. The book subsequently seeks to construct and estimate IUIs that the Pakistan government in particular and governments in general can use to formulate policies targeted at stimulating industrial upgrading in the textiles and clothing industry.

The theoretical framework shown in Figure 4.1 explains the constructs and technological upgrading pillars used in the study, while the in-depth use of this framework along with the specific analytic frameworks developed from there are presented in Chapters 5, 6, and 7.

Towards a Taxonomy of Capabilities

The formulation of technological capabilities and organizational and management capabilities trajectories of textiles and clothing firms require a profound assessment of taxonomies on the industry (e.g., Figueiredo, 2003; Rasiah, 2004a; Dutrénit, 2006), and that not all firms start at the entry level, though most micro and traditional firms have their origins from there. There are then phases with four classified as catch-up phases differentiated by the initial, mid, critical transition, and frontier phases. Whereas Figueredo (2003), Rasiah (2004a), and Dutrénit (2006) focused on technological capabilities, also included here are organizational and management capabilities.

The data and methodology used in Chapter 4 was explained in broad terms. This chapter adapted the work of Figueiredo and Cohen (2019), Rasiah (2010), and Rasiah (2003) to formulate a taxonomy by trajectories of industrial upgrading in textiles and clothing firms (see Table 4.1).

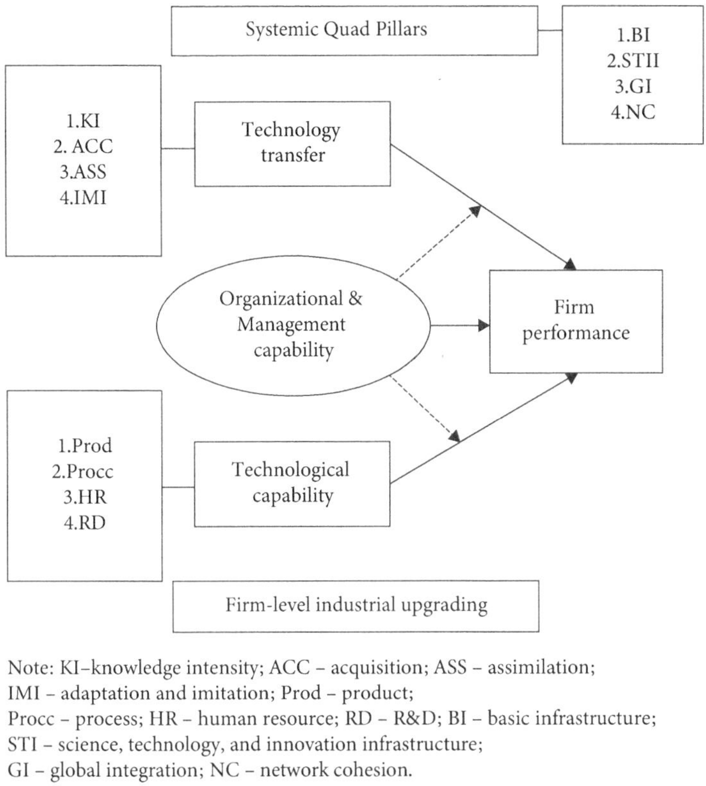

Figure 4.1 Industrial upgrading—dimensions, drivers, and embedding pillars

Note: KI—knowledge intensity; ACC—acquisition; ASS—assimilation; IMI—adaptation and imitation; Prod—product; Procc—process; HR—human resource; RD—R&D; BI—basic infrastructure; STI—science, technology, and innovation infrastructure; GI—global integration; NC—network cohesion.
Source: Developed by the authors.

Firm-level knowledge development focuses on specific industry parameters and the level of complexities vary with the scale of operations and the sub-category of operations (e.g., spinning and weaving in textiles, and stitching in clothing) (Rasiah, 1995; Nelson, 2008; Kim & Lee, 1987). To ensure that the production structure template is followed, we develop an industry firm-specific taxonomy based on knowledge accumulation in the textile and clothing firms, which helps the mapping of the firm-level catching-up trajectories to capture the way firms upgrade from one level to another.[1] It has to be noted that the evolutionary notion of learning as an adaptive process subsumes innovation in all the production stages, and not just at the R&D stage,

[1] A further differentiation of taxonomies by clothing and textile firms can also be done. We chose not to do it because some of the firms are vertically integrated.

Table 4.1 Firm level taxonomy by trajectory of technological, and organizational and management capabilities, textile and clothing industry

	Technological Capabilities			Organizational and Management Capabilities	
Level	Human Resource	Process Technology	Product Technology		Level
1	Dexterity and learning by doing. Supervisory command	Largely clothing firms using labour-intensive production.	Simple activities Cut, make, and trim operations using contractor specs with supplies going to firms functioning at levels 2 and above.	Simple functional management structure. critical use of supervisors.	1
2	Technical Development work, in–house training sessions and performance Rewards	Minor process adaption, machinery, layouts, techniques, material and problem solving	Minor improvements Freight-on-board operations with autonomy to determine inputs and suppliers but orders use contractor specs	Beginnings of knowledge Management and motivational approaches, inter-firm coordination, Learning from buyer-supplier firms. Pursuit of modern management principles. Time motion studies	2
3	Emphasis on training and retraining: staff with training responsibility.	Major process adaptation and production reorganization	Major improvements Routine QC to maintain existing standards. Begin product adoption for functional diversification to create additional values for customers		
4	Hiring of engineers/technicians for process control and adaptation activities	Inventory Management systems. Process adaptation and production layouts, equipment and techniques and Designing	Engineering-focused improvements OEM capabilities, product quality enhancement, focus on automated systems to raise precision engineering routine Product adaptation Minor adaptations to meet clients' requirements.	Modern quality control systems (QCCs). Materials Requirement Planning (MRP1). Path dependence and on-line services like inquiry of order status, delivery time, video conferences, product knowledge, customer inquiries and new order booking characterize firm operations.	3

5	Human resource focused on in-house product adaptation and development activities, Preliminary technical assessments.	Process development capabilities: layouts, machinery and equipment, materials and processes using SPC and TPM capabilities. Auto-scanning of outgoing fabric by textile firms, and in-coming fabric by clothing firms.	Early R&D Early designing capability via partnerships.		
6	Consultations to learn from industry-specific sponsored chairs, collaborative research and development projects, and commercialization of innovation.	Enhanced process development capability, (upgrade capacity for), process materials, layouts, machinery and equipment and methods that lead to a reduction of manufacturing costs.	Intermediate applied R&D Product differentiation capability, apply in-house concepts for new product development.	Learning of organizational values to facilitate constructive changes. Absorption of international best practices in management. Beginnings of divisional firms to differentiate activities as firms integrate vertically. Participation in telemonitoring with buyers, strategic linkages with buyers and suppliers.	4
7	Enhanced skills to produce desired fabric shade or finish.	Central control automated systems. R&D that leads to intermediate manufacturing cost reduction and higher production yield	Sustainable innovation capacity through applied research and major exploratory development with market results such as time to market.		

Continued

Table 4.1 *Continued*

	Technological Capabilities			Organizational and Management Capabilities	
Level	Human Resource	Process Technology	Product Technology		Level
8	Technical Education and Vocational Training for staff with a focus on digitalization and automation skills Hiring of R&D technologists to support process and product technologies. Collaborative R&D knowledge sharing. Contract IP lawyers.	Increased R&D that leads to major internal manufacturing cost reduction. Competitive production yield in the industry (Designs for manufacturing principle to foundries system) Joint process R&D with public and university labs to automate, computerize and design inventory flow, and machinery handling.	Close to technology frontier Advanced functional diversification involving cross disciplinary knowledge, rich product portfolio and service offerings. Capability to fill up obsolete capacity to achieve scale effect. Applied research. Exploratory Development and begin advanced development with customers to develop prototype for production, market results, and feedback. New fibre and fibre and fabric mix development capability, ODM original brand manufacturing capability with customers and suppliers via strategic alliance. Potential for Brand sharing	Partnerships with strategic national firms, including fashion houses, R&D centres, and machine tool firms, and management of process and product technologies. Preferential shares for executives to build bonding with firm. Internationalization to circumvent tariffs and quotas. MRP11 and TQM systems. Cross-industry strategic alliances among national firms, including R&D partnerships. Strong coordination with R&D consortias, incubators in national public and university labs.	5

9	Exposure to IR4.0 skills—coding, programming, and handling of robots, digital links related to big data analytics, and cloud computing, strategic R&D thinking and strategizing capabilities, including long-term and medium-term planning	Robots displacing most tasks, including sowbot in clothes stitching. Material resource planning. Either through strategic collaboration or through own subsidiaries strong focus on machine tooling, and robotization.	Joint Technology Leader In-house generation capabilities to launch new cycles of innovation. Basic Research capability to drive industry's migration to new manufacturing methods to replace industry's development of new production and product with few taking on original brand Manufacturing (OBM) capability. New material development, such as BCI yarn, organic yarn (including bamboo yarn), synthetic yarn, and various mix of cotton). Filing of patents to protect proprietary knowledge.	Partnerships with strategic international firms, including fashion houses, R&D centres, and machine tool firms with robotic support for marketing, logistics, and management of process and product technologies. Strong focus on corporate social responsibility practices, including green practices. Cross-industry and -country complementary strategic alliances, including R&D partnerships. Strong coordination with international R&D consortias, incubators in public and university labs.	6

Note: Drawn from interviews with 30 industry experts engaged in strategic management strategies and planning from the 50 experts interviewed for the estimation of the industrial upgrading index.
Source: Authors' classification.

which is why the taxonomy used here does not create a template each for production and innovation. The chapter also explains in detail the construction of the capability accumulation taxonomy to explain the learning interfaces undergone by Pakistan's textile and clothing firms within a trajectory that includes the lead manufacturing firms located abroad. Chapters 5 and 6 rely on firm-level data from where the firms' responses were classified under nine categories of technological capabilities and six categories of organizational and management capabilities. The rationale behind the classifications is explained in this section.

Given that the textiles and clothing industry have evolved over time, and they differ with locations, the previous in-depth mapping by Rasiah (2009) is somewhat outdated to embrace Nelson's (2008) evolutionary argument, i.e., the learning trajectory that we eventually map is expected to differ from earlier taxonomies. Consequently, the decision to develop a new knowledge accumulation taxonomy by trajectories is appropriate as it provides a better picture of the nature of integration between firm-level technological capabilities, and growth of vertical linkages, as well as inter-sector exchange of knowledge among the interconnected economic components of the textiles and clothing firms in Pakistan.

Technological Capabilities

Within the four phases, nine distinct technological capability levels were identified that firms go through from the entry level to reach the technology frontier. Such a trajectory was constructed using both firms abroad, including frontier manufacturers, such as TAL, Everest Textiles, and Toray. Rajah Rasiah undertook a thorough visit to study the entire factory floor and R&D departments in selected subsidiaries of the TAL and the Toray, while an expert with profound knowledge of Everest Textiles was engaged to draw information from that firm.[2] The following sub-section explains the nine technological capability levels.

Level 1

At level 1 of technological activities, firms largely specialize on cut, make, and trim operations to supply to other firms domestically that sell in the domestic market (Rasiah, 2009). This is the phase before firms' attempt to stimulate technological upgrading where entrepreneurs use their embodied

[2] The expert is Hemant Kedia. The authors also accessed the website of Everest Textiles to map its activities in detail.

expertise to manage supervisors to instruct workers about the tasks they perform. Given that scale is essential for textile manufacturing, such as fibre production, spinning, weaving, and knitting, only clothing firms are expected to participate in level 1 activities. Training is undertaken on-the job with strong use of supervisors to ensure yields are met with little defects. Operations are labour-intensive and no pronounced inventory and quality control systems are in use while the machinery used is largely outdated.

Catch-up Initial Phase

The technological catch-up phase in the textiles and clothing industry begins at level 2. Firms begin to acquire and evolve technology development capability through in-house training sessions and performance rewards. Firms also begin to engage in minor adaptations to processes, machinery, layouts, techniques, material, and problem-solving activities. Unlike in level 1, firms in level 2 enjoy freight-on-board operations with the autonomy to determine inputs and suppliers, though they still use contractors' specs to meet the orders (Table 4.1). It is at level 3 that emphasis on training and retraining starts with staff enjoying training responsibility. Major process adaptation and production reorganization takes place at this level.

At technological capability levels 2 and 3 technological capability is accumulated in a unidirectional way starting from buyer firms placing orders with their specs. Buyers play a critical role in firms' upgrading of human resource, and process and product technologies. Significant flows of knowledge take place to upgrade human resource skills (including time-motion studies) and process technologies. No significant attempt is made to adapt product technologies as production is confined to the specs provided by buyers in this initial catch up phase.

Catch-up Mid-Phase

At technological capability level 4, firms strengthen further their process, machinery, layout, and product adaptation capabilities to begin product adaptation for functional diversification to create additional value for owners. Firms hire engineers and more technicians to support process control and adaptation activities. Process engineers assist with inventory management systems through the use of software tools. Also, engineers and technicians undertake adaptation of layouts, equipment, and inventory control systems, such as materials requirement planning.

Human resource planning and execution have a higher intensity when a focused human resource department is added at level 5 that exposes employees to in-house product adaptation and development activities, and preliminary technical assessments. While skilled workers in stitching, for example, still need dexterity skills, they also require exposure to the technical change interface with incoming and out-going material flow. At the level 5 end of the mid-phase of catch-up, firms also enjoy strong process development capabilities to modify layouts, machinery and equipment, materials and processes using statistical process control (SPC) and total preventive maintenance (TPM) capabilities. Firms at this level have the capability to participate in fabric and clothing designs.

Critical Transitionary Phase

At technological capability levels 6 and 7, the OEMs and ODMs integrate with external sources of knowledge with their internal knowledge to strengthen their capacity to design products and process technologies suitable to meet customer demand. Furthermore, participation in inter-firm collaboration has to be successive and constantly upgraded to progress to higher levels of technological capabilities. Indeed, inter-firm and firm-organization collaboration (which is a major source of knowledge accumulation for latecomers) hardly exists among Pakistan's textiles and clothing firms.

At technological capability level 6, firms access consultations with external experts to learn from industry-specific sponsored chairs, collaborative research and development projects, and commercialization of innovation. In other industries, such as construction, some even engage foreign consultants endowed with tacit knowledge (Zahra, 2005). Firms also enjoy enhanced process development capability for further upgrading in the use of materials, layouts, machinery and equipment, and methods that lead to a reduction in internal manufacturing costs and shortening of throughput time. Level 6 firms are engaged in product differentiation capability and are capable of applying in-house designs for new product development.

The RBV theories emphasize that the firm is the source of knowledge and that this knowledge is accumulated and embodied in firms as tangible and intangible assets (Penrose, 1959; Nelson & Winter, 1982). The transition to technological capability levels 6 and 7 where firms are engaged profoundly in R&D activities have evolved since Schumpeter's (1939, 1942) advocacy of the large firms as initiators of R&D and new business cycles. As we have argued earlier, the emergence of knowledge networks with laboratories in universities and those held publicly, and incubators in science and technology parks have enabled small firms to connect with them to participate in the creation of new stocks of knowledge. However, latecomers begin innovating by learning from imports and subsequently adapting technologies from abroad to stimulate upgrading their own technological capabilities (Amsden, 1989,

1991; Lall, 1992; Rasiah, 2004a) before their embedding knowledge networks evolve. Consequently, in countries where such networks connecting firms with science, technology, and innovation infrastructure (STI) organizations are underdeveloped as in Pakistan, most textiles and clothing firms acquire technologies through turnkey projects. These firms hardly interact with other textiles and clothing firms, but link with manufacturers from whom they purchase machinery and equipment. Often the initial contact is through international exhibitions and seminars but once purchases are made, sellers offer operational training and service repair support. Hence, if in Taiwan, firms have already connected with the critical STI organizations by the time they upgraded from level 5 technological activity to levels 6 and 7, Pakistan's firms in technological levels 6 and 7 have largely evolved such capabilities without significant support from the domestic STI infrastructure. This explains why only 31 of the 503 firms that responded to the surveys were engaged in levels 6 and 7 technological levels in Pakistan in 2018.

Several large firms in Pakistan have upgraded to include cutting-edge quality and inventory control systems and the launching of computerized control in production planning. However, to cope with the instable political situation of the country, and to appropriate synergies from producer-user relationships, the advanced firms have mostly installed order-tracking systems, wastewater plants and CCTV cameras for international buyers to keep them updated about the status of their order, and to meet ethical conditions, manufacturing standards and, work environments (Nabi & Hamid, 2014). Besides, large firms (particularly in woven clothing) have invested in modern washing systems. Few firms have updated their equipment to include computer-controlled Jacquard knitting machines) to manufacture patterned knitwear with Global Organic Textile Standard manufacturing certification. In this regard, firms need to be consistent to understand and integrate beneficial knowledge in their operations to upgrade to higher value-added segments of textiles and clothing production (Carlile & Rebentisch, 2003; Ferdows, 2006).

Technical workshops become important at level 7 as firms focus on the development of enhanced skills to produce desired fabric shade or finish. Firms at this level emphasize that all technical and direct workers are always looking to improve process and product technologies creatively and continuously throughout the process flow chart. The R&D department focuses on manufacturing cost reduction and raising production yields. Engineers focus on experimental and exploratory R&D with strong interface with the global marketing brandholders, including targeting towards greening the environment. At this stage, firms emphasize knowledge accumulation through linking with knowledge networks, including through their tangible and intangible assets, which then has a bearing on firms' performance (Penrose, 1959; Nelson & Winter, 1982). While latecomers begin by importing and adapting much of their technological capabilities to accumulate and eventually grow their technological capabilities (Amsden, 1989, 1991; Lall, 1992; Rasiah, 2004a), in countries where there are few linkages between the science, technology, and innovation infrastructure and firms, as in Pakistan, most textiles and clothing firms acquire technologies through turnkey projects. Also, these firms hardly interact with other textiles and clothing firms, though they enjoy strong links with manufacturers of the machinery and equipment purchased from them. Often the initial contact is through international exhibitions and seminars, but once purchases are made, sellers do offer operative training and service repair support.

At levels 6 and 7, firms enjoy strong telecommuting links with brandholders and supermarkets. Especially in locations equipped with the digital infrastructure, firms do not just enjoy user–producer linkages in such key areas as telemonitoring the production process and interactively coordinating production to meet demand from brandholders and supermarkets.

Frontier Phase

Unlike in some industries where catch-up firms seek to leapfrog incumbents (e.g., semiconductors), the textiles and clothing industry is characterized more by firms catching up to join the frontier firms. Furthermore, brandholders tend to have a strong say in the sale of branded garments but work with subcontractors demonstrating strong technological capabilities and linkages with suppliers and logistics clients. Examples include Levis, Adidas, Nike, GAP, Louis Vuitton, and JC Penney.

Within level 8 of the frontier phase, firms largely hire graduates from advanced technical education and vocational training institutes who have been exposed to digitalization and automation skills, and R&D technologists to support process and product technology development. The focus on R&D is deepened to lead major internal manufacturing cost reduction and further improvements in competitive production yields. Firms also establish joint process R&D activities with national public and university labs to automate, computerize, and design inventory flow, and machinery technology advancement. Exploratory development and joint product and process development are extended to clients with prototyping for production of marketable products with strong producer–user feedback links. Textile firms at this level also enjoy new fibre- and fabric-mix development capability to support ODM capability with customers and suppliers via strategic alliances.

At level 9 technological capability levels, several textiles and clothing firms are internationally integrated through strategic alliances and or via equity sharing with brandholders, fashion houses, and premier R&D centres, including at universities and public laboratories. In this regard, brandholders and fashion houses have devolved considerable power in the clothing value chain to the frontier manufacturers (such as TAL, Taiyuan Garments, and Everest Textiles) that specialize in R&D targeted at both improving designs and reducing costs.

Firms' cross-specialization capabilities also stimulate product-centred firms with original brandname manufacturing (OBMs) capability with R&D corporations to co-develop latest product technologies. Everest Textiles in Taiwan, Toray in Japan, and TAL in Hong Kong are among the frontier firms that show level 9 technological capabilities in textiles and clothing. In addition, TAL and Everest are also strongly engaged in logistic activities to complement their exports to reach the big supermarkets with brandholders, such as POLO, GAP, and Nike. Being a textile firm, the Toray group of companies directly sell their fabric to clothing firms, apart from having subsidiaries that design and manufacture the machinery and equipment they use. Although the level 7 Pakistan firms reported having the potential to participate at such a level, none of them reported participation at levels 8 and 9 technological capability activities in 2018.

Firms at technological capability level 9 are also strongly integrated in digital platforms with employees exposed to IR4.0 skills—coding, programming, and handling of robots with digital links related to big data analytics, and cloud computing. Given the joint involvement in the development of complementary materials, software programs, and machines, some firms even manufacture these items through the creation of subsidiaries, including synthetic and synthetic/organic fibres, machines (e.g., air-jet looms by Toray since the 1980s) and the development of robots through strategic partners (e.g., Everest Textiles). In addition to the deployment of robots, firms at the frontier also utilize material resource planning inventory control systems to better monitor demand–supply coordination. In-house new knowledge generation capabilities are evolved at this stage to launch new cycles of innovation in the textiles and clothing industry. Basic research capability is evolved to drive firms' migration to new manufacturing methods to replace old organizational and management structures with new ones to support new processes and products with some taking on original brand manufacturing (OBM) capability but through share acquisition from brandholder firms or through strategic collaboration with them. New material development is also undertaken at this level, such as better cotton initiative (BCI) yarn, organic yarn (including bamboo yarn), synthetic yarn, and various cotton-mix). The BCI yarn is focused on sustainable farming of cotton right till its harvesting and manufacturing. Indeed, frontier textiles and clothing firms, whether driven by markets or by governments responding to sustainable development goals launched by the United Nations, are focused on greening operations. Some firms seek share purchase in brandholder firms to control demand. Firms also engage in filing patents to protect proprietary knowledge, although they are far less frequent than in the semiconductor and pharmaceutical industries.

Everest Textiles (Taiwan), Toray (Japan), and TAL (Hong Kong) are among the frontier firms that show level 9 technological capabilities in textiles and clothing. Firms with levels 8 and 9 have in-house facilities to support smartification of manufacturing operations, including the deployment of robots in both textiles and clothing manufacturing. Given the nature of technologies deployed in textiles and clothing, firms typically only join rather than leapfrog industry leaders, even if it means leapfrogging firms falling behind. Consequently, in both textiles and clothing more than a few industry leaders operate. Strategies used by these lead firms at level 9 technological level include vertical integration, and blue ocean strategies that result in the integration into more than one market to appropriate collective market synergies (see also Kim & Marbourgne, 2005; Rasiah, 2022). No Pakistan firm reported participation at levels 8 and 9 technological activities.

Organizational and Management Capabilities

Through the adaptation and adoption of frameworks that were reviewed in Chapter 4 and using data collected from a fresh survey, a taxonomy trajectory of firm-level accumulation of technological, and organizational and management capabilities is constructed by trajectories towards mapping industrial catch-up in Pakistan's textile and clothing firms (see Table 5.1). The proposed framework also takes account of R&D characteristics presented by Amsden and Tschang (2003), that is, the five R&D categories of: (1) pure science; (2) basic research; (3) applied research; (4) exploratory development; and (5) advanced development. Technological capabilities at the firm-level take on a different set of categories with the research content and pure science aspects coming last. Consequently, the taxonomy by trajectory used in this study also takes account of contributions from Rasiah (2004a, 2007) and Figuieredo and Cohen, 2019). The survey of the firms and interviews for estimating the IUI are based on responses by 503 of the 600 firms approached, and the 50 industry experts respectively. Both sets of questionnaires were tested with 20 pilots before they were finalized for the study.

We identify five major phases in the trajectory of technological catch-up in the textiles and clothing industry, viz., the entry phase, initial catch-up phase, the mid catch-up phase, the critical transitionary phase, and the frontier phase (see Table 4.1). The essential aspects of organizational and management structures and practices are similar in these five phases.

Level 1

The management structure in the entry phase is functional with some functions jointly handled by the managers, while supervisors are critical for meeting targets. Where the focus is on cut, make, and trim operations at level 1 technological activities, not only do these firms rely on contractor specs with supplies going to firms operating at levels 2 and above, but also the material inputs are specified and often supplied by the purchasers (Table 4.1).

Firms at this level have little understanding of organizational and management functions of firms to evolve knowledge capabilities (including core competencies) to support technological progress to the frontier technological capabilities activities (see Prahalad & Hamel, 1990; Nahapiet & Ghoshal, 1998; Teece, 2007). Without the use of modern personnel and process flow capabilities, such firms largely do not show exports, though their inputs are purchased and transformed into output at levels 2 and 3.

Level 2

Firms for the first time start knowledge management and motivational approaches in the initial catch-up phase at technological levels 2 and 3, while focusing on inter-firm coordination, and learning from buyer-supplier firms. In this regard, Mathews (2006) had argued that latecomers can 'begin' learning at the point of insertion into a GVC as they face lower-technological requirements but inserting into GVCs offers them the opportunity to move to level 2 of organizational and management capability, which is the initial catch-up phase. Firms in this phase begin to adapt technologies using knowledge management approaches and focus on inter-firm coordination and learning from buyer-supplier firms. Organizational and management structures are still functional and are driven by deliberate attempts to deploy modern operational principles.

At level 2, firms also focus on inter-firm coordination and learning from buyer-supplier firms. In addition, firm strategies at this level emphasize modern management principles and the use of time and motion studies to monitor worker performance. At this initial catch-up phase, decision-making on technology adoption and strategies to manage knowledge in firms lies with the owners rather than modern professional managers.

Despite attempts to acquire technology, however, the bulk of the textiles and clothing firms until they reach organizational and management capability level 3 in Pakistan have not systematically accumulated and appropriated technological capabilities—tangible and intangible. Indeed, these firms still lack sufficient understanding of the organizational and management functions of firms to evolve knowledge capabilities to support purposeful technological progress (see Prahalad & Hamel, 1990; Tecce, et al., 1990; Nahapiet & Ghoshal, 1998).

Level 3

Level 3 organizational and management capability firms emphasize knowledge embodied in human resources to improve existing technologies (Rasiah, 2004a). Consequently, firms use modern quality control systems (QCCs), especially to monitor throughput time, such as materials Requirement Planning (MRP1). Path dependence and online services like inquiry of order status, delivery time, product knowledge, customer inquiries, and new order booking characterize firms' operations. In-house training to support changes in process flow to strengthen the use of scientific management increases as firms move to the mid-catch-up phase.

Level 4

It is at this mid catch-up phase that latecomers start participating in focused technology-related connections and partnerships with other firms and organizations in production networks. For instance, the intermediary meso-organizations that include associations of businesses that are established through both private and government initiatives, as well as alliances with big buyers from abroad play critical roles to stimulate efficiency improvements, and shortening of lead times in firms (Rasiah, 1995; Polidano, 2001; Stiglitz, 2002). Among such roles are efforts to seek from human capital and training organizations support to enhance firm-level skills development (Rasiah, 2010). At this stage knowledge starts to move from outside to inside and inside to outside. Level 4 firms participate in the early developmental stages to start with continuous improvement (*kaizen*) activities but without substantial technological capabilities.

The critical transition phase of level 4 organizational and management capability connects with technological capability levels 6 and 7, which are the stages before catching up to the manufacturing frontier takes place.

Thus, it is critical to understand this 'critical transition' phase as latecomers close the technology gap with the front-runners. At level 6, firms evolve sound innovative capability, which distinguishes them from latecomers who are not capable of transmitting knowledge due to the absence of a myriad of sources, such as in-house knowledge-intensive research, engineers, capital resources for sustainable R&D activities, and networking linkages (Figueiredo, 2014). Firms seek to gain momentum in levels 6 and 7 prior to reaching levels 8 and 9. The notion of gaining momentum have been used to study organizational path-shaping moments (Sydow et al., 2009) and organizational crisis-construction that drive technological learning at critical stages (Kim, 1997, 1998). Level 6 ensures that even latecomer firms can transmit knowledge as they move to compete with larger incumbent firms. This includes learning interfaces between original OEMs and their networking agents, who start to change considerably as knowledge acquisition moves in two important ways where firms establish R&D collaboration activities with networked customers or collectively evolve with networked agents such activities to deliver expertise and knowhow in process technologies.

Organizational and management capability level 4 firms also begin to restructure divisionally to differentiate activities as firms integrate vertically. Some firms retain the same organizational structure even after integrating vertically. Strategic partnerships with big international buyers evolve from this phase. Firms begin to use telemonitoring but with greater control by the buyers, having in place representatives globally to handle logistics with buyers and suppliers to support sales and purchases.

Through strategic collaboration, firms at this phase largely handle the shipment of fabric from textiles firms, and garments to malls, including the packaging of clothes. Some firms contract out these services to specialist logistics firms but enjoy strong control of the activity. Lead firms in Pakistan, such as Nishat Chunian and Sapphire Textiles, are at this level but have not evolved beyond only because of the lack of the requisite embedding ecosystem support to move into level 5 OMC activities.

Level 5

In the penultimate frontier phase, firms establish strategic partnerships with firms in complementary industries but among national and foreign firms to participate jointly in the designing and manufacture of robots and other inputs, including materials. Similar collaboration is also strong among national firms to supply national and regional markets OBM textiles and garments.

Integrated materials requirement planning (MRP11) and total quality management (TQM) systems are used to lower throughput times and improve quality. However, lead times can still be high as sea transport is the main mode in textiles and clothing trade. At organizational and management capability level 5, firms engage in advanced functional diversification activities involving cross-disciplinary knowledge sharing, rich product portfolio, and service offerings. Firms also attempt to optimize space and other resources to appropriate scale effects.

Firms emphasize strongly the evolution of organizational values to facilitate constructive changes by absorbing international best practices in management. A number of firms experience a restructuring to divisional firms to differentiate activities as firms integrate vertically. Horizontal participation in telemonitoring with buyers and strategic linkages with buyers and suppliers takes place at this level. Firms also own corporate offices in buyer markets to handle marketing, tecommonitoring, and logistics.

Level 6

At the frontier organizational and management capability level, the management and control of textiles and clothing value chains evolve horizontally where lead manufacturing firms establish strong partnerships with big international brandholders and fashion houses, often through acquisition of equity. On the one hand, lead manufacturers get to share control to reduce uncertainty, while on the other hand, brandholders and fashion houses reduce volatile fluctuations in investment returns through capital injections from the lead manufacturers. Moreover, this collaboration helps strengthen demand–supply coordination, including streamlining consumer taste for both parties.

Partnerships also emerge strongly between lead manufacturing firms and international fashion houses, R&D centres, and machine tool firms equipped with robotic support for marketing, logistics, and management of process and product technologies. Preferential shares are offered to executives to build bonds with firms. While internationalization still occurs to circumvent tariffs and quotas, firms also focus strongly on corporate social responsibility practices, including green practices, cross-industry and -country complementary strategic alliances, including strong coordination with R&D consortias, and incubators in public and university labs. Frontier manufacturing firms, such as the TAL, Toray, and Everest Textiles have evolved to level 6 organizational and management capabilities.

Locating Lead Firms in the Capability Taxonomy

A number of firms have begun introducing robots in textiles and clothing manufacturing. In the United States for example, automated sewing research began[3] at Georgia Tech's Advanced Technology Development Center before 2008. This technology began to take shape following a collaborative agreement with Walmart Foundation, which subsequently received a research grant of USD1.25 million[4] from the Defense Department's (DARPA) tech innovation centre. Chinese owned Tianyuan Garments took advantage of this development to acquire and use this robot-driven sewbot technology in its Arkansas plant in 2018 (Device Plus, 2018). While many frontier firms exist in the textiles and clothing industry (especially in the developed countries), a few were chosen from Asia for the purpose of benchmarking technologically Pakistan's firms against these frontier firms. Everest Textiles, Toray, and TAL are among the frontier firms that show level 9 technological capabilities and level 6 organizational and management capabilities in textiles and clothing. While Everest Textiles is a vertically integrated firm engaged in both textiles and clothing manufacturing, Toray is a conglomerate engaged in various activities other than just textiles but is not involved in clothing manufacturing. TAL is engaged in clothing manufacturing.

Everest Textiles

Everest textiles is a vertically integrated textile and garment firm headquartered in Tainan, Taiwan, which is focused on greening the whole process of fabric manufacturing with manufacturing subsidiaries in Shanghai (China), Ratchanaburi (Thailand), North Carolina (United States), Awassa (Ethopia), and Caracol (Haiti) in 2021.[5] The firm is engaged in textiles manufacturing from yarn texturizing, weaving, knitting, post-finishing to clothing, and produces for the famous brands, such as Nike, POLO, GAP, Decathlon, North Face, Lululemon, and Patagonia. This firm is at the frontier in introducing environment friendly process technologies, and launching new mixes

[3] https://www.fastcompany.com/40454692/this-t-shirt-sewing-robot-could-radically-shift-the-apparel-industry.

[4] https://www.roboticsbusinessreview.com/security/softwear_automation_wins_1-25m_darpa_contract_for_sewing_robots/.

[5] In addition to interviews with Hemant Kedia of Rincon (an Indian textile firm located in Malaysia), information was also drawn from Everest Textiles website, accessed on 30 October 2021 from http://www.everest.com.tw/_english/00_site/01_edit.aspx?MID=16.

of materials in fibre production, as well as focusing on continuous innovation throughout the value chain with significant support from R&D activity. Advantech is a key partner that supports the smartification of manufacturing by Everest Textiles, including in the development of robots that Everest increasingly deploys on its production floor.

Toray Group of Companies

With the headquarters located in Ishikawa (Japan), Toray is a textiles conglomerate engaged in the manufacture of synthetic fibres, yarn texturization, weaving, dyeing, and finishing of fabric. The firm was among the earliest to introduce air-jet looms in textile weaving in the 1980s (Rasiah, 1995). As a conglomerate it also manufactures chemicals and machinery and equipment, while its subsidiaries are located in a wide range of countries. In addition to polyester and carbon fibres, as well as spinning that also uses cotton, the firm has profound frontier R&D facilities.[6]

TAL Group

TAL Apparel Limited is headquartered in Hong Kong with clothing manufacturing operations in China, Thailand, Vietnam, and Vietnam. It had plants in Malaysia but closed them down in 2020. The group is also engaged in wholesale, logistics, and consulting activities, with well-known capabilities for producing new designs. While much of its manufacturing is targeted at export markets using brandholder's names abroad, it also has its own designs sold in the Asian market. The firm has profound R&D operations focused on product design to engage strongly in strengthening process and product technologies. Its frontier innovative activities include strong participation in handling global logistics operations that have allowed the firm to undertake packaging, transport, and the distribution of branded garments right to the shelves at foreign malls.[7]

A knowledge accumulation taxonomy was developed on the basis of technological capabilities, and organizational and management capabilities. This was followed by an equation used to examine the relationship between technology transfer and technological capabilities, and firm performance

[6] In addition to interviews with Lee Ow Kim, the former managing director of Penfabric, information was also drawn on 31 October 2021 from https://www.toray.com/global/network/.

[7] In addition to interviews with its former managing director, Tan Yik Huay, other information was drawn on 31 October 2021 from https://www.talapparel.com/en/tal-group/apparel-manufacturer.

with the mediating role of organizational and management capabilities on this relationship using the PLS-SEM statistical method. Finally the IUI was developed by adopting Rasiah's (2019) systemic quad model, Saaty's (1990) Analytical Hierarchical Procedure (AHP) method, and Simon's (1977) Decision-Making Process method. Survey responses were used to construct a knowledge accumulation taxonomy for textiles and clothing firms in Pakistan that captures both technological capabilities, and organizational and management capabilities separately.

Technology transfer (TT) was examined by measuring embodied knowledge from imports of inputs and machinery (KI), technology acquisition (ACC), technology adaptation and imitation (IMI), while technological capabilities (TC) were measured by product (PROD) and process (PROC) technologies, R&D (RD), and human resource (HR) capabilities. The same method was used to measure organizational and management capabilities (OMC). Firm performance was measured by using Likert scale score assessments (1–5) of competitive advantage (COMP), export (EXP), productivity (PRO), and innovation (INN). Finally, the IUI was measured using selected proxies that constitute basic infrastructure, Science, Technology, and Innovation (STI) infrastructure, global integration, and network cohesion.

Nine levels of technological capabilities were differentiated vertically to locate firms in the technological capability trajectory, and six levels of organizational and management capabilities. The influence of the embedding ecosystem variables of the systemic quad was subsequently captured through Likert scale score ratings (1–5) to develop the IUI. Data collection was divided into two phases. The first phase involved a cross-sectional data collection process on textiles and clothing firms, which was used to develop the knowledge accumulation taxonomy by technological, and organizational and management capability trajectories in Chapter 5. Subsequently, Likert scale score ratings (1–5) to measure technology transfer (TT), firm performance (PERF), technological capabilities (TC), and organizational and management capabilities (OMC) using trajectories of sophistication by nine and six levels respectively, which are used in Chapter 6 to test the hypotheses and the relationships between TT and TC and PERF with OMC as a mediator.

The second fieldwork phase was set up to gain insights into the embedding ecosystem factors that influence technological, and organizational and management upgrading capabilities in the textiles and clothing firms, which was then used to develop the IUI. However, instead of reaching the surveyed firms, 50 textiles and clothing experts were identified to select the dimensions and sub-dimensions of the embedding ecosystem that impact on industrial upgrading in the textiles and clothing firms by using the systemic quad model.

The IUI was measured using selected proxies that constitute the four pillars of the systemic quad, i.e., basic infrastructure, STI infrastructure, global integration, and network cohesion. Likert scale score ratings (1–5) were used to obtain ratings from experienced experts from industry (30), academia (10) and government (10) who are strongly involved in strategies, research, and policies on industrial upgrading in the textiles and clothing industry.

Representative Firm Sample

A combined qualitative and quantitative approach is appropriate for this study, although its purpose is to gather and analyse data from a large pool of firms from the population to assess, analyse, and confirm the validity of the model used. The approach allows the use of analytical frameworks using data rather than just to interpret industrial upgrading but without attempting to predict or forecast, which is consistent with evolutionary understanding that industries are always evolving. The approach enables the achievement of the first objective, which is to locate firms in the taxonomy by knowledge trajectories, the impact of the independent variables, that is, technology transfer, technological capability, and organizational and management capability on firm performance to address the second objective, and the influence of the broad systemic quad variables to meet the third objective. The survey approach through the use of a questionnaire was utilized to collect data, and it was sent to 600 firms, which is more than the required numbers. The questionnaire carried detailed questions on technological, and organizational and management capabilities, and firm performance.

Characteristics of Firms

The textiles and clothing industry of Pakistan is generally divided into three size categories of small, medium, and large firms. However, since small firms are dominated by micro family firms that function informally using traditional technologies, these firms were excluded from the study. Small firms were also excluded because several of them operated informally and were largely incessable owing to a lack of registration with the formal textiles and clothing organizations. Furthermore, small textile and clothing companies in Pakistan largely operate as home industries, which are characaterized by traditional management, and focused on meeting local demand using low capital investment, and with little linkages with the medium and large firms. Moreover, officials from APTMA noted that small firms in Pakistan generally do not keep record of production, sales, and exports. Hence, only firms with employment size of over 50 employees were selected. The sampled firms were drawn from the Securities and Exchange Commission of Pakistan (SECP), All Pakistan Textile and Manufacturing Association (APTMA), Chamber of Commerce listing, and Pakistan Stock Exchange (PSX) (formerly Karachi Stock Exchange, KSE), which are the state associations of the registered firms. The firms were categorized according to the definition provided by the State Bank of Pakistan, SMEDA, and the Organization for Economic Cooperation and Development (OECD).[8]

Therefore, this research focuses on only medium and large textiles and clothing firms, which contributed over two-thirds of the total output of the industry in Pakistan in 2016 (Wadho & Chaudhry, 2016). The total number of registered textile and clothing firms in 2016 was 4458 with their provincial location amounting to 2687 in Punjab (primarily in Lahore and Faisalabad), 1592 in Sindh (mainly Karachi), 128 in Khyber Pakhtun Khwa (mainly in Peshawar), and 51 in Balochistan (mainly in Quetta) (Table 4.2). The provinces with the highest density of textiles and clothing firms were chosen for this study, that is, Punjab and Sindh.

From the two provinces chosen, the three main textiles and clothing cities of Pakistan were targeted for this study, viz., Karachi, Lahore, and Faisalabad as the textile and clothing sector is mostly concentrated in these big cities of Pakistan. The three cities together had a total of 2745 textiles and clothing firms in 2016: viz., 1511 firms in Karachi; 1128 firms in Lahore; and 466 firms in Faisalabad respectively (Table 4.3).

Using a stratified random sampling method the survey was performed in Karachi, Lahore, and Faisalabad from April 2016 to July 2017, and all data

Table 4.2 Provincial distribution of textiles and clothing firms, Pakistan, 2016

Province	Number of Firms	% of Total Population
Punjab	2687	60.3
Sindh	1592	35.7
KPK	128	2.9
Baluchistan	51	1.1
Total	4458	100.0

Note: KPK—Khyber Pakhtun Khwa; this population exceeds the 2745 we have used because we dropped micro and small firms as officials from the textiles and clothing associations of Pakistan neither held records of these firms with many of them operating informally.
Source: Wadho and Chaudhry (2016).

[8] The State Bank classified small firms as having employment up to 50 employees and medium firms up to 51–250 employees).

Table 4.3 Distribution of Firms by City, 2016

District	Number of Firms
Karachi	1511
Faisalabad	1128
Lahore	466
Hyderabad and Jamshoro	68
Gujranwala	246
Kasur	219
Sheikhupura	167
Sialkot	141

Source: Wadho and Chaudhry (2016)

were subsequently updated to 2018. The two criteria used for stratification were size and location between the three cities. No attempt was made to differentiate firm selection by textiles and clothing categories because several big firms in Pakistan had integrated textiles and clothing operations and we lacked ex ante knowledge of the actual operations of the firms. The survey questionnaires were distributed to 600 firms targeted at CEOs, members of top management, middle management and lower management (see Dess and Robinson in 1984). The sample was based on 2745 textiles and clothing firms, which were drawn from the 2015 census), with 95 per cent confidence interval and a margin of error of below 4 per cent. Based on Krejcie and Morgan (1970) estimations, for a total population of 2745, a sample of 498 is adequate with a 95 per cent confidence level and a margin of error of 5 per cent is sufficient to undertake a statistically significant analysis. The total complete and reliable questionnaires received from the participants were 503, which was helped by Nazia Nazeer's close association with officials in the textiles and clothing industry. The 83.8 per cent response rate easily passed the Cronbach alpha sample validity rate of 70 per cent (Hair et al, 2014). The questionnaires were delivered and collected by Nazia Nazeer and her enumerators in person. All firm respondents were also personally called by Nazia Nazeer before the questionnaires were collected. The interviews with the 50 textiles and clothing experts were continued till April 2018 with all data updated to December 2018. While the number of questionnaires sent (21.9 per cent) and responses received (18.3 per cent) more than met the percentage required for large populations from the last enumerated firm population of 2745 firms using the 2015 census of medium and large firms, the responses also met the Cronbach alpha sample validity test of 70 per cent. The sample breakdown against the population is presented in Table 4.4.

Table 4.4 Firm sample size

City	Total Firms	%	Required size	Selected Size
Faisalabad	1128	47	169	175
Lahore	466	16	70	85
Karachi	1151	41	259	345
Total	2745	100	498	600

Source: Prepared by the authors

The approach taken took account of survey approaches to gather financial data, which always raises reliability issues. Moreover, errors can also arise from different accounting measures used by firms (Dess & Robinson, 1984). Denison and Mishra (1995) deployed a three-year time span to minimize the effect of short-range fluctuations in performance records. In addition, this approach was preferred with the assumption that whatever errors that arise from the data collected will be cancelled out. This approach is also consistent with Kangis et al. (2000) who deployed an 'average corporate performance' measure over three years to avoid fluctuations that might result from problems involved in single reporting records. Thus, we deployed a three-year time-span of firm performance in the survey.

Pilot Test

Given the evolutionary approach used in the study, the questionnaires were first pilot tested to ensure that the appropriate questions were asked, and that firms' officials were on the same page with us with regard to the interpretation of the questions and the responses for all three objectives of the study (Chapters 5, 6, and 7). Importantly, it helped the finalization of questions (Zikmund, 2003). The pilot tests were conducted in Karachi, Lahore, and Faisalabad to examine the validity, reliability, and relevance of the variables in the study. In addition, for the expert interviews used for the construction of the IUI (Chapter 7), the first draft of the questionnaire was shown to five experts that specialize on technology and innovation issues in Pakistan's textiles and clothing firms, who interactively validated each item in the questionnaire by considering the theoretical foundation of the study against the embedding ecosystem institutions and organizations. Following their feedback some constructs were deleted, while some were added or rephrased to ensure that the data collection instrument and the constructs defined were appropriate to Pakistan's textiles and clothing firms. Consequently, the number of constructs selected was trimmed down from 82 to 61. The modified

Table 4.5 Pilot study results

Constructs	Cronbach's Alpha	No. of Items
Technology Transfer (TT)	0.84	12
Technological Capability (T)C	0.90	24
Organizational and Management Capability (OMC)	0.89	28
Firm performance (PERF)	0.86	29

Source: Authors' estimations

questionnaires were then sent to 50 recognized professionals in textiles and clothing firms (30), academia (10), and government (10). The expert professionals gave advice on the study questionnaire but were not involved in the main firm-level survey involving the 600 firms selected. The questions related to locating firms in the technological, and organizational and management capabilities trajectories for firms to tick the level their firm is best placed in the tables based on nine technological capability levels, and six organizational and management capability levels (see Chapter 5). For Objective 2, the findings of the descriptive statistics show that the questionnaire was adequate for final use with no abnormality issues. Table 4.5 shows the results of the pilot study used to address Objective 2.

The interviews used Likert scale score ratings (1–5) of 50 experts in the construction of the IUI, while the experts were drawn from those carrying the right tacit and experiential knowledge on textiles and clothing manufacturing.

Data Collection Instruments

The data collection instruments and the respondents are discussed in this sub-section. While the information on firms collected for Chapters 5 and 6 were drawn from the firm questionnaire, the interviews with textiles and clothing experts were conducted from 50 experts for Chapter 7.

Firm-level Questionnaire

A close-ended questionnaire was developed (see Appendix A) after reviewing the extant literature, discussions with experts with substantial experience in undertaking research on the industry, and officials from the textiles and clothing industry. In addition, the questionnaire also benefited from the work of others, such as Khan (2011) and Shujaat et al. (2016). The questionnaire was prepared in the English language and reviewed by the experts and industrial officials to minimize ambiguous phrasing of concepts for all the constructs. Self-completion and face-to-face meetings were the two approaches adopted for the survey. As the respondents were professionals from industry, it would perhaps become hard to expect or demand a long time from them. Most questionnaires were filled up by the respondents in their free time.

Five sections characterized the firm questionnaire. Section 1 focused on company's demographics. Section 2 sought information on technology transfer knowledge. Section 3 focused on the nine technological capability levels, including process and product technologies used, along with R&D and human development practices, while section 4 sought information on organizational and management capabilities. Section 5 drew information on firm performance.

Likert scale score ratings (1–5) were deployed for intensity questions (Zikmund, 2003), ranging from 1 (Strongly disagree), 2 (Disagree), 3 (neutral), 4 (Agree), and 5 (Strongly agree) were used. Table 4.6 describes the variables, their dimensions, and the number of items used in data collection to achieve Objectives 2 and 3.

The firm-level survey questionnaires were sent to CEOs and members of top management, middle management, and lower management members among the 600 sampled firms with an official cover letter to guarantee confidentiality of the survey, and that individual firms will not be identified. A wide range of communication routes were used to encourage participation in the survey, including calls, and direct visits to some of the sampled firms. Enumerators were used for firms that could not be reached by us. The initial respondents for this work were the CEOs and members of top management of the firms, but we had to extend the target group to include middle management and lower middle management personnel to increase the response rate, viz., technical and operations, quality, processing and production, and human resources. In total, the breakdown for the responding personnel for the 503 firms were: 128 (25 per cent) top management, 303 managers (60 per cent) middle management, and 72 (15 per cent) assistant managers, and supervisors from lower management (Table 4.6).

Expert Interviews

The expert interviews were conducted with 50 experts, which was determined by a division of 3:1:1 ratio as advised by officials of the APTMA. Consequently, the study obtained participation from 30 industry experts

Table 4.6 Textiles and clothing firms survey, by management level and size, Pakistan, 2018

Characteristics		N	%
Occupational Position	CEO or Top Management	128	25
	Middle Management	303	60
	Lower Management	72	15
Firm Size	Up to 250 employees	183	36
	More than 250 employees	320	64

Source: Authors' survey.

from textiles and clothing firms engaged in strategic decision-making on technological, organizational, and management development, 10 academics in universities and institutes who undertook research on textiles and clothing firms, and 10 government officials who carried the responsibility of promoting textiles and clothing firms.

Overall, a total of 503 questionnaires were received satisfactorily from the 600 sent, representing a 83.8 per cent response rate. The 97 firms that were excluded include those that supplied incomplete responses. The construction of the IUI relied on a different set of data, which was drawn from 50 expert opinions from industry (30), academia (10), government (10), and textiles and clothing related focus carrying strong tacit and experiential knowledge on the textiles and clothing industry. The empirical data for Chapters 5 and 6 are drawn from this survey, while the empirical data for Chapter 7 is drawn from the 50 expert interviews. Meanwhile, the taxonomy by trajectory categorizations of the nine-level technological capabilities, and the six-level organizational and management capabilities undertaken in this chapter will be used in Chapters 5 and 6.

Summary

This chapter described the broad conceptual and methodological framework, along with primary research undertaken to address the three objectives of the book. A conceptual framework was developed to construct a taxonomy of technological, and organizational and management capabilities and formulate the critical variables appropriate for the textile and clothing industry of Pakistan. However, the specific methodologies for each of the three objectives of the book are discussed in analytical Chapters 5, 6, and 7 as they address somewhat different issues.

The first part of the methodology focused on knowledge accumulation at the firm level that leads to industrial upgrading, which is presented in greater detail in Chapter 5. The study identifies nine levels of technological capabilities and six levels of organizational and management capabilities to locate the 503 firms in that trajectory. The questions used in the questionnaire related to firms' location in the industrial upgrading trajectory are captured in the attributes described at each technological, and organizational and management capability level without specifying the trajectory order so as not to bias the responses.

The second part established the broad methodology for testing the influence of technology transfer and technological capabilities on firm performance by using organizational and management capability as the mediating variable using the sample of 503 firms. The specific details of the PLS-SEM model used to test the relationships are discussed in Chapter 6.

The third part focused on formulating the IUI using the assessment of 50 experts on the textiles and clothing industry by deploying Saaty's (1990) Analytical Hierarchical Procedure and Simon's (1977) decision-making approach, which is developed as an index to prioritize the shaping and molding of the embedding ecosystem factors through the assignment of weights to all dimensions and sub-dimensions using Rasiah's (2019) systemic quad model that will be discussed in greater detail in Chapter 7. The IUI is expected to offer policy-makers an instructive policy instrument to lay the path for industrial upgrading to the frontier in Pakistan in particular, and the other countries seeking to stimulate upgrading in the textiles and clothing industry in general.

5 Technological, and Organizational and Management Capabilities

Introduction

Since Marx (1867) and Schumpeter (1912, 1934, 1942) initiated the first profound argument over the critical role of technology in driving economic growth, the concept has evolved significantly, albeit truncatedly. Mainstream works have used growth accounting and subsequently computable general equilibrium models to focus on total factor productivity (Solow, 1957; Romer, 1994). Despite the glaring problems of this methodology, which among others, is because of its inability to capture tacit knowledge (Dosi, 1995; Rasiah, 1995), it has continued to dominate assessments of technology and economic development. In fact, Young's (1994) claim using this methodology that the East Asian economies grew through factor inputs, and hence, their growth would eventually stall, has without any doubt been proven wrong. Hence, we deploy the embodied technology approach pioneered by Rosenberg (1982) to examine technological, organizational, and management capabilities in this chapter.

While the technological capability framework recognizes the significance of tacit knowledge, not all of it can be measured over a period of time as humans react differently over different situations, including the same experts often show variations in outcomes for their efforts. Nevertheless, the technological, organizational, and management capabilities' approaches offer the most significant mapping of industrial upgrading as the specificity of industry allows a more focused measure of embodied technologies and strategies.

As explained in Chapter 3, industrial upgrading has been achieved by South Korea and Taiwan through firm-level technological capability building via technology transfer and the mediating role of organizational and management capabilities as national firms inserted into global production networks (Kim, 1997; Rasiah & Lin, 2005). Indeed, South Korean and Taiwanese firms, such as Samsung, and TSMC have by the turn of the millennium leapfrogged the global incumbents to shape the technology frontier in memory and

Industrial Upgrading in the Textiles and Clothing Industry. Nazia Nazeer and Rajah Rasiah, Oxford University Press.
 DOI: 10.1093/9780198961697.003.0005

logic chips respectively (Rasiah & Yap, 2019). However, given the specificity of industries, this chapter uses the nine-level technological capabilities, and six-level organizational and management capabilities to locate Pakistan's textiles and clothing firms in the taxonomy trajectory developed in Chapter 4.

Since technological upgrading of diverse industries varies with location and time, several methodological frameworks have been adapted to suit specific industries (Rasiah, 2003, 2007; Figueiredo, 2014), which is an appropriate practice to develop frameworks that combine firm-level taxonomies of industrial upgrading with catch-up trajectories that takes account of industry type, timing, and location. All knowledge-intensive industries are managed and moulded by their own staffs' tacitness, independence, and complexity, which is unique to particular industries (Nelson & Winter, 1982). In the assembly model, manufacturers provide the parts for simple assembly to garment sewing plants, while in the OEM model the buyer–seller linkage between foreign merchants and local manufacturers allows national firms to learn about tasks in the upstream and downstream divisions of the textiles and clothing chain (Gereffi, 1999).

The organization of the chapter is as follows: The first section describes the specification of the analytical framework based on firm-level knowledge accumulation targeted at catch up in textile and clothing firms. The second section outlines the methodology used for this research. The third section describes the outcomes that constitute mapping of firm-level technological capabilities using particular indicators to examine their catch-up trajectories, which is then finished with the chapter summary. Also, examined in the mapping process are organizational and management capabilities as they correspond to their level of technological capabilities. However, organizational and management capabilities are primarily used in Chapter 6 as a mediating variable. Not only that the intensity of capabilities involving organizational and management capabilities are difficult to capture precisely as a considerable aspect of it involves competence, it appears best to use this approach from the perspective of firms.

Analytic Framework

The taxonomy by trajectories for locating textiles and clothing firms in the technological, and organizational and management capabilities was developed in Chapter 4 (see Table 4.1), while the exercise in this chapter is to locate the 503 firms in the taxonomy by technological trajectories (see Table 5.1).

While firms can jump stages in both the technological, and organizational and management trajectories, it is typically common only in the early stages.

Table 5.1 Textiles and clothing firms by technological capability, Pakistan, 2018

Level	Location			Size		Total
	Karachi	Lahore	Faisalabad	Large	Medium	
1	33	18	87	41	97	**138**
2	18	8	8	18	16	**34**
3	55	9	15	25	54	**79**
4	58	12	36	51	55	**106**
5	56	11	19	52	34	**86**
6	18	8	3	22	7	**29**
7	23	7	1	30	1	**31**
Total	**261**	**73**	**169**	**239**	**264**	**503**

Note: Figures represent the most advanced level of participation only.
Source: Authors' survey.

Also, it is important to note that the buyer-driven industry of clothing is largely driven by brandholders who have outsourced stages of manufacturing to sub-contractors. The most sophisticated clothing manufacturers in Pakistan largely operate as OEMs, though some have ventured into using their own brand names, *viz*., Diners, Limelight, Sana Safinaz, Khadi, Zelbury, and Generation.

The trajectory classifications by technological, and organizational and management capabilities are also used in Chapter 6. Firms responded in each of the categories through the description of activities that they enjoyed. The capability levels were not numbered so as not to bias firms' replies. Nazia Nazeer followed up with careful interviews to ensure that their questionnaire replies matched what they meant in their replies.

Firms in the Technological Capability Trajectory

The taxonomy by trajectory shown in Table 5.1 is based on firms' highest technological capability levels attained with the focus of the important activities undertaken in each of the stages. Like most small firms in Pakistan, a number of medium clothing firms were also only specializing largely on cut, make, and pack operations and supplying entirely to the domestic market. The catch-up phase starts with adaptations in product and process technologies from level 2. Table 5.1 shows the different levels of technological capabilities achieved by Pakistan's textiles and clothing firms in the sample by the year 2018.[1]

[1] Although the survey was begun in 2017, all responses were updated in 2018.

Table 5.2 Textiles and clothing firms by organizational and management capability, Pakistan, 2018

	Organizational and Management Capabilities					
Level	Karachi	Lahore	Faisalabad	Large Firms	Medium Firms	Total Firms
1	33	18	87	41	97	138
2	73	17	23	43	70	113
3	114	23	55	103	89	192
4	41	16	4	52	8	63
Total	261	74	169	239	264	503

Source: Prepared by the authors.

Entry Level

Of the 503 firms surveyed, the maximum number of 138 firms only reported participation in technological capability level 1 activities where the major technological activity focused on simple activities (Table 5.2). Whereas the bulk of these firms are in Faisalabad (87), Karachi and Lahore had 33 and 18 firms respectively. Although these firms were medium and large sized, they engaged in cut, make, and trim activities only. Firms at level 1 were not engaged in exports and were primarily supplying firms ahead in the trajectories through subcontract activities.

Catch-up: Initial-Phase

The initial and catch-up phases start from levels 2 and 3 when minor improvements are made on product and process technologies. The 34 firms that reported participation in level 2 activities had mastered cut, make, and trim operations, but were also engaged in adaptions and other forms of incremental innovations. At levels 2 and 3, the machinery and equipment used are dated with both levels of firms lacking original equipment manufacturing (OEM) capabilities. At levels 2 and 3, firms use quality control circles. Minor improvements have been the prime source of innovations undertaken by level 2 and 3 firms.

Catch-Up: Mid-Phase

Levels 4 and 5 constitute the mid-phase of catch-up. Latecomer OEMs raise revenue through inserting themselves into GVCs directly rather than indirectly through the main subcontractors, creating and building stronger linkages that support ramping up of firm-level capabilities. Level 4 firms in Pakistan have training functions, but the focus is on skills enrichment rather than on the acquisition of cognitive and programming knowledge. Whereas at level 4 technological capability, firms show engineers in their payroll, they do not have separate training departments. Nevertheless, level 4 firms participate in product and process adaptation activities. While market experience, knowledge, and processes through which companies develop their knowledge are crucial to understand their performance and spread internationally, such expertise is often accessed through external consultants, while most of these firms are engaged in modular and relational activities in GVCs.

Large textile and clothing firms in Pakistan were mostly involved at levels 4 (51) and 5 (52) technological capability activities with participation in early designing capability with collaboration with buyers and suppliers, including in colour mix, yarn, and fabric among textile firms. Meanwhile, medium-sized firms numbered 55 at level 4 and 34 at level 5 and are engaged in adapting used machinery and equipment acquired from large firms.

Catch-up: Critical Transition Phase

The critical transition stages are the levels when textiles and clothing firms acquire the capabilities to undertake high value-added manufacturing operations, including OEM capabilities but do not have the capability to undertake new material development to meet global demand, introduce autonomous robots, and strong ownership and knowhow linkages with leading brandholders, R&D organizations in specialized universities, and fashion houses. Among the two critical transition catch-up phase levels of 6 and 7, 22 large firms and seven medium firms reported level 6 technological capabilities, and another 30 large firms and one medium firm showed level 7 technological capability. Also, based on sophistication, firms in Karachi dominate levels 6 (18) and 7 (23). These firms use product-related technologies, including 30 large and one medium-sized firm that show designing capabilities to participate in functional design and diversification in products through trust and cooperation with their main customers. A few firms used their own brands but sold their garments in the domestic market. Khaadi, Limelight, Sapphire, and Diners are some examples. The 30 large firms and one medium size firm that participated in level 7 technological activities conduct basic to intermediate research through affiliations with universities, such as the Textile University in Faisalabad, and Textile Institute, Pakistan

(TIP) in Karachi, and small training institutes under provincial boards of technical education. However, these firms reported facing poaching problems, and hence, have not managed to retain most of the trained graduates. The government also encouraged technological upgrading to penetrate and take full advantage of China's market, especially after the third Textiles and Apparel Policy (2020–2025) was launched. However, the macroeconomic collapse since 2019 following a ballooning of external debt has undermined these initiatives. Consequently, no textiles and clothing firm demonstrated participation in levels 8 and 9 technological capabilities.

Overall, entry level 1 and mid-catch-up level 4 dominated the technological capabilities of Pakistan's textiles and clothing medium and large firms respectively in 2018. Also, firms in Karachi dominated technological levels 2–7. Most medium-size firms were at entry levels 3 and 4 technological capabilities, while most large firms were at levels 4 and 5 technological capability activities. Indeed, none of the textiles and clothing firms were at the frontier phase, though technologically they show the potential to reach levels 8 and 9.

Firms in the Organizational and Management Capability Trajectory

The taxonomy shown in Table 5.1 is based on firms' highest organizational and management capability levels attained with the focus of the important activities undertaken in each of the stages. A number of the firms were also only specializing in levels 1, 2, and 3 organizational and management capabilities

Entry Level

Given the traditional nature of operations and the lack of export quality capabilities, 138 firms were engaged in simple operations, though these firms were large and medium-sized (Table 5.2). Whereas Faisalabad had the most number of firms operating at the entry level with functional management capability and supervisors dominating operations (87), Karachi and Lahore had 33 and 18 firms respectively. Of these firms, 41 were large firms and another 97 were medium-sized firms. Most of these firms were engaged in producing uniform clothing for schools, the military, police, and government officials.

Catch-up: Initial Phase

The breakdown of firms enjoying level 2 organizational and management capabilities were 113 firms overall in the initial catch-up phase with 73 from Karachi, 17 from Lahore, and 23 from Faisalabad of which 43 firms were large and 70 firms were medium-sized. Pakistan's firms at level 2 organizational and management capability have put in place a knowledge development focus towards improving the quality and delivery times of items among level 3 firms. Supervisors were still used to handle quality control and meeting targets.

Catch-Up: Mid-Phase

The sampled textiles and clothing firms were dominated by organizational and management capability level 3 with 192 firms and a breakdown of 114 in Karachi, 23 in Lahore, and 55 in Faisalabad. The breakdown by size was 103 large firms and 89 medium-sized firms. Connected in GVCs, these firms learn and adapt considerably from international buyer-supplier links. Engineers help achieve the standards required to meet the specs supplied by international buyers. Firms introduce MRP1 practices to reduce throughput time, but Pakistan's firms are often saddled with fluctuations in delivery times owing to poor transport facilities faced by firms in Faisalabad and Lahore.

Level 4 constitutes the mid-phase of catch-up. The breakdown of organizational and management capabilities enjoyed by firms locate in Karachi, Lahore, and Faisalabad were 41, 16, and 4 and by large and medium-sized firms were 52 and 8. These firms enjoy collaboration with textile institutes, training centres, and support from textile organizations but lack the links with state of the art labs at universities abroad, participation in international logistics activities, and alliances with brand holders to penetrate major foreign markets to engage in higher value-added activities, such as designing for these markets. They are also not engaged in consortias within Pakistan to share research activities.

While the level 4 firms expressed ambition to catch up with the frontier organizational and management capabilities of 5 and 6, these firms noted that the embedding environment in Pakistan does not offer them a level playing field to compete with frontier firms abroad.

Summary

This chapter updated significantly the taxonomy used in the past on the textiles and clothing industry following the evolutionary tradition of looking at industry-specific developments, location and timing of the evaluation. This new taxonomy helped the identification of nine levels of technological capabilities, and six levels of organizational and management capabilities. In doing so the taxonomy takes account of some of the leading global firms that are located abroad, e.g., TAL, Toray, and Everest Textiles.

The exploration into the 'forest' of textile and clothing firms to examine the 'trees' produced an interesting account of the nuts and bolts of the industry in Pakistan. Although some firms have reached technological capability level 7 in the trajectory of the industry, the bulk of the large and medium firms are still at levels 1–5 activities, which explains why the industry's exports have largely stuck in low and medium value-added activities despite enjoying strong natural resource endowments and a long period of export experience. Also, Pakistan's textiles and clothing firms only show level 4 organizational and management capabilities when the frontier textiles and clothing firms are level 6.

Yet, despite concentration of firms in relatively low technological, organizational, and management capability levels, the progress of some national firms to technological capability levels 6 and 7 suggest that the potential is there for upgrading to technological capability levels 8 and 9 and organizational and management capability levels 5 and 6. A profound evaluation of the experience of Everest Textiles, TAL, and Toray in reaching level 9 and level 6 technological, organizational, and management capability levels can offer Pakistan's national firms the direction to catch-up with these firms.

This chapter provided the empirical start to locate Pakistan's firms in the technological, and organizational and management capability trajectories, which is followed by an assessment of the drivers of firm performance in Chapter 6.

6
Drivers of Firm Performance

Introduction

The acquisition of technology is a critical factor to raise firm performance (Desai, 1984; Lall, 1992; Bell & Pavit, 1995; Rasiah, 2004). Also, Rasiah (2004) had emphasized the importance of technological capabilities on export success among East Asian countries. Whereas Figueiredo (2003) determined the impact of learning processes on technological capability in firms, Rasiah (2004a) found technological capabilities to affect positively firm performance in African, Asian, and Latin American countries. Specifically, there is evidence that industrial upgrading is largely achieved through changes in organizational and management, and process and product technological capabilities, including incremental innovations, with a major source of it originating from technology transfer from abroad (Amsden, 1991; Rasiah, 1995; Kim, 1997). Although the growth and impact of technological capabilities has been examined extensively (see Lall, 1992; Rasiah, 1995; Kim, 1997), there are gaps in the way the concept has been used to analyse firm performance. Much of the problem arises from the difficulty in measuring technology owing to its dynamic public goods properties, and the wide variance in the way it evolves in different industries and sectors.

In addition, several works emphasize the importance of organizational and management practices in the development of technological capabilities and improvements in firm performance (e.g., Barney. 1991; Hamel & Prahalad, 1993). Indeed, organizational and management capabilities have increasingly become important in driving firm-level competitive advantage (Prahalad & Hamel. 1990). However, the extant literature does not offer an exhaustive account of how organizational and management capabilities mediate the relationship between technology transfer and technological capabilities, and firm performance. Consequently, this chapter seeks to examine its relationship in the textiles and clothing industry of Pakistan. Unlike most other works on technology transfer and technological capabilities, and firm performance, this chapter examines the mediating role of organizational and management capabilities in that relationship.

Industrial Upgrading in the Textiles and Clothing Industry. Nazia Nazeer and Rajah Rasiah, Oxford University Press.
 DOI: 10.1093/9780198961697.003.0006

While tacit knowledge is impossible to measure exhaustively, organizational and management capabilities provide some approximation of its potential aspects, which include firm strategies, inventory and quality control systems, promotional activities, and buyer–supplier relationships, and external R&D support. The inclusion of these firm-level instruments is critical to connect the micro-level influences with the meso- and macro-level influences to stimulate industrial upgrading.

The chapter starts with the premise that the lack of industrial upgrading in Pakistan is both a consequence of little domestic accumulation of technological, organizational, and management capabilities, as well as a lack of technology transfer from abroad. Hence, this chapter examines the relationship between technology transfer and technological capabilities on firm performance using organizational and management capabilities as a mediating variable in the textile and clothing firms in Pakistan. The following section explains the methodology deployed in the study, while the subsequent sections describe the findings and analysis of outcomes against the hypothesis developed in the chapter, followed by a summary of the overall findings.

Methodology

The methodology for examining the link between technology transfer and technological capabilities on firm performance, and the mediating effects of organizational and management capabilities on this relationship uses structural equation model (SEM), which is suitable as several factors collectively account for the outcomes, and it is also ideal when the evidence available is from a cross-sectional data set.

Structural Equation Modelling

While the methodology for the construction of the taxonomies by trajectories is explained in Chapter 4, we used SEM by deploying the Smart-Partial Least Square (PLS 3.0) software to examine the relationships. This SEM has two sub-models: the inner model (structural model), which shows the relations among the latent variables (independent and dependent), and the outer model (measurement model), which shows the relations among these latent or unobserved variables with their observed indicators. The exogenous variable contains path arrows indicating outwards and not directed towards, while the endogenous variable contains path directing towards it, indicating the effects of other variables.

Although SEM has different approaches, the widely used approaches are the covariance-based SEM (CB-SEM), which use software packages, such as AMOS, LISREL EQS, and MPlus. The other is the Partial Least Squares (PLS), which emphasizes the examination of variance by using PLS-Graph, SmartPLS, VisualPLS, and WarpPLS.

Partial Least Square

Smart Partial Least Square (PLS) structural equation modelling can be traced back to Wold's (1985) initial work on principal component analysis. Some scholars recently refined Wold's (1985) work on PLS (e.g., Lohmöller, 1989; Chin, 1998; Chin & Newsted, 1999) to use computer packages for its wider use. Besides, the previous literature on SEM was developed only with reference to co-variance-based SEM (e.g., Arbuckle, 1996; Enders, 2006).

PLS is similar to ordinary least squares (OLS) regressions, but, as a component-based structural equation model it deals simultaneously with the measurement and structural paths (Lohmöller, 1989). The PLS-SEM technique and its framework are explained in the subsequent sections. Smart PLS is similar to semi-parametric regression techniques in that it does not need the distribution of data to be normal, though specific models address issues associated with distribution. The component-based approach was preferred over covariance-based approaches, because the latter methods only support reflective constructs, while PLS not only supports reflective constructs but also allows the evaluation of formative constructs (Chin, 1998b). One important advantage to use this method is its ability to handle multicollinearity issues and to solve convergence issues (Fornell & Cha, 1994). Lastly, PLS does not require assumptions regarding the population and measurement scales, and hence, works easily with ordinal, interval, and nominal classification of variables (Fornell & Cha, 1994).

Fundamentals of PLS-SEM

The PLS-SEM involves two distinct types of outer models, i.e., reflective and formative (Diamantopoulos & Siguaw, 2006). The former shows causal relations between the latent variable and its indicator variable whereas the latter shows causal relations between manifest or indicator variables towards its latent constructs.[1] The PLS methodological approach needs separate estimation of all constructs. The sequence starts with an examination of the measurement model to confirm the uni-dimensionality and validity of all constructs to be tested (Fornell & Cha, 1994). If the indicator items of a construct do not link with their related construct, it has to be modified prior to the structural estimation process, which is carried out using confirmatory factor analysis (CFA) (O'Cass & Grace, 2003). Furthermore, the assessment of the measurement model takes place independently in all high-order constructs (Wilson, 2010). The structural measurement or the estimation of the inner model relations can be done once the measurement model is fit. Structural assessment provides an estimation of nomological validity (Fornell & Cha, 1994; Chin, 1998; Tenenhaus et al., 2005).

Reflective and formative estimations of indicators of the relationships between technology transfer and technological capabilities and firm performance, and the mediating effect of organizational and management capability in that relationship were carried out. Reflective indicators are used to estimate second-order factor models because all independent variables that were included in this study have their respective first- and second-order model constructs.

PLS Model Evaluation

As explained earlier, a systematic estimation of PLS is conducted through a two-step procedure, that is, through an assessment of the measurement model and the structural model. Reflective and formative models have been differentiated and used to make the estimations in the measurement models. The following steps were followed while performing the assessment of the measurement model.

Assessment of Reflective Models

Reflective models involve uni-dimensionality, reliability, internal consistency, indicator reliability, convergent, and discriminant validity, which are explained below:

[1] Reflective indicators are viewed as the 'effects' of the latent variables. In other words, these latent variables form the indicators (Chin, 2010). All the reflective indicators change if the latent variable changes. Also, all the reflective indicators must be positively correlated. Formative indicators are considered as the cause variable that shows the forms in which the latent variable is identified (Chin, 2010). Moreover, a formative indicator for a similar latent variable does not necessarily have to be correlated (Bollen, 1989; Rossiter, 2002).

Loadings on Uni-dimensionality

Loadings show relationship whereas the indicators show the construct, which can be estimated using confirmatory factor analysis (CFA). The coefficient of loading is normally considered high when it exceeds 0.6, while its values are considered low when it is less than 0.4 (Gefen & Straub, 2005).

Internal Consistency

Internal consistency can be estimated using the Cronbach's alpha and composite reliability tests (Cronbach, 1951; Henseler & Fassot, 2010). Because the Cronbach's alpha presumes that each indicator is equally reliable, therefore, it underestimates the internal consistencies of reliability of all latent constructs used in PLS-SEM, while the composite reliability test presumes that all indicators have changed loadings (Henseler & Fassot, 2010). Therefore, it is not important what reliability coefficients are utilized, which is considered as satisfactory when the value of internal consistency reliability is more than 0.7 in the initial stages and over 0.8 in the later stages of the analysis (Nunnally & Bernstein, 1994).

Indicator Reliability

The indicator reliability is a tool to observe the loadings of all reflective indicators used to evaluate indicator reliability. Usually, the indicator reliability measures the amount of indicators variance through their related latent variables. The indicator reliability is a tool to observe the loadings of all reflective indicators used to evaluate indicator reliability. Usually, indicator reliability measures the amount of indicators variance through their related latent variables. Loadings above 0.708 are suggested, as they specify that the construct clarifies more than 50 per cent of the indicator's variance, and can provide satisfactory reliability (Chin, 2010). Consequently, the convergent validity, discriminant validity, and loading significance tests were undertaken to ensure their reliability for use in the analysis.

Convergent Validity

The convergent validity or Average Variance Extracted (AVE) to measure convergent validity was proposed by Fornell and Cha (1994), which reflects the extent to which the single items load on their labelled constructs. A value of 0.5 shows the acceptable amount of convergent validity, which means that latent variables can explain half of its indicator variance on average.

Discriminant Validity

Cross loadings are examined to assess discriminant validity. If correlations are not present between measures of separate constructs, it shows that discriminant validity exists. In other words, the measure must load properly upon their intended variable or construct rather than with other associated constructs (Agarwal & Karahanna, 2000; Chin, 1998).

Loading Significance

The assessment of parameters or loading significance is done through bootstrapping or jack- knifing option methods (Chin, 1998). The two-options estimate t-statistics, which could result in decisions made based on parameter significance. For this study, critical ratios to choose parameter significance were assessed through the method of bootstrapping (Efron & Tibshirani, 1994). The sample numbers for bootstrapping were fixed at 500, which is well beyond the recommended number of 200 that was proposed by Chin (1998). The directional hypothesis' deploying one-tail tests were utilized and the value of 1.65 was set to reject the null hypothesis at the significance level of 0.05 and 2.33 at significance level of 0.01.

Assessment of Formative Measurement Model

Henseler and Fassot (2010) proposed two levels to estimate the validity of formative constructs, that is, one for the indicator and other for the construct, which are explained below:

Indicator Level

To estimate the validity of the indicators in the formative constructs, it is necessary to observe the significance of their weights using a bootstrapping technique (Efron & Tibshirani, 1994) or a jack-knifing technique (Miller, 1974). A 0.05 significance level shows that the indicators are significant and have a satisfactory level of validity. Furthermore, the issue of multicollinearity among all the formative indicators shall be estimated through the assessment of the variance inflation factor (VIF) (Cassel et al., 2000), which demonstrates the degree of the indicator's variance that is illuminated through other indicators of a similar construct. It is to be noted that values less than 10 thresholds indicate that multicollinearity is not a problem, and the model can be accepted (Gujarati, 2003; Diamantopoulos & Siguaw, 2006).

Construct Level

The assessment of the construct level is necessary to test the support of nomological validation, which refers to a set of hypotheses, in which the formative construct performs as a predictor. As a result, the relationships among the constructs in the model must be strong and significant (Henseler, 2010; Diamantopoulos & Riefler, 2011). In case, the correlation among the formative and other constructs in the model are less than 0.7, the construct contrasts satisfactorily as compared to the other constructs (Bruhn, Georgi, & Hadwich, 2008). When the measurement model has been validated, the structural model can be fit for further analysis.

Assessment of the Structural Measurement Model

The most important parameter to evaluate the PLS model is the coefficient of determination (R^2) or multiple determinations of all dependent constructs. The R^2 calculates the predictive variance of latent variables related to their overall variance. An R^2 of PLS-SEM path models is considered strong (0.67), moderate (0.33), and weak (0.19) (Chin, 1998).

The Size Effect f^2 and Q^2

At this stage, the structural model can be evaluated by assessing the regression coefficients among the validated latent constructs. The regression coefficient specifies the strength of the relationship between two latent constructs. Some studies claim that regression coefficients must exceed 0.1 to provide a significant effect in the model (e.g., Henseler & Fassot, 2010). Additionally, regression coefficients need a minimum significance level of 0.05. Resampling techniques, such as jack-knifing or bootstrapping tests are normally deployed to determine the significance level (Miller, 1974; Efron & Tibshirani, 1994).

Lastly, the estimation of the structural model includes the capacity of the model to predict. For this purpose, the predictive significance of the structural model is evaluated by means of Q^2 Stone-Geisser's statistics, which is measured through a blindfolding technique (Tenenhaus et al., 2005). The size effects of f^2 and Q^2 predicts the model fitness and robustness.

Specification of Variables

The variables to be examined in this chapter are technology transfer (TT), Technological Capabilities (TC), and organizational and management capabilities (OMC), and firm performance. Table 6.1 shows the variables, dimensions, and their sub-dimensions.

Technology Transfer

Knowledge inflow from imported inputs and machinery (KI), acquisition (ACC), assimilation (ASS), and adaptation and imitation (IMI) are used to estimate technology transfer.

Table 6.1 Variables, dimensions, and measurement

Variable	Dimensions	Measurement
TT [exogenous variable]	• KI • KM • ACC • ASS • IMI	**KI** Access to external technological knowledge in imported inputs and machinery, the use of latest acquired technological knowledge, and firm's internal knowledge development (No to both—0; Yes to one—1; Yes to both—2) **KM** If firm has knowledge management activities ((No-0; Yes—1). **ACC** Acquisition of latest technical knowledge, techniques, designing methods, skills development, improvement and modification of technologies (No—0; Yes—1) **ASS** The assimilation of technology through absorption and internalization of transferred technology (No—0; Yes—1). **IMI** When adaptation and imitation of product and process technologies take place in innovation and reverse engineering (No—0; Yes—1)
TC [exogenous variable]	• HR • RD • PROC • PROD	**HR** Training functions using external staff—1; training functions through training staff internally—2, training department with training programmes—3; share of skilled, technical, and professional staff in total staff (per cent). **RD** R&D estimated using R&D Expenditure in sales (per cent). **PROC** Participation in process innovation (No—0; Yes—1) **PROD** Participation in product innovation (No—0; Yes—1)
OMC	• **KM** • **MC** • **SP**	**KM** Participation in knowledge management (No—0; Yes—1) **MC** Participation in marketing of products (No—0; Yes—1) **SP** Participation in strategic planning (No—0; Yes—1)

Continued

Table 6.1 *Continued*

Variable	Dimensions	Measurement
PERF [endogenous variable]	• INN; • COMP • EXP • PRO	**INN** Firm's innovation capability in process and product technology (1—new to the firm; 2—new to the country; 3—new to the universe **COMP** Competitiveness achieved by firms, measured as national markets 1, regional markets 2, and global markets 3. **EXP** Export share in gross output (per cent). **PRO** Productivity was measured as gross output divided by gross inputs.

Source: Authors.

$$TT = (KI, ACC, ASS, IMI)$$

Technological Capabilities

Human Resource (HR), Research and Development (RD), and Process (PROC) and Product (PROD) technologies were used to estimate technological capabilities as shown below:

$$TC = (HR, RD, PROC, PROD).$$

Organizational and Management Capabilities

Knowledge Management (KM), Learning by Doing (LD), Strategic Planning (SP) and Marketing Capabilities (MC) were used to estimate organizational and management capabilities as shown below:

$$OMC = (KM, LD, SP, MC).$$

Firm Performance

Innovation (INN), Productivity (PRO), Export (EXP), and Competitiveness (COMP) were used to estimate firm performance (PERF) as follows:

$$PERF = (INN, PRO, EXP, COMP).$$

Table 6.2 Indicators used in the analysis

Construct	Item used	Loadings
ACC	ACC1	0.746
	ACC2	0.764
	ACC3	0.891
	ACC4	0.769
ASS	ASS1	0.831
	ASS2	0.830
	ASS3	0.855
	ASS4	0.852
COMP	COMP1	0.807
	COMP3	0.804
	COMP4	0.861
EXP	EXP1	0.735
	EXP2	0.778
	EXP3	0.772
	EXP4	0.725
	EXP5	0.813
	HR3	0.784
	HR4	0.735
	HR5	0.765
	HR6	0.777
	HR7	0.771
	HR8	0.768
INN	INN6	0.767
	INN7	0.832
	INN8	0.864
	INN9	0.823
	INN10	0.869
KM	KM1	0.831
	KM2	0.861
	KM3	0.833
	KM4	0.824
	KM7	0.853
MC	MC3	0.763
	MC4	0.863
	MC5	0.828
	MC6	0.811
PRO	PRO1	0.788
	PRO2	0.881
	PRO3	0.893
	PRO4	0.843
PROC	PROC1	0.829
	PROC2	0.905
	PROC3	0.754

Continued

Table 6.2 *Continued*

Construct	Item used	Loadings
PROD	PROD1	0.898
	PROD2	0.881
	PROD4	0.848
RD	RD1	0.751
	RD3	0.819
	RD4	0.766
	RD5	0.846
SP	SP1	0.710
	SP3	0.786
	SP4	0.868

Note: Items having loading < 0.50, i.e., if AVE was less than 0.50.
Source: Authors' estimations.

Smart PLS-3 was deployed to analyse the data from the 503 firms surveyed. Technology transfer and technological capabilities were used as explanatory variables, and firm performance as the dependent variable, with organizational and management capabilities as the mediator.

Specification of the Statistical Model

Two steps were taken to validate the measurement model through confirmatory factor analysis and to fit the structural model through path analysis with the latent variables. The loading for each variable is shown in Table 6.2.

Assessment of Measurement Model

The measurement models deal with the relationship between latent and observed variables, which constitute (a) composite reliability (CR), (b) individual indicator reliability, and (c) average variance extracted (AVE). Additionally, the Fornell-Larcker Heterotrait-monotrait (HTMT) and cross-loadings were deployed to assess the discriminant validity through PLS logarithm, which is the criteria used to assess the measurement model based on formative and reflective constructs. Indicators reflecting a loading lower than a threshold value of 0.7 were deleted as a rule of thumb (see Table 6.3).

Table 6.3 Results of convergent validity

Constructs	Cronbach's Alpha	Composite Reliability	Average Variance Extracted (AVE)
Technology acquisition	0.802	0.871	0.621
Technology assimilation	0.853	0.908	0.708
Competitiveness	0.761	0.854	0.66
Export share in output	0.829	0.883	0.552
Human resource	0.847	0.892	0.534
Innovation	0.878	0.919	0.682
Knowledge intensity	0.888	0.878	0.714
Knowledge management	0.886	0.924	0.705
Learning by doing	0.806	0.876	0.649
Marketing Capability	0.834	0.888	0.678
Product technology	0.864	0.915	0.707
Process technology	0.795	0.873	0.681
R&D	0.802	0.864	0.645
Strategic planning	0.727	0.835	0.577

Source: Authors' estimations.

Table 6.3 shows the Cronbach alpha statistics and composite reliability threshold values as suggested by Nunnally and Bernstein (1994). The composite reliability results show that most of the values lie between 0.831 and 0.928, which denotes that less than 50 per cent of an indicator's variance was a result of errors. Additionally, the AVE is more than 0.5 for all constructs. Every construct in the model shows a high degree of internal consistency reliability and all the indicators are suitable for their relevant variables or constructs. Hence, all the reliability tests provide an indication of uni-dimensionality, and hence, show that all the constructs are appropriate for further examination.

A higher outer loading of constructs indicates that every item is strongly related to their respective constructs as the outer loadings are over 0.708, which is above as the rule of thumb. Thus, the results in Table 6.3 above verify that the constructs' measurements have a higher level of convergent validity with acceptable internal consistencies. In other words, the indicators of measurement for every construct estimated for relevance of construct is satisfactory.

Discriminant Validity

The Fornell-Larcker criterion (1981) was used to assess discriminant validity and heterotrait-monotrait ratio of correlations (HTMT) method.

Cross-Loadings

To assess discriminant validity through cross-loadings of the indicators, the indicator's outer loading on the related construct must be higher than all of its loadings on other indicators in every item row (Hair et al., 2014). The results of cross-loadings show that every indicator of the constructs is higher than their specified constructs. Hence, the results validate the discriminant validity of all the constructs.

Average Variance Extracted

The AVE values were compared for all constructs based on the square of the correlation between the two constructs (Fornell & Larcker, 1981; Brady & Robertson, 2001). Table 6.4 indicates that AVE for all constructs is above the squared correlations between the constructs, which verify that the square root of the AVE is above the inter construct squared correlation values for all variables. The convergent validity and discriminant validity give a satisfactory sign of model fit, and hence, the model is robust to examine the relationships between the constructs in the structural model.

Assessment of Structural Models

The evaluation of the structural model focuses on the relationships in the hypothesized model (Hair & Anderson, 1995) to test the model and the hypotheses relationships between the constructs established. This section evaluates the results of the structural model that represents the underlying concept of the path model.

The research model used for Objective 2 needs to be analysed using a method that captures the estimation of their scores. Therefore, a PLS algorithm was first performed on the model to estimate loadings of the indicators and their weights (path coefficients). The strength of the structural model was then evaluated using a bootstrapping procedure with 500 re-samples (Chin 1998). The results are discussed in the subsequent subsection.

Table 6.4 Results of multicollinearity test

Construct	Item	VIF
TT	ACC	1.135
	ASS	1.113
	KI	1.073
TC	HR	1.017
	PROD	1.075
	PROC	1.038
	RD	1.084
OMC	KM	1.256
	MC	1.032
	SP	1.050
PERF	COMP	1.279
	EXP	1.236
	INN	1.502
	PRO	1.429
Second order		
Technological Capabilities		1.076
Technology Transfer		1.172

Source: Authors' estimations.

Multicollinearity

SPSS 22 Statistics software was used to run multiple regressions to examine multicollinearity issues by using VIF values (Table 6.4). All VIF values were below the suggested cut-off point of 0.1 level (Tabachnick & Fidell, 1996).

Structural Model Path Coefficients

The structural model is the next step of SEM analysis, which provides the particular information of the relations between independent and dependent variables (Ho, 2006; Hair et al., 2014). Partial Least Squares (PLS) was used to test the hypotheses. In the first model, the effect of both independent variables of technology transfer and technological capability was evaluated on firm performance. With a bootstrapping process using 503 responses, Figure 6.1 shows the results of the path model without taking account of organizational and management capabilities as a mediator.

Table 6.5 presents t-value estimates of the model without the mediator, which shows that technological capabilities enjoyed a stronger association

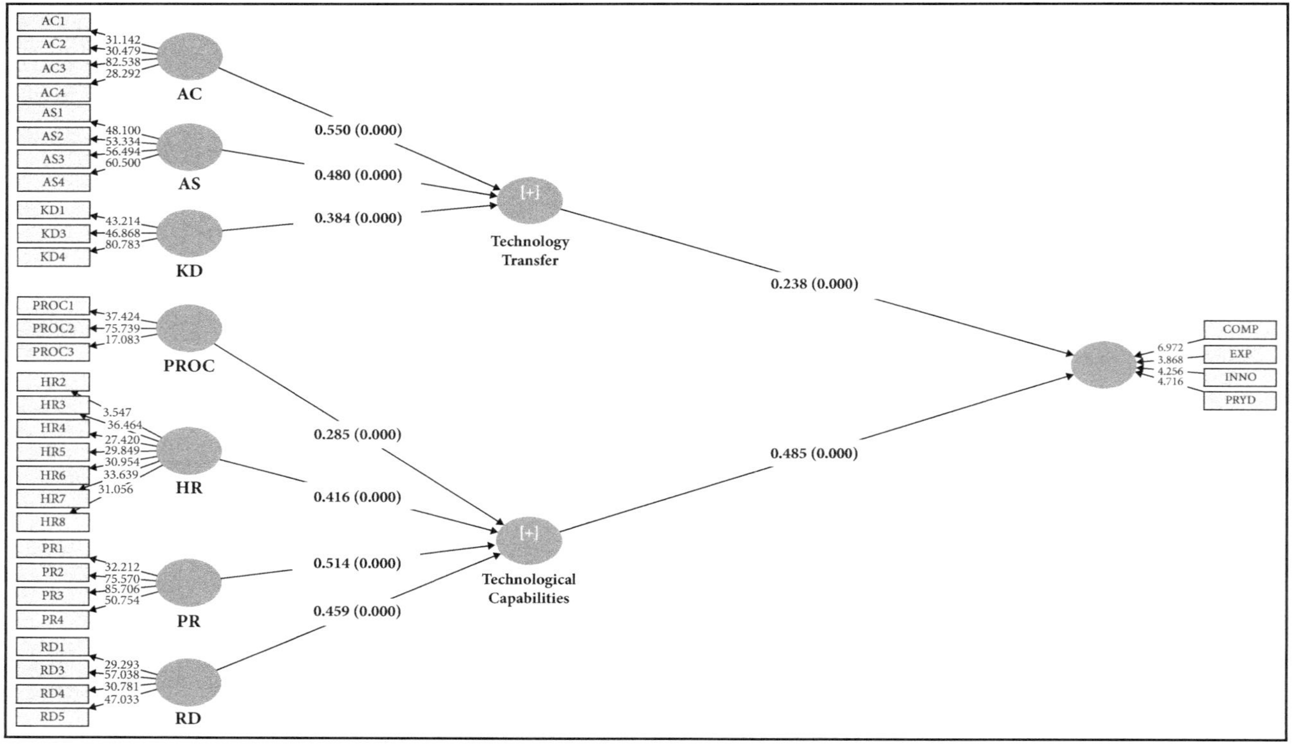

Figure 6.1 Structural model path coefficients

Source: Authors' estimations.

Table 6.5 Results of the structural model path coefficients

Path	Beta	SD	t-stat	*P* -Values
TC → PERF	0.465	0.036	12.465	0.000
TT → PERF	0.228	0.045	6.089	0.000
ACC → TT	0.552	0.028	18.084	0.000
ASS → TT	0.485	0.038	12.899	0.000
HR → TC	0.426	0.054	6.679	0.000
KI → TT	0.339	0.035	11.696	0.000
PROD → TC	0.513	0.037	13.392	0.000
PROC → TC	0.287	0.052	6.618	0.000
RD → TC	0.451	0.035	11.758	0.000

Source: Authors' estimations.

with firm performance (12.46) than technology transfer (6.08). Viewed by dimensions of the respective constructs on firm performance, technology acquisition contributed most to t-values (18.08), followed by technology assimilation (12.90), product technology (13.39), R&D (11.76), knowledge inflow (11.70), HR (6.68), and process technology (6.62) respectively.

Mediating Effect of Organizational and Management Capabilities

The relationship between the independent and dependent constructs may not directly affect each other but can be influenced by other intervening variables (Latan & Ghozali, 2014). It is for this reason the organizational and management capabilities (OMC) variable was introduced as the mediator in the relationship between technological transfer and technological capability, and firm performance (see Figure 6.2). The mediation effect divides the correlation of the constructs into three different ways in structural equations modelling:

- Direct effect of the independent variables on the dependent variable.
- Indirect effects of the independent variables on the dependent variable by introducing more variables.
- Total effects (the sum of direct and indirect effect).

As shown in Table 6.6, the mediating effect of OMC on TT and TC is both significant with TC stronger than TT (see t-ratios). The same is observed in

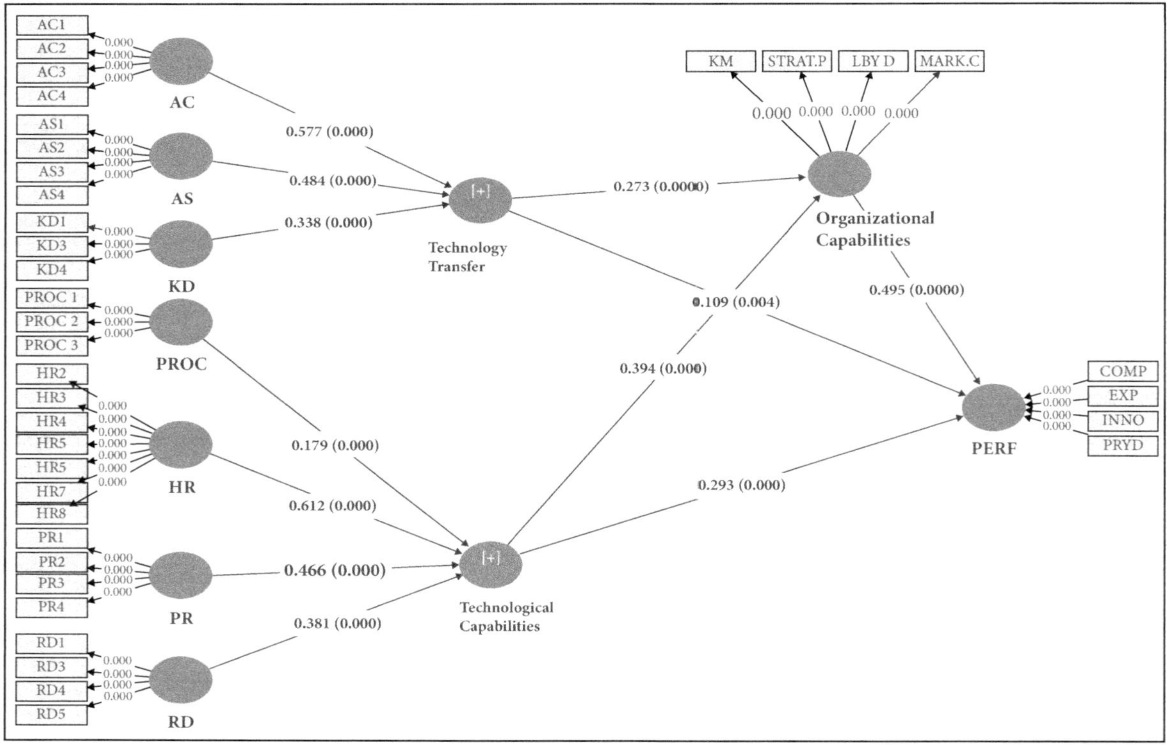

Figure 6.2 Measurement Model Using Mediating Effect of Organizational and Management Capabilities

Table 6.6 Results of the measurement model

Path Path a	Beta	SD	t-Stat	p-values
TC → OMC	0.375	0.033	11.839	0.000
TT → OMC	0.283	0.044	5.595	0.000
Path b				
OMC → PERF	0.498	0.037	6.676	0.000
Path c'				
TT → PERF	0.111	0.033	4.807	0.004
TC → PERF	0.297	0.035	12.356	0.000

Source: Authors' estimations.

Table 6.7 Test of mediation effects using bootstrapping

Path	Beta	SE	t-value	P-value
TT → OMC → PERF	0.132	0.016	8.25	0.000
TC → OMC → PERF	0.190	0.018	10.55	0.000

Source: Authors' estimations.

the relationship between TT and TC, and PERF. While TC shows a stronger impact on PERF than OMC, the latter shows a stronger influence on PERF than TT.

Table 6.7 shows the direct and indirect effect of TT and TC on firm performance. The results show a positive and significant effect on firm performance after introducing the mediating variable of OMC. Similarly, the results of OMC show a positive and significant influence on firm performance. Hence, organizational and management capability partially mediated the relationship between technology transfer and technological capabilities, and firm performance. The results also show that higher levels of technology transfer and technological capabilities will raise firm performance. However, TC shows a stronger relationship than TT even after the introduction of the mediator of organizational and management capabilities.

Table 6.8 shows the effects of second-order constructs of technology transfer and technological capabilities on firm performance. Technology Transfer and its three first-order constructs ACC, ASS, KI are significant (0.45, 0.36, 0.32), which means that these constructs validate a substantial effect in the relationship between technology transfer and firm performance. Similarly,

Table 6.8 Second-order construct after mediation

Construct	Dimension	Path Co-efficient value
TT	ACC	0.451
	ASS	0.364
	KI	0.321
TC	PROC	0.187
	HR	0.605
	PROD	0.476
	RD	0.321

Source: Authors' estimations.

Table 6.9 Results of hypothesis testing

Hypotheses	t-value	Inference
H1: TT has a positive relationship with PERF	($t = 2.90$; $p < .05$)	Supported
H2: TC has a positive relationship with firm performance.	($t = 13.344$; $p < .05$)	Supported
H3: OMC mediates positively the relationship between TT and PERF.	($t = 6.49$; $p < .05$)	Supported
H4: OMC mediates positively the relationship between TC and PERF.	($t = 10.738$; $p < .05$)	Supported
H5: OM Chas a positive relationship with PERF.	($t = 7.65$ $p < .05$)	Supported

Source: Authors' estimations.

technological capabilities and its first-order constructs HR, PROC, PROD, and RD are also significant (0.60, 0.19, 0.48, 0.32), which means that these constructs validate the strong relationship of technology capabilities on firm performance.

The hypotheses of the study were tested by analysing the path estimate of critical t-values. Each hypothesis is supported by considering critical values less than 0.05 level of significance and t-value equal to 1.96. Values less than 1.96 are considered insignificant in which case the hypothesis concerned is not supported (Hair et al., 2014). The five hypotheses tested were all supported as shown in Table 6.9.

Coefficient of Determination

The results for the inner structure of the model were estimated from the value of adjusted R^2 for all endogenous variables. The adjusted R^2 is shown because of its strong predictive properties. The values of 0.25, 0.40, and 0.75 of adjusted R^2 indicate weak, moderate, and strong predictive power, respectively. The adjusted R^2 was used compared to R^2 because the value of an additional value of the exogenous construct may necessarily change, that is, either increase or reduce.

In PLS 3, variance explained (R^2) is used to assess the model fit. However, existing research has included predictive relevance Q^2 (Stone-Geisser'sQ^2) (see Tenenhaus, Vinzi, Chatelin, & Lauro 2005) for endogenous constructs measurement, which is usually known as predictive sample reuse (Geisser, 1974).

Some researchers (e.g., Chin, 1998; Tenenhaus et al., 2005) have recommended that R^2 and Q^2 be used to investigate the fitness of the model. Table 6.10 shows that 25 per cent of variance in organizational and management capabilities can be explained by the proposed model, which, though weak, is highly significant as its predictive relevance statistic is more than zero. Also, the findings show that 52 per cent of the variance in firm performance can be explained by the empirical model, which is moderately strong but also highly significant as its predictive relevance statistics (Q^2) is higher than zero.

Following Chin (1998) $f^2$was deployed to measure the model's fitness. The guidelines for assessing f^2 are: if value is below 0.02, 0.15, and 0.35 the effects of the exogenous variables will be small, medium, and large respectively (Cohen, 2013). The significance of f^2 indicates that the size effect of organizational and management capability is higher (0.349) than the other independent variables. Similarly, the size effect of technological capabilities is higher (0.207 and 0.148) than technology transfer (0.095 and

Table 6.10 Results of model fitness test

Latent Variables	R^2 Adjusted	Q^2	Predictor	OMC	Performance f^2
OMC	0.248	0.152	OMC-PERF		0.349
PERF	0.524	0.129	TC-PERF	0.207	0.148
			TT-PERF	0.095	0.027

Source: Authors' estimations.

0.027). Hence, the size effect of organizational and management capability has a larger predictive relevance impact on firm performance, while technological capabilities show a higher size effect of predictive relevance on organizational and management capability, and medium effect on firm performance. Technology transfer shows a medium effect on the predictive relevance of organizational and management capability and a small effect on firm performance. Meanwhile, technological capabilities, and organizational and management capabilities show a medium effect on predictive relevance, but technology transfer produced a small effect on predictive relevance.

Overall, while TT is positively correlated with firm performance, TC and OMC enjoy stronger association with firm performance. Indeed, TC and OMC show as a medium effect while TT only shows a small effect on the predictive relevance of the PLS-SEM model.

Summary

Using firm-level data, this chapter examined the direct and indirect effects of technology transfer and technological capabilities on firm performance through the mediating effect of organizational and management capabilities. The statistical results showed that technology transfer and technological capabilities have had a direct and significant effect on firm performance. However, technological capabilities (0.29) had a higher impact than technology transfer (0.11) on firm performance. The coefficient values show that the HR dimension (0.61) impacted the highest with process technologies (0.17) having the lowest impact among the components of technological capabilities.

The chapter also showed the critical role of organizational and management capabilities as a mediator on the relationship between technological capabilities and technology transfer, and firm performance. Although organizational and management capabilities do not capture tacit knowledge exhaustively, being the closest to track embodied competence levels it does to some extent demonstrate the significance of organizational and management strategies and practices in stimulating technology transfer and technological capabilities and driving firm performance. These results are consistent with the findings of Helfat and Peteraf (2003: 1004), that organizational and management capabilities depend on the ability of managers to work in sync with firms' objectives as different managers in different firms may make different decisions. That is to say that the mediating role of organizational and management capabilities differs among firms depending on their understanding and implementation of strategies. Similarly, the results also support the findings of Rasiah (2003, 2004, 2005) that technological capabilities have a positive and significant relationship with firm performance. Pakistan's textiles and clothing industry is no exception in this regard.

7

Embedding Ecosystem and Industrial Upgrading

Introduction

Industrial upgrading undeniably has been the driver of economic progress as it fuels productivity growth and structural change. Indeed, the latecomer catch-up experiences of the United States, Germany, Japan, South Korea, and Taiwan were very much based on the transfer of foreign technologies (Hamilton, 1791; List, 1885; Amsden, 1989; Wade, 1990), as well as in-house R&D development eventually. International technology transfer is recognized as a major channel through which firms raise their technological capabilities (Reisman, 2005). The challenge in this chapter is to understand the ecosystem instruments that are important and common to promote technological upgrading among latecomer countries. These factors vary by phases in the development trajectory, viz., initial, developmental, and maturity.

Much of the existing technology-based indices that denote location in the technology trajectory are focused on a limited set of industries, such as semiconductors and automotive products (e.g., Rasiah, 2003), and steel and ships (Figueiredo, 2003; Dutrénit, 2006). Missing are the critical industry-based evolutionary characteristics, such as the embedding environment at the location, nature of technological dynamics at the time of the catch-up process, and the specific industry involved. In addition, existing attempts to show technological upgrading in firms have been confined to small sample sizes and with little inclusion of the embedding instruments in the measurement methodologies used (cf. Figueiredo 2003; Rasiah, 2003; Dutrinet, 2006). This shortcoming may explain why little efforts have manifested in policy instruments developed for industrial promotion. Therefore, while there is a dearth of conceptual publications on technological capabilities, there are little empirically incisive works that use representative samples to assist policy-makers when diagnosing gaps in institutional support structures to design catch up strategies.

Industrial Upgrading in the Textiles and Clothing Industry. Nazia Nazeer and Rajah Rasiah, Oxford University Press.
 DOI: 10.1093/9780198961697.003.0007

This chapter seeks to fill that lacuna by using 50 experts endowed with experiential and tacit knowledge from Pakistan to construct the IUI for the textiles and clothing industry, which can then serve as a guiding tool for policy-makers in Pakistan specifically and among the developing economies generally. Past works on Pakistan have identified glaring shortcomings in intermediary support from technical and vocational training, and higher education institutes, which has undermined the capacity of firms to adapt novel practices in the industry (Wadho & Chaudhary, 2016). There is, therefore, a need to evaluate the embedding institutions and organizations to construct an IUI that policy-makers can deploy to govern industrial upgrading in Pakistan specifically and the developing countries generally.

Hence, the aim of this chapter is twofold, viz., to explain the critical factors that are important for the development of the IUI that affect technological upgrading with a focus on the transfer of foreign sources of knowledge, technological capability building, and organizational and management capabilities; and to disentangle the level of institutional support firms face in Pakistan. The identification of the institutional drivers would be useful to policy-makers seeking to design policies to stimulate industrial upgrading and structural change from low to high value-added activities. Specifically, this chapter relies on experts' opinions to prioritize factors that are critical for stimulating industrial upgrading in the textiles and clothing industry. The rest of the chapter is structured as follows. The next section introduces the systemic pillars facing firms in the textiles and clothing industry followed by the methodology and data deployed. The AHP and decision-making methods, as well as the measurement of systemic pillars, are examined in this section. The subsequent section analyses the results. The final section presents the summary.

Systemic Pillars Facing Firms

This section focuses on the specific nature of the four systemic pillars embedding Pakistan's textiles and clothing firms (Table 7.1). It starts with an assessment of ecosystems facing the lead firms of TAL, Toray, and Everest Textiles. Such an assessment will provide a picture of institutional support facing the lead firms in their respective nations and firms in Pakistan.

The impact of basic infrastructure (BI) organizations on firms is both direct and indirect. BI can be considered a general requirement for all economic activities, but much of it is only important where the firms are located. Whilst transport, telecommunications, power, and water supply bear direct effects that could disrupt production and stretch lead times, the indirect ones include education, health, access to finance, security, and macroeconomic and political stability. According to officials from the APTMA the embedding ecosystem facing textiles and clothing firms in Pakistan rate far below the support the lead firms abroad get in Hong Kong, Japan, Taiwan respectively. Also, power failures have often disrupted production in Pakistan. In fact, Pakistan had 81.1 per cent of firms reporting electrical outages in 2013 (World Bank, 2023). Consequently, some large firms, such as Nishat Chunian in Lahore have installed their own coal-powered generators to overcome supply disruptions.

Also, TAL, Toray, and Everest Textiles are located at sites with superior STI infrastructure. Whereas the Hong Trade and Development Council, which was formed in 1966, had its research focus expanded when the Hong Kong Research Institute of Textiles and Apparel (HKRITA) were launched in 2006 (Chan & Lee, 2022). Foreign technology was critical with increasing diffusion domestically to evolve national innovation capabilities. Hong Kong had nevertheless enjoyed considerable transfer of technology as an entrepot since British colonialism. TAL, Toray, and Everest Textiles enjoy strong links with intermediary organizations to solve collective problems associated with their innovation activities, including as strong facilitators to build and stimulate knowledge flows between firms and support organizations. These firms are highly integrated in mature systemic pillars of BI, STI infrastructure, global integration, and network cohesion.

TAL, Toray, and Everest Textiles have long moved to environment and energy-friendly textiles and clothing, and bio-degradable fibres, such as organic cotton, soy fibre and ahimsa silk as fashion holders, such as Levis, Adidas, Nike, GAP, Louis Vuitton, JCPenney, Stella McCartney, H&M, Zara, Ralp Lauren, ASOS, and Quicksilver have imposed stringent process technology upgrading conditions which require the use of new technologies with micro-organisms over water-intensive dyeing to reduce heavy chemicals and heating (EPA, 2004).

The key government organizations that were launched by Japan and Taiwan to drive industrialization were MITI (1949) and the ITRIs (1974) respectively with the former playing a direct entrepreneurial role and the latter organized along industries to support technological upgrading. The Taiwan Textile Research Institute (TTRI) focuses on the development of textile materials, functional apparel, home textiles, high value-added technical textiles, environment-friendly and energy-saving textiles, and textile testing and certification (Chen-Chiu, 2009; Huang et al, 2017 . Whereas Japan's MITI also performed the trade promotion role, the Taiwan External

Trade Development Council, which was founded in 1970, undertook the promotion of trade in Taiwan. These organizations helped build the ecosystem to facilitate the emergence and catch-up of national firms.

In addition, the ecosystem in Hong Kong, Japan, and Taiwan have evolved a strong machinery and equipment industry to support frontier operations. Taiwan's government-funded Machine Tools Technology Centre focuses on machinery and equipment development. Everest Textiles jointly developed an automated multi-tasking system incorporating 3D smart vision technology that shortened textile and garment sample proofing time from 7–10 days to 1–3 days (Fibre2Fashion, 2019). ITRI's anti-reflective 3D vision guiding module helps determine fabric material feeding positions on different sizes of T-shirts to relay the positions to robotic arms, which then executes material loading and unloading by stitching and thermos-printing machines, thus integrating separate steps of processes into a one-stop operation.

Japan's textiles and clothing firms have since the 1970s been developing new fibres with advanced materials and are now increasingly focusing on green and health-friendly products with extensive support from R&D in manufacturing and engineering. Japan's Advanced Textiles Association acts as a facilitator for Japanese textiles firms, which are globally dispersed with R&D access to reputed universities. Toray, Kanebo, Teijin, Toyobo, and Mitsubishi focus on smart textiles using R&D support from both government and private funds (Japan, 2004).

While STI organizations have already been launched in Pakistan, in contrast to the stellar STI infrastructure facing firms in Hong Kong, Japan, and Taiwan, firms in Pakistan face weak and under-funded organizations. Significant promise emerged following the launching of the Textiles and Apparel Policies, which include the allocation of funds for installing solar panels and designing but the limited funds have not helped its spread across all firms. Given the low level of development and indebted nature of the Textile Research Institute, Textile University, and textile training institutes in Pakistan, it will take a long time before the STI infrastructure could be developed to match the achievements of Hong Kong, Japan, and Taiwan, which is made worse by frequent balance of payment problems and external exposure to debt. Hence, the empirical evidence in Pakistan is expected to attract low firm-level ratings on the embedding STI infrastructure facing them.

As to how networked are the firms with the BI and STI infrastructure, and how integrated they are with export and investment, and technology (including human capital) sources abroad can either be captured by firm-level investigation, or through a careful assessment by industry experts. While the former was used by Rasiah, Shahrivar, and Yap (2017), the second is more appropriate here owing to knowledge gaps expected from firms far down in the technological capability trajectory that characterize textiles and clothing firms in Pakistan.

Nevertheless, while firms in Pakistan are significantly disadvantaged in their links with BI and STI infrastructure, firms with good internet links have managed to connect with export markets, though power outage problems and lack of R&D support have denied them access to cutting-edge IR4.0 technologies. Also, firms located in Lahore and Faisalabad face longer lead times owing to the distance required to reach the Arabian sea.

As explained above, Hong Kong, Japan, and Taiwan enjoy world-class basic and STI infrastructure, and strong export and innovation linkages with major suppliers and intermediary organizations located abroad, including R&D linkages with globally renowned universities. Not only are their intermediary organizations supported well through both government and private funds but are also reviewed frequently to ensure that the networks are increasingly more efficient and effective. Having examined the ecosystem facing firms in Hong Kong, Japan, Taiwan, and Pakistan in general terms, the remaining chapter examines the ecosystem support faced by Pakistan's textiles and clothing firms.

Methodology and Data

Unlike deductive methodologies, this inductive exercise requires the use of a stylized framework to construct the IUI. The empirical basis for the construction of the IUI is drawn from what experts from the industry view as the critical factors that impact on firm performance. Whereas the trajectory dimension is critical for locating textiles and clothing firms in the nine-level technology trajectory and the six-level organizational and management capability trajectory, the IUI is focused on the four pillars of the systemic quad that are critical as the ecosystem to support firms' industrial upgrading.

Industrial Upgrading Index

The systemic quad (Rasiah, 2007, 2019) was adapted to determine the factors that influence industrial upgrading in the textiles and clothing firms in Pakistan by identifying the dimensions and sub-dimensions for the development of the index. In doing so, this model is preferred over Porter's (2000) cluster diamond, and Best's (2001, 2018) productivity triad because of the emphasis on the critical external influences that impact on firm-level industrial upgrading. Furthermore, the model draws on experts' assessment of critical influences that are fundamental to industrial upgrading.

The decision-making process (Simon, 1977) and the Analytical Hierarchy Process (AHP) (Saaty, 1990) are then used to develop the IUI, which is based on the following three major steps: (1) problem identification, (2) selection, and (3) prioritization. Of the three stages of intelligence, design, and choice, the first two are qualitative while the third is quantitative (Simon, 1977) (Figure 7.1).

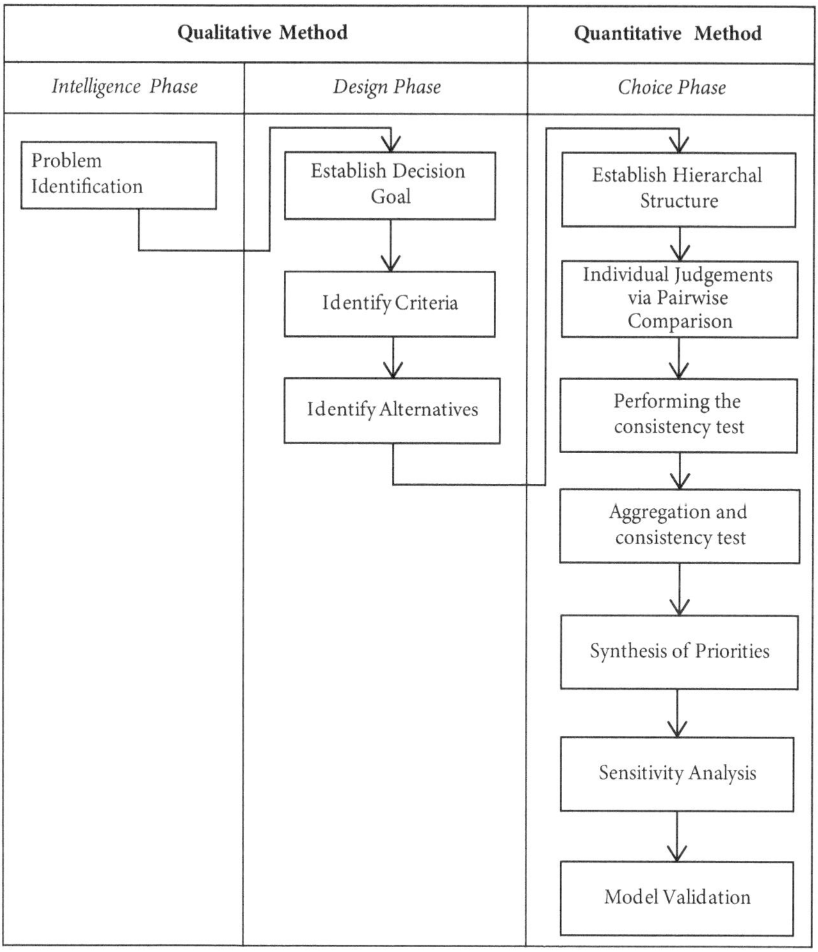

Figure 7.1 Development of industrial upgrading index

Source: Adapted from Simon (1977) and Saaty (1990).

Expert Interviews

The development of the IUI starts with in-depth interviews. Fifty experts were selected to answer questions face-to-face to identify the dimensions and sub-dimensions of IUI associated with the critical organizations and instruments drawn from the systemic squad. The responses were then typed and resent to the respondents to re-evaluate their original answers. This practice of evaluation and re-evaluation enabled the quantification of experts' opinions with the second tool, that is, the AHP, which was used to prioritize and assign weights to dimensions and sub-dimensions that were identified in the first step to form the structure of the IUI for textile and clothing firms in Pakistan. AHP is an influential and comprehensive approach aimed at facilitating decision-making, which quantifies the subjective judgements using a pairwise comparison approach. The central principle of the analysis is the probability of linking information and knowledge to make decisions (Saaty & Vargas, 2001). Its aim is to capture the goals, values, desires, and objectives of decision-makers. It remains a popular and extensively deployed decision-making instrument (Lin et al., 2007) as it handles complicated, multi-valued, and economic and political decision problems enabling organizations to develop suitable strategies (Saaty, 1990). AHP and its related analytic techniques give a logical frame to facilitate organizations and individuals to make rational decisions in difficult circumstances through a hierarchal order.

Against the above backdrop, the application of AHP is intended to support textile and clothing firms in Pakistan to determine the ecosystem factors that influence successful industrial upgrading. Besides, the AHP is superior to other decision-making methods because of its capacity to observe consistencies through which decision-makers build their judgements (Roper-Lowe & Sharp, 1990).

Dimensions and Sub-dimensions

Following Rasiah (2019), 30 variables were identified in which six were overlapping variables that constitute the dimensions, which affect directly industrial upgrading in textile and clothing firms. The relevant dimensions and sub-dimensions were initially identified through in-depth interviews. These dimensions and sub-dimensions were then synthesized to establish relative priority of each dimension and sub-dimension.

Table 7.1 Systemic quad

Pillars	Institutions and Organizations
BI	Access to finance
	Government incentives and other basic infrastructure support
	Information communication Technology
	Transport
	Health
	Political stability
STII	Environment for stimulating Innovation
	Environment for stimulating technology adaptation and imitation
	IPR framework
	Research & Development incentives and grants
	University-industry linkages
	Supply of human capital
GI	Global production networks
	International management strategies, Competition
	FDI
	Cross-border access to human resource and technologies
NC	Firm-government coordination Councils
	Knowledge flows from external organizations
	Producer-user relationships
	Inter-firm coordination councils
	Trust and loyalty

Source: Compiled by authors.

Dimensions and Sub-dimensions

Since dimensions are important to measure performance in the AHP method, their selection is crucial for decision-making (Simon's Stage 3). To finalize the dimensions and sub-dimensions, four considerations were made consisting of completeness, non-redundancy, operationality, and the number of criteria:

a) ***Completeness***

Three major steps could help in the logical assessment of dimensions and sub-dimensions to confirm completeness. Initially, every dimension at the second level was studied to ensure that all the key classifications are incorporated. For this connection, the value tree hierarchy model or a layered chart was a valuable instrument adopted. Last of all, the main dimensions (level 2) and the sub-dimensions (level 3) were rechecked to confirm that all necessary characteristics are captured to attain the overall goal (level 1).

b) ***Non-redundancy***
In this stage, dimensions that were judged irrelevant or as duplicative shall be eliminated at an early stage. However, the omission of any dimension or sub-dimension should be handled with intent.

c) ***Operationality***
To consider that all dimensions are profound, including after judging them against each dimension.

d) ***Number of Dimensions***
This stage needs a final confirmation that the number of dimensions was not larger than what is required. Because many dimensions cause analytical difficulties in calculating input data and addressing outcomes of the analysis, the hierarchy could not be exceeded by more than seven components. Within this condition, a rational evaluation can be done to confirm consistency (Saaty, 1990).

Sampling

It is widely acknowledged in academic research that small sample sizes often give unrepresentative clues for interpretation. But, in the Analytical Hierarchical Procedure (AHP) approach, it is not essential to include a large number of experts in the study. Opinions from key experts or executives are adequate to generate useful and reliable results. Sometimes important decisions include opinions of just one expert like a managing director of a firm rather than a survey of an entire list of managers from that firm.

The expert sampling technique was adopted, which assumes a non-probabilistic sampling approach, to gather experts' opinions and to give appropriate weights for the dimensions and sub-dimensions of industrial upgrading index in the context of textile and clothing firms in Pakistan. Expert sampling falls in the category of purposive sampling methods, which allows the investigator to depend on his or her tacit and personal knowledge to choose the sampling population for analysis. This includes the sample of individuals with some long experience along with expertise in a specific field (Guarte & Barrios, 2006). This technique was adopted as the study focuses on experts engaged in state organizations, academics, and industry, especially because the population of these expert categories is not known. Additionally, experts' opinions with specific experience and expertise in their related fields require thoughtful selection of sample members.

The experts' sampling exercise was started with their categorization into three groups, viz., experts from the textile and clothing industry, government

Table 7.2 List of experts interviewed

Categories	Organizations/Firms	Numbers	Total Numbers
Industry			30
	Textiles	*10*	
	Clothing	*10*	
	*Integrated**	*10*	
Academics			10
	Universities	*6*	
	Technical Board	*2*	
	Technical Institutes	*2*	
Government			10
	APTMA	*6*	
	Export Promotion Bureau	*2*	
	SMEDA	*2*	

*Firms had integrated textiles and clothing operations.
Source: Authors' compilation.

executives, and academicians. Data from industry and institutional experts were collected through personal contacts. The initial pilot involved eight experts with four experts from the textile and clothing industry, two experts from government officials from the Ministry of Textiles and Clothing (MTC), and another two from among academicians specializing on textiles and clothing technology and markets. A total of 50 experts were then chosen from these three groups. Survey questionnaires were used to collect the information to undertake the AHP comparisons. A list of possible participants having at least 10 years of experience in their respective categories was drawn. The breakdown of the 50 experts by categories is shown in Table 7.2, viz., 30 from textiles and clothing firms, 10 from academics focused on textiles and clothing research, and another 10 from government organizations engaged in textiles and clothing policies and administration. The focus for academics—involved research on the textiles and clothing industry, for government officials—involved participation in the development of textiles and clothing sector policies, and for industry—involved in strategic management (middle and top) of textiles and clothing firms.

Application of the Decision-making and AHP Approaches

The following section describes the application of the decision-making (Simon, 1977) and AHP (Saaty, 1990) approaches in the development of the IUI.

Simon's Qualitative Method

The methodological framework advanced by Simon (1977) helps track closely the factors that influence technological upgrading in more detail in the textile and clothing sector of Pakistan. The following sections describe the qualitative steps introduced by Simon (1977).

In-depth Interviews

Simon's (1977) intelligence phase was used to establish a deeper view of the problem to explain the problem accurately and to give the experts an opportunity to understand and discuss the problem statement. Simon's second phase, that is, the design phase was drawn through identification and drafting of a list of appropriate dimensions and sub-dimensions related to the textiles and clothing industry. The design phase was extended to involve the definition of the objective due to the strong link between the objectives and criteria as the list of dimensions might be influenced by the defined objective. The interview procedure provided the opportunity to establish harmony between the objectives.

The exercise was started with initially eight experts as the pilot face-to-face from the three categories of industry (four), academics (two), and government (two). These experts helped recommend experts with credible knowledge of the textiles and clothing industry to attract cooperation from them. In-depth face to face interviews was conducted at the intelligence and design phase using the decision-making procedure of Simon (1977). As recommended by Simon, the questions focused strongly on the most relevant dimensions and sub-dimensions involved for constructing the IUI of the textiles and clothing industry in Pakistan. All interviews were conducted at mutually agreed locality between Nazia Nazeer and the appointed enumerators, and the experts. Each interview lasted for 1–3 hours but sometimes exceeded the normal period owing to unforeseen circumstances. The interviews were transcribed and rewritten by Nazia Nazeer after consultation with Rajah Rasiah, and subsequently presented to the experts to re-examine their original answers. The experts were also interviewed on the relevance of the dimensions and sub-dimensions that were originally identified from the systemic quad (2019) in a series of open-ended questions.

The experts were encouraged to include or exclude any dimensions or sub-dimensions of factors from the original systemic quad (Rasiah, 2019). From the data collected from the in-depth interviews a final list of dimensions and sub-dimensions was developed, which was again showed to the experts to get their final approval. All experts concurred that each dimension and sub-dimension that they finally defined covered the domain of industrial upgrading, with the experts only revising through additions and deletions of some sub-dimensions.

Quantitative Method: Choice Phase

Saaty's (1990) AHP and Simon's (1977) decision-making process are appropriate to establish and weight of the critical external drivers of firm-level industrial upgrading (Dyer & Forman, 1992). Although, studies reveal that the AHP can be applied in all stages of Simon's decision-making process, this approach is deployed here only for the choice phase. An expert choice software, which is a multi-purpose decision support instrument that relies on the AHP, was deployed for establishing a hierarchy through a laddering method to compute the weights from the experts' responses. The strength of the AHP approach lies in its capacity for framing complex multi-dimensional problems in the hierarchy tree to examine every level individually, and to combine the results at all stages of analysis.

Prioritization Using Analytical Hierarchical Procedure

To prioritize the dimensions and sub-dimensions the AHP approach allots weights according to their significance. As discussed earlier, AHP is a multi-dimensional method used for decision-making and deals with complex problems. Therefore, it is important to evaluate all dimensions and sub-dimensions. AHP provides pairwise comparison techniques to estimate different alternatives, which shows the comparative importance of every alternative with reference to all the dimensions—to help the AHP obtain weights according to the importance of every dimension. The dimensions and sub-dimensions take numerical values, which are then used to define the priorities. Lastly, these priorities were used as the basis to make the final decisions. Saaty (1990) had explained the four steps to utilize the AHP

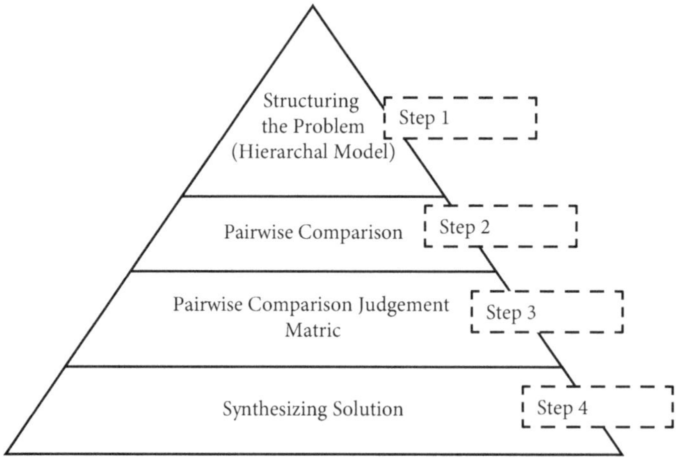

Figure 7.2 Steps in the analytical hierarchical procedure
Source: Adapted from Saaty (1990).

method, which include construct problem, collection of data, computation of normalized weights, and consolidation of results (finding a solution to the problem). Figure 7.2 shows the step-by-step procedures of the AHP.

Problem Construction Using the Analytical Hierarchical Procedure

During the design phase after in-depth interviews, a list of criteria was developed to construct a suitable hierarchical structure of the AHP model containing the goals, dimensions, and the sub-dimensions. Saaty (1990) highlighted that the AHP construction is useful for decision-makers by offering a whole representation of multifaceted relations built into the conditions for judgement development.

The factors of all dimensions and sub-dimensions should be correlated. The first hierarchy level is the goal or problem, while the second and third levels contain the dimensions and sub-dimensions used to assess the relative preferences for all the alternatives. When all dimensions and sub-dimensions or factors are structured in a stratified order, the setting up of an overall stratified hierarchical cluster for the objectives can then be finalized. A pairwise comparison of the dimensions and sub-dimensions utilized in all the three levels of the AHP model were then performed. To assess this pairwise comparison, all dimensions in every level were subsequently compared with

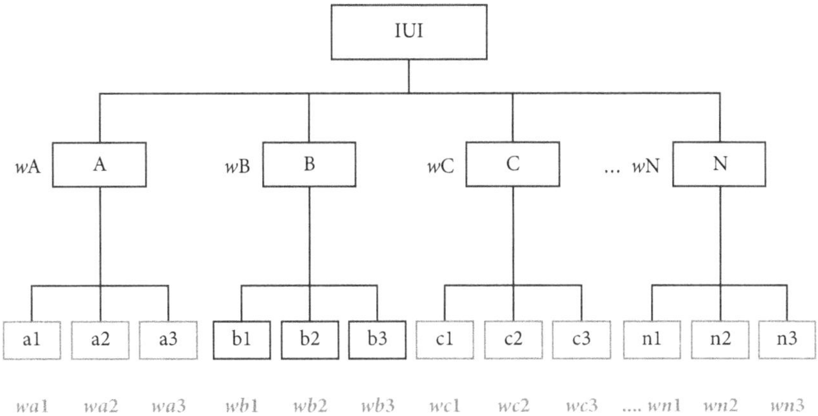

Figure 7.3 Analytical hierarchical procedure

Note: IUI refers to overall industrial upgrading index; A, B, C, and N refer to the dimensions of IUI; a, b, c, and refer to the sub-dimensions of IUI; and *w* shows the weights of the dimensions and sub-dimensions.
Source: Adapted from Saaty (1990).

respect to each single parent dimension placed above one level. The hierarchical structure of the dimensions and sub-dimensions in the AHP is depicted in Figure 7.3.

Data Collection

Once the hierarchical clusters were organized using the experts' responses, the next step led to the measurement and collection of data. Likert scale scores were deployed in the questionnaire designed by following the scale of comparison between 1 and 9 (Table 7.3) established by Saaty (1990). The questionnaire is shown in Appendix B.

The questionnaires were sent to 50 industry, academic, and government experts on the textiles and clothing industry targeted at pair-wise comparisons of all factors among each other. Experts were required to compare all the dimensions of the systemic squad for industrial upgrading with other dimensions first, and then to compare the particular sub-dimensions with each other within the main dimensions. Nobody among the experts possessed prior understanding of pairwise comparison and hence, AHP had to be firstly explained to the experts and specifically the comparison matrices that they were needed to fill out. We provided them an example and explained the concept of AHP. This process lasted till every factor was compared with

Table 7.3 Judgement scores of preferences, dimensions, and sub-dimensions

Verbal Judgement	Numerical Rating	Explanation
Extremely Important/Preferred	9	Decision criterion extremely more important than the other
Very much more Important	7	Decision very much more important than the other
More Important	5	Decision more important than the other
Moderately More Important	3	Decision moderately more important than the other
Equally Important	1	Decision equally important
Intermediate Judgement Values	2,4,6,8	Judgement values between equally, moderately, more, much more, and extremely important

Source: Saaty (1990).

each other. Along these lines, the comparisons among all factors in the hierarchy were taken out. Reminders were sent to the participants on a weekly basis before the data were received.

The questionnaires were then utilized for the formulation of priorities for the entire dimension for assessment in the different levels. The completed matrices were further evaluated for consistencies. Some marginal inconsistencies were observed initially, which is to be expected as the AHP was new to the experts interviewed but were eventually reconciled through further discussions with the experts so that the final consistency tests carried out to assess the robustness and inconsistency ratio (IR), as required by Saaty (2001), did not exceed 0.1.

Computation of Normalized Weights

The relative significance of all factors by means of their contribution was then determined to obtain the overall objective (Saaty, 1990). The data collected from the questionnaire are then processed through the pairwise comparison judgement matrices (PCJMS), for assessing the normalized weights. The judgement scale provided by Saaty (2001) in Table 7.4 was utilized for the pairwise comparison of the dimensions and sub-dimensions.

To calculate the weights of different criterion and sub-criterions, a pairwise comparison matrix P was established. In the P-matrix of '$n \times n$', the symbol n denotes the number of dimensions used to evaluate. Every record of the P-matrix denotes the relative importance of *w*th dimensions when comparing with the *l*th dimensions. Suppose *awl* > 1, then the *wth* dimension is more important as compared to the *l*th dimension, while if *awl* < 1, then the *wth* dimension is less important when compared to the *l*th dimension. Likewise, if *awl* = 1 then both dimensions have equal importance. Noticeably, *aww* = 1 for all *w*. The records *awl* and *alw* attenuate the following constraint:

$$awl \,.\, alw = 1. \tag{4.1}$$

$$P = \begin{array}{c} \\ D_1 \\ D_2 \\ D_3 \\ D_4 \\ D_5 \\ D_6 \\ . \\ D_n \end{array} \begin{array}{c} \begin{array}{ccccccccc} D_1 & D_2 & D_3 & D_4 & D_5 & D_6 & . & D_n \end{array} \\ \begin{pmatrix} 1 & a_{12} & a_{13} & a_{14} & a_{15} & a_{16} & . & a_{2n} \\ a_{21} & 1 & a_{23} & a_{24} & a_{25} & a_{26} & . & a_{2n} \\ a_{31} & a_{32} & 1 & a_{34} & a_{35} & a_{36} & . & a_{3n} \\ a_{41} & a_{42} & a_{43} & 1 & a_{45} & a_{46} & . & a_{41} \\ a_{51} & a_{52} & a_{53} & a_{54} & 1 & a_{56} & . & a_{51} \\ a_{61} & a_{62} & a_{63} & a_{64} & a_{65} & 1 & . & a_{61} \\ . & . & . & . & . & . & 1 & . \\ a_{n1} & a_{n2} & a_{n3} & a_{n4} & a_{n5} & a_{n6} & \dots & 1 \end{pmatrix} \end{array}$$

Whereby:

n is the number of dimensions
D represents the relevant dimension up to the nth level.

Once the construction of the P matrix is done, the next step is to develop a matrix which represents normalized pairwise comparison. This can be calculated by taking the sum of all the records in every column, which equals to 1. This means each entry $\bar{a}\,wl$ of matrix *Pnorm* is calculated as:

$$\bar{a}_{wl} = \frac{a_{wl}}{\sum_{z=1}^{m} zl}. \tag{4.2}$$

Finally, the records of each row of *Pnorm* were averaged, which is used to develop the criteria weight vector k.

The following equation represents this process:

$$k_w = \frac{\sum_{z=1}^{m} \bar{a}_{wz}}{m}. \tag{4.3}$$

The sub-criteria matrix is vector column C where each record of C_{ij} of C denotes the score of the *i*th selection related to *j*th dimension. To determine the scores, the pairwise comparison matrix T^j of all the g dimensions, j = 1, 2, 3...g was done. The T^j matrix is m × m real matrix; the symbol m represents the sub-dimensions' numbers used to evaluate. Every record $h_{qx}^{(j)}$ of the T^j matrix indicates an estimation for the qth option compared with *x*th option with regard to the *j*th criterion. Similarly

In case $h_{qx}^{(j)} > 1$, option *q*th is better than option *x*th.
In case $h_{qx}^{(j)} < 1$, option *x*th is better than option *q*th.
In case $h_{qx}^{(j)} = 1$, both options have equal importance.

Therefore $h_{qx}^{(j)}$ and $h_{xq}^{(j)}$ attenuate in the given equation below:

$$h_{qx}^{(j)} \cdot h_{xq}^{(j)} = 1$$

$$h_{qq}^{(j)} = 1 \quad [\text{for all } q]$$

Similarly, the same two-step process, which is applied to the P-matrix, is used for processing the C-matrix. By dividing each entry with the sum of similar column records, then the average calculated of each entry in each row shall give the score vectors $y^{(j)}, j = 1...g$.

Thus, the $y^{(j)}$ vector has the scores of all measured sub-criteria with respect to the jth criterion.

Lastly, the score Y matric $y^{(j)}$ is calculated as follows:

$$Y = \left[y^1 \cdots y^m\right].$$

Once the computation of the score matrix **Y** and weight vector ***k*** is done, the next stage is to find global scores. The overall global scores are obtained by multiplying the weight vector ***k*** by the score matrix **Y**.

$$\text{Y.k} = \text{u}.$$

The *i*th record of **U** shows the global scores, using the AHP for the *i*th option. A ranking of dimensions is then done through collating the global scores in descending order with respect to the priorities.

Determining the Consistency Index

As the AHP approach is based on judgemental decision-making, to check consistencies for all the opinions or judgements is crucial for robustness, reliability, and accurateness of the AHP technique for decision-making.

While doing pairwise comparisons, the outmost problem usually faced is inconsistency. The problem of inconsistency denotes that the experts are not consistent with their responses for the comparison of the factors. In simple terms, the consistency assumption can be explained as follows:

$$\text{In case } A > B, \text{ and } B > C, \text{ then } A > C.$$

The consistency index (CI) is obtained through calculating the vector '*x*', as an average of the scalar factors vector whose *j*th factor is the ratio of jth element of the P.*k vector*, with the corresponding factor of the *k vector*.

Hence

$$\frac{CI}{RI} < 0.1.$$

Whereby n represents the number of evaluation criteria

Saaty (1990) recommended the consistency ratio (CR) statistic to evaluate the experts' consistency. All t outcomes of pairwise comparisons shall fill up the reciprocal matrices to measure the Eigenvalue and vector. The CI is acceptable if it exceeds 0.1 (Saaty, 1990). If CI is equal to zero, then the decision-making is considered perfectly consistent.

For more accurate measurement, the CI is divided by the Random Index (RI), and the results are shown in Table 7.4. To obtain aggregate consistency of the combined judgements, the geometric mean technique has been widely used with the AHP, which helps to aggregate individual preferences among the number of experts that took part in the decision-making. All judgements collected were found to be consistent and therefore were accepted for further analysis.

Synthesis of Analytical Hierarchical Procedure

The synthesis includes finding a solution for the derivation of IUI. Once, the procedure of combining priorities and weighting the whole model (including

Table 7.4 Random index values

M	2	3	4	5	6	7	8	9	10
RI	0	0.58	0.90	1.12	1.24	1.32	1.41	1.45	1.51

Note: Random index values for problem from 2 to 10.
Source: Estimated by the authors.

the dimensions and sub-dimensions), they are considered as normalized with priority weights for every PCJM that has been computed. All normalized weights of the dimensions and sub-dimensions are then summed up to derive the hierarchical ranks to obtain the global combined priority weights. The preferred dimensions shall be the one with the highest priority.

Specification of Variables

This section focuses on the systemic quad variables and their estimations. The specification of the variables constituting the four pillars of the systemic quad model is undertaken in this section.

Basic Infrastructure

Some of the proxies used by Rasiah (2019) to estimate the strength of basic infrastructure were dropped following the 50 experts' views, which include basic education and customs coordination. Basic infrastructure (BI) was measured by focusing on government incentives and other forms of basic support for business operations (GoV), information communication technology (ICT) infrastructure, transport (T), health (H), and political stability (PS).

$$\mathrm{BI} = (\mathrm{Gov}, \mathrm{ICT}, \mathrm{T}, \mathrm{H}, \mathrm{PS})$$

Science, Technology, and Innovation Infrastructure

The science, technology, and innovation infrastructure (STII) was estimated using the components of environment for innovating (I), environment for technology acquisition (TA), legal framework of intellectual rights (IPR), training programmes (TP), universities (U), R&D incentives and grants (RDIG), and skilled workers (SW).

$$\mathrm{STII} = (\mathrm{I}, \mathrm{TA}, \mathrm{IPR}, \mathrm{TP}, \mathrm{U}, \mathrm{RDIG}, \mathrm{SW}).$$

Global Integration

Globalization has brought not only challenges but choices to the firms, which explains firms' shifting of standards from a domestic to global standard. Likewise, significant interactions have played a key role to address inter-border pecuniary and non-pecuniary flows of economic gains and knowledge—human resource (HR), material, knowledge transfer, finance, and technological resources—that are important in explaining firm-level technological upgrading. Global integration (GI) was estimated by considering global production networks (GPN), management strategies (MS), competition (COMP), FDI, and human resource practices and process technologies (HRPT).

$$GI = (GPN, MS, COMP, FDI, HRPT).$$

Network Cohesion

The synergy between industry agents (government and non-government organizations) and firms is influenced strongly by connectivity and coordination between firms, and between firms and organizations, and the pulse rate of these interactions should be high to ensure that producer-user and firm-organization relations are at their best.[1] Strong network cohesion (NC) through a blend of competition (including the market prices) and cooperation, can ensure that textiles and clothing firms will enjoy strong positive synergies from the supporting role of institutions and organizations. In doing so, we included the roles of government-industry coordination councils (GCC), firm-business chamber links (FCC), firm-government-university (FGU) linkages, and knowledge flows (KF) from external organizations and firms, and producer-user relationships (PUR). In addition, given the importance of trust and loyalty (TL) in the overall ecosystem, TL was included in the estimation of NC.

$$NC = (GCC, FCC, FGU, KF, PUR, TL).$$

Industrial Upgrading Index

Once in-depth face-to-face interviews were completed with the eight experts, a few dimensions and sub-dimensions were combined and reviewed while some were deleted. The overall objective of this exercise was to determine the factors which are important for technological upgrading in the textiles and clothing industry. Hence, 23 sub-dimensions were selected for the four pillars of the systemic squad. The questionnaire was then sent to 50 selected experts with a strong relationship with the textiles and clothing industry.

[1] Elements of this were discussed by Vernon (1966) and Lundvall (2010).

Since the aim of this chapter is to construct a reliable and valid mechanism to measure the factors needed for technological upgrading, the Analytic Hierarchical Process (AHP) framework was adapted for use (Figure 7.4). At the top of the hierarchy is the overall goal of technological upgrading. The hierarchy is constituted at the second level by the dimensions of basic infrastructure, STI Infrastructure, global integration, and network cohesion, which was then

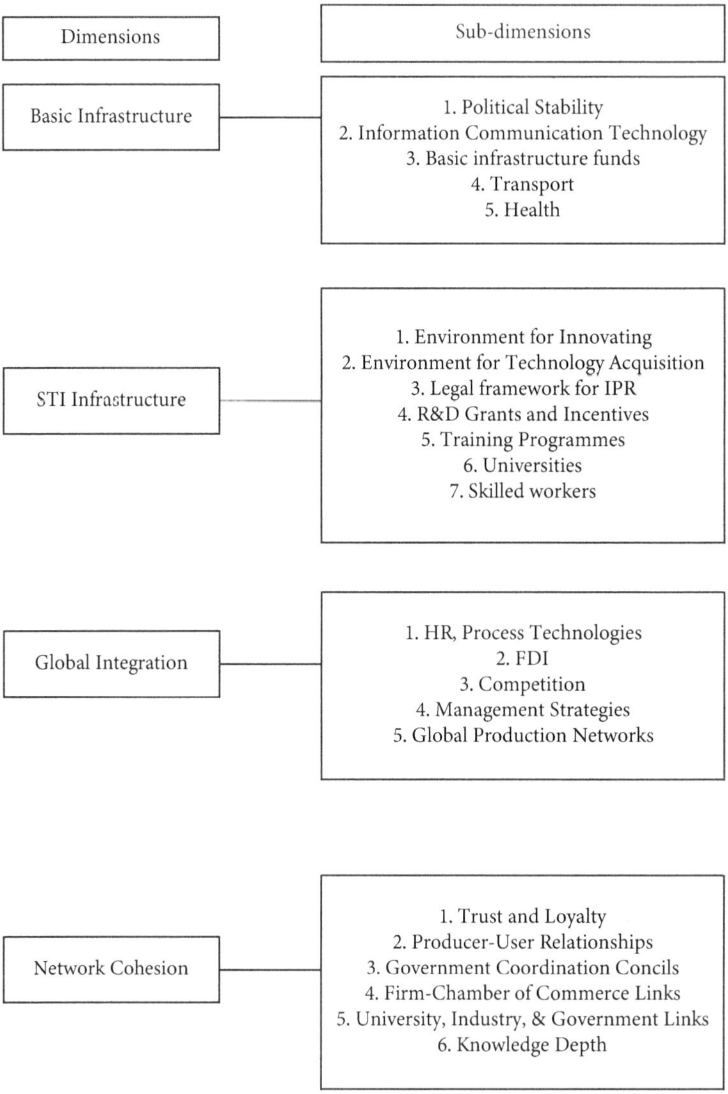

Figure 7.4 Industrial upgrading index, dimensions, and sub-dimensions

Source: Prepared by authors.

followed at the third level of the hierarchy with all related sub-dimensions under each pillar or dimension. Overall, 23 sub-dimensions were selected. For basic infrastructure, the five dimensions of Gov, ICT, T, H, and PS were considered. For STI infrastructure, the seven sub-dimensions of IE, TE, IPR, TP, U, RDIG, and SW were selected. For global integration, the six sub-dimensions of GPN, MS, COMP, FDI, HRPT were selected. For network cohesion, the six sub-dimensions of GCC, FCC, FGU, KF, PUR, and TL were selected.

Constructing the Industrial Upgrading Index

Once the AHP is established after identifying the related dimensions and sub-dimensions, pairwise comparison judgement matrices (PCJM) are developed using the AHP methodology. Consolidated PCJM values were then estimated to develop the IUI after the consistency ratios were estimated and the conditions of the consistency index were met. The AHP approach validates the contents of a developed hierarchy which is based on judgement consistency. If the expert judgements are consistent, the hierarchy should be considered valid and if they are inconsistent, the hierarchal validity of the model should be re-examined (Saaty, 1990). In other words, it gives details of how much of what the experts have explained has been consistent when giving rank to one criterion over the others.

The results in Table 7.5 show that the CR values of all the PCJM are statistically significant as they are below 0.10, and hence, the respondents' assessments are consistent in the comparisons made.

Table 7.5 Consistency indices of dimensions by expert groups

	Industry	Government	Academic	Total
IUI	0.08***	0.03**	0.02**	0.070***
BI	0.03**	0.02**	0.01*	0.03**
STII	0.03**	0.04**	0.01*	0.03**
GI	0.02 **	0.02**	0.03 **	0.05**
NC	0.06***	0.04**	0.01*	0.04**

Note: The figures*, ** and *** show significance at 1 per cent, 5 per cent and 10 per cent levels respectively.
Source: Computed by authors.

Table 7.6 Pairwise comparison of judgement matrices by dimensions

	BI	STII	GI	NC
BI	1	1.78	1.14	1.43
STII	1	1	1.86	1.31
GI	0.877	0.537	1	1.45
NC	0.699	0.763	0.689	1
				CR = 0.07

Source: Computed by authors.

Table 7.7 Pairwise comparison of judgement matrices, basic infrastructure by sub-dimensions

	Gov	ICT	T	H	PS
Gov	1	1.29	1.94	1.03	1.69
ICT	0.775	1	1.93	1.75	1.81
T	0.515	0.518	1	1.53	1.73
H	0.970	0.571	0.653	1	1.57
PS	0.591	0.552	0.578	0.636	1
					CR = 0.03

Source: Computed by Authors

The composite results of the PCJM matrices of the overall sample are presented in Table 7.6, while Tables 7.7, 7.8, 7.9, and 7.10 present the results of every sub-dimension of the four dimensions. Table 7.6 presents the composite results of the industrial upgrading index.

Table 7.11 shows the composite results of the dimensions and sub-dimensions along with their local weights and global weights.

Application of the IUI Index

Three steps are required to apply IUI for obtaining the level of technological upgradation of any industry.

Step 1 Questionnaire-based data: For using the above prioritization as an index, all the sub-dimensions were translated into a statement, forming a close-ended questionnaire. The close-ended questionnaire provided the basis for estimating the influence of the four dimensions of basic infrastructure, STI infrastructure, global integration, and

Table 7.8 Pairwise comparison of judgement matrices, STI infrastructure by sub-dimensions

	IE	TA	IPR	TP	U	RDIG	SW
IE	1	1.03	1.44	1.09	1.07	1.29	1.18
TA	0.9708	1	1.22	1.96	1.81	1.93	1.93
IPR	0.694	0.819	1	1.82	1.33	1.66	1.82
TP	0.917	0.510	0.549	1	1.78	1.89	1.71
U	0.934	0.552	0.751	0.561	1	1.89	1.7
RDIG	0.775	0.518	0.602	0.529	0.529	1	1.86
SW	0.847	0.518	0.549	0.584	0.588	0.537	1
							CR=0.03

Source: Computed by authors.

Table 7.9 Pairwise comparison of judgement matrices, global integration by sub-dimensions

	GPN	MS	COMP	FDI	HRPT
GPN	1.00	1.62	1.99	1.78	1.92
MS	0.617	1	1.59	1.99	1.55
COMP	0.502	0.628	1	1.93	1.92
FDI	0.561	0.502	0.518	1	1.31
HRPT	0.520	0.645	0.5208	0.763	1
					CR=0.05

Source: Computed by authors.

Table 7.10 Pairwise comparison of judgement matrices, network cohesion by sub-dimensions

	GCC	FCC	FGU	KF	PUR	TL
GCC	1	1.96	1.22	1.57	1.55	1.82
FCC	0.510	1	1.26	2.32	1.85	1.33
FGU	0.819	0.793	1	1.36	1.92	1.36
KF	0.636	0.431	0.735	1	1.77	1.69
PUR	0.645	0.540	0.520	0.564	1	1.72
TL	0.549	0.751	0.735	0.591	0.581	1
						CR=0.04

Source: Computed by authors.

Table 7.11 Industrial upgrading index, local, and global weights

Dimensions	Local weights	Sub-dimensions	Local weights	Global weights
Basic infrastructure	0.207	Gov	0.189	0.039
		ICT	0.227	0.047
		T	0.146	0.031
		H	0.144	0.030
		PS	0.293	0.061
STI infrastructure	0.23	IE	0.139	0.032
		TE	0.21	0.048
		IPR	0.096	0.022
		TP	0.149	0.034
		U	0.100	0.023
		RDIG	0.129	0.030
		SW	0.177	0.041
Global integration	0.308	GPN	0.250	0.077
		MS	0.291	0.090
		COM	0.151	0.046
		FDI	0.139	0.043
		HRPT	0.169	0.052
Network cohesion	0.255	GCC	0.203	0.052
		FCC	0.155	0.039
		FGU	0.139	0.035
		KF	0.129	0.033
		PUR	0.251	0.064
		TL	0.123	0.031
Overall				**1.000**

Source: Computed by authors.

network cohesion along with their sub-dimensions. The questionnaire was sent to the 50 experts on the textile and clothing firms of various sizes, across various sub-national territories of Pakistan to get their levels of technology upgradation.

Step 2 Aggregation of responses and computation of dimension level: Responses from all the experts were aggregated to obtain a mean value (MV) for every sub-dimension as presented in Table 7.12 under the heading MV. The MVs were then multiplied by the global priority weights (GPW) to compute the actual position of each sub-dimensions.

Step 3 Consolidation and synthesis: All the values obtained from multiplying MV with GPW were added (see also Mubarik et al., 2018) to get the value of overall IUI. The results are shown in Table 7.12,

Table 7.12 Industrial upgrading index, local and global priority weights

Dimensions	Local weights	Sub-dimensions	Local weights	Global priority weights	MV of textiles and clothing	IUI value
		Gov	0.189	0.039	3	0.117
		ICT	0.227	0.047	4	0.187
BI	0.207	T	0.146	0.031	2	0.060
		H	0.144	0.03	1	0.029
		PS	0.293	0.061	3	0.181
		IE	0.139	0.032	2	0.057
		TE	0.21	0.048	2	0.086
		IPR	0.096	0.022	2	0.039
STII	0.230	TP	0.149	0.034	3	0.092
		U	0.1	0.023	2	0.041
		RDIG	0.129	0.03	3	0.080
		SW	0.177	0.041	3	0.109
		GPN	0.25	0.077	4	0.207
		MS	0.291	0.09	3	0.180
GI	0.308	COMP	0.151	0.046	3	0.093
		FDI	0.139	0.043	3	0.086
		HRPT	0.169	0.052	2	0.069
		GCC	0.203	0.052	3	0.126
		FCC	0.155	0.039	2	0.064
NC		FGU	0.139	0.035	3	0.086
	0.255	KF	0.129	0.033	2	0.053
		PUR	0.251	0.064	3	0.155
		TL	0.123	0.031	2	0.050
IUI						**2.260**

Source: Computed by authors.

which specifies the industrial upgrading index in the textile and clothing industry for Pakistan. GPN (0.207) and MS (0.180) from the GI dimension show the highest influence, followed by PUR (0.155) and GCC (0.126) from the NC dimension, and SW from the STII dimension. The results of the index can vary between 1 (lowest) to 5 (highest), as noted by Mubarik (2015) and Mubarik et al. (2018). Pakistan's IUI is 2.26, which reflects that the industry has a low level of industrial upgrading (see Table 7.13).

Based on the interpretations shown in Table 7.13, an IUI value of 2.260 is low. Hence, that there are firms operating at level 7 of technological capabilities,

Table 7.13 Interpretation of IUI values

1–1. 99	Very low
2–2.99	Low
3–3.99	High
4–5	Very high

Source: Mubarik et al. (2018).

and level 4 of organizational and management capabilities, suggests that improvements to the IUI will stimulate the upgrading of several textile and clothing firms in Pakistan to enjoy levels 8 and 9 of technological capabilities and level 5 and 6 organizational and management capabilities. Indeed, strong integration with national and international fashion houses and globally renowned R&D centres at universities and government public laboratories abroad can stimulate catching up to the frontier by Pakistan's textiles and clothing firms.

Findings and Discussion

This section attempts to capture the strength of the four dimensions facing textile and clothing industry in Pakistan. The emphasis in this section is on the factors that impact on successful technological upgrading in textiles and clothing firms in Pakistan. Using the data collected from the industry, government, and academic experts, the factors were prioritized based on dimensions and sub-dimensions. The three groups' data were compared with each other before the results were consolidated. The IUI is based on the composite results.

Basic Infrastructure

As shown in Table 7.14, ICT is superior to the others among the BI sub-dimensions with a weight of (0.293) followed by PS (0.227). Gov came next with a weight of 0.189, which is superior to transport and health.

Science, Technology, and Innovation Infrastructure

As shown in Table 7.15 TE enjoyed superior priority with a weight of 0.210, followed by skilled workers (0.177) in the STII dimension. The experts then

Table 7.14 Synthesis of results, basic infrastructure

Basic Infrastructure	Priority
ICT	0.293
Political stability (PS)	0.227
Govt support (G)	0.189
Transport (T)	0.146
Health (H)	0.144

Source: Computed by authors.

Table 7.15 Synthesis of results, STI infrastructure

	Priority
TE	0.210
SW	0.177
TP	0.149
IE	0.139
RDIG	0.129
U	0.100
IPR	0.096

Source: Computed by authors.

prioritized TP (0.149), IE (0.139), and RDIG (0.129), which are close to each other with marginal difference in weightage. The sub-dimension of U showed a weightage of 0.100, which was slightly higher than IPR (0.096).

Global Integration

As shown in Table 7.16 under global integration, the sub-dimension of MS obtained the highest priority of 0.291 while global production network, HR, process, and product technology, competition, and FDI, received lower weights of 0.250, 0.169, 0.151, and 0.139 respectively.

Network Cohesion

Under the network cohesion dimension shown in Table 7.17, PUR obtained the highest score among the sub-dimensions with a priority of 0.251. GCC ranked as the second most important factor with the weightage of 0.203. FCC

Table 7.16 Synthesis of results, global integration

	Priority
MS	0.291
GPN	0.250
HRPT	0.169
COMP	0.151
FDI	0.139

Source: Computed by authors.

Table 7.17 Synthesis of results, network cohesion

Networking cohesion	Priority
PUR	0.251
GCC	0.203
FCC	0.155
FGU	0.139
KF	0.129
TL	0.123

Source: Computed by authors.

enjoyed a weightage of 0.155, which is superior to FGU with a weight of 0.139. KF (0.129) while TL (0.123) received the lowest priority.

Factors Influencing Successful Industrial Upgrading

Based on matrix comparisons, global integration emerged as the foremost prioritized factor among the four pillars (dimensions) of the systemic quad that influenced successful industrial upgrading in the textile and clothing firms of Pakistan (Table 7.18).

Besides, among all sub-criterion, management strategies appear as the most prioritized factor (Table 7.19).

Overall, global integration has been the most influential factor for industrial upgrading in the textile and clothing firms of Pakistan with a priority weightage of 0.308 from the overall total weight of 1.000. This is understandable as the exporting firms need strong links with importers from abroad. Network cohesion ranked second with a priority weightage of 0.255 followed by the STI infrastructure, which received a weightage of 0.230 and basic infrastructure last with a priority weightage of 0.207.

Table 7.18 Prioritization of dimensions for industrial upgrading index

Dimensions	Priority
GI	0.308
NC	0.255
STII	0.230
BI	0.207
Total	1.000

Source: Computed by authors.

Table 7.19 Industrial upgrading index components

Sub-dimensions	Priority (global weight)
Management strategies (MS)	0.097
Global production networks (GPN)	0.068
Producer-user relationships (PUR)	0.066
Training expenditure (TE)	0.059
Information communication technology (ICT)	0.053
Trust and loyalty (TL)	0.053
Skilled workers (SW)	0.050
Human resource and process technology (HRPT)	0.046
Political stability (PS)	0.043
Environment for innovation (IE)	0.042
Competition (COMP)	0.041
Firm-Coordination Council (FCC)	0.040
Training programmes (TP)	0.039
Foreign direct investment (FDI)	0.038
R&D incentives and grants (RDIG)	0.036
Firm-government university links (FGU)	0.036
Government support for basic infrastructure (GOV)	0.035
Knowledge flows (KF)	0.034
Government coordination councils (GCC)	0.032
Universities (U)	0.028
Legal framework for Intellectual Property Rights (IPR)	0.027
Transport (T)	0.026
Health (H)	0.025
Total	1.000

Source: Computed by authors.

With regards to sub-dimensions, MS (0.097) ranked highest followed by GPN (0.068) as the most influential factors supporting industrial upgrading in Pakistan's textile and clothing firms. It is interesting to observe that almost all experts rated PUR (0.066) strongly, while TE received a priority weightage of 0.059. From basic infrastructure, ICT received the highest ranking (0.053). Among the network cohesion dimensions, PUR ranked highest followed by TL (0.053). The SW score of 0.050 from STI infrastructure is higher than HRPT (0.046) from global integration as cutting-edge technologies need skilled employees to adapt and operate them. It is striking to note that PS (0.043), which refers to security and peace has been ranked higher than the STI infrastructure sub-dimensions of IE (0.42) and U (0.028), suggesting that improving the political environment to attract investors appears more important than focusing on the latter two now.

The results also show that the network cohesion sub-dimension of FCC links enjoyed higher priority (0.040) over the STI infrastructure sub-dimension of TP (0.039) and the global integration sub-dimension of FDI (0.038). One of the main barriers for effective industrial upgrading reported in past studies has been the lack of a stable flow of funds and incentives to support R&D (see Chapter 3). Both the STI infrastructure sub-dimension of RDIG (0.036), and the network cohesion sub-dimension of FGU linkages (0.036) had a low score. The basic infrastructure sub-dimension of Gov (0.035), and the network cohesion sub-dimensions of KF (0.034), and GCC (0.034 received low priority. Also, the STII sub-dimensions of U (0.032) and IPR (0.0.27 received low-priority weightage. Finally, the basic infrastructure sub-dimensions of transport (0.026) and health (0.025) showed the lowest prioritization.

Summary

This chapter applied the Saaty (1994), Simon (1997), and Rasiah (2019) approaches to locate and assess the factors that influence successful technological upgrading in the textile and clothing industry in Pakistan by drawing on the four systemic pillars recommended by Rasiah (2019), that is, basic infrastructure, STI infrastructure, global integration, and network cohesion. In-depth interviews with experts were then conducted to identify the problem, and to evaluate the dimensions and sub-dimensions. The validated dimensions and sub-dimensions were confirmed and reconfirmed by eight experts from the three critical groups of industry, academics, and government officials. Following the confirmation, the validated dimensions and sub-dimensions were then sent to 50 experts from industry professionals, academicians, and state officials who were approached for pairwise comparisons as required in the AHP approach through bipolar questionnaires. To assess the robustness of the IUI all the pairwise comparisons were scrutinized using consistency indices. The purpose of applying the AHP method is to find out the relative importance of the factors that influence successful industrial upgrading in Pakistan's textile and clothing firms.

The systemic pillar (dimension) of global integration got the highest priority weightage of 0.308, exceeding all others. The sub-dimension results place management strategies with the highest priority weightage of 0.097 followed by global production networks at 0.068, and producer-user relationships at 0.066. These findings are consistent with the assessments made by Rasiah (2009), and Kumar, Luthra & Haleem (2015). However, because the factors influencing successful technology transfer varies from country to country owing to the specificities associated with the systemic pillars' dimensions, any attempt to generalize must be done carefully as the active instruments in the ecosystems vary with industry, location, and timing. Hence, the IUI obtained for Pakistan's textiles and clothing industry should apply well for the federal government and local governments of the country to focus on strengthening them to stimulate industrial upgrading. Similar IUIs should be computed for other locations, different industries, and at different times for it to be a useful guide for strengthening the ecosystem to promote industrial upgrading.

8 Textiles, Clothing, and Late Industrialization

The extant literature on latecomer economic catch-up has enlightened us about the significant role of technology transfer and technological, and organizational and management capabilities in technological catch-up and economic performance. Although the link between tacit knowledge and organizational and management capabilities is not exhaustive its use in this study is arguably the closest undertaken to capture its role quantitatively by deploying a large data set. Three analytical chapters anchored the analysis and findings. The first of the analytical chapters (Chapter 5) began with the construction of a taxonomy of catch-up trajectories to locate firms by technological capabilities, and organizational and management capabilities. The second analytical chapter (Chapter 6) examined empirically the relationship between technology transfer and technological capabilities, and firm performance with organizational and management capabilities as a mediating variable. The third and final empirical chapter (Chapter 7) developed an industrial upgrading index (IUI) for the textiles and clothing industry of Pakistan. The focus of this concluding chapter is to synthesize the findings, and to draw implications for theory and policy.

Empirics of Catch-Up

The study subjected the economic theory of catch-up and leapfrog to empirical evaluation by targeting its mechanics and links between firms, and between firms and intermediary organizations that are necessary to solve collective action problems, and the institutional change essential to stimulate industrial upgrading in textiles and clothing firms in Pakistan. The findings help illuminate three major areas of industrial upgrading: first, locating firms in the technological, and organizational and management capability trajectories from the starting stage to the final stage; second, the importance of technology transfer and technological capabilities in

Industrial Upgrading in the Textiles and Clothing Industry. Nazia Nazeer and Rajah Rasiah, Oxford University Press.
 DOI: 10.1093/9780198961697.003.0008

driving firm performance and to establish the significance of the mediating role of organizational and management capabilities on this relationship; third, the role of the embedding ecosystem in supporting firm-level upgrading.

Location in Capabilities Trajectory

Consistent with evolutionary theorizing, the focus of this book was on drawing a cutting-edge template of technological, and organizational and management capabilities to build a contemporaneous taxonomy by trajectory of the different levels as textiles and clothing firms move up the industrial ladder from technological capability level 1 to level 9, and organizational and management capability level 1 to 6 (Chapter 4). In doing so, the mapping included the identification of firms that are at the technology frontier globally among textiles and clothing firms. Everest Textiles, Toray, and TAL were identified as lead firms in the global textiles and clothing manufacturing with level 9 technological capabilities and level 6 organizational and management capabilities. The differentiation of textiles and clothing firms by levels 1–9 was determined through opinions of senior employees who carried extensive tacit knowledge in the industry from firm visits. The template produced eventually helped upgrade the one Figueiredo (2014) had developed using the level 1–9 framework earlier, and the one Rasiah (2012) had used to differentiate technological capabilities embodied in human capital, process technology, and product technology in the textiles and clothing industry (Chapter 4). This study also extended the Rasiah (2012) study, which presented one with fewer technological capability levels in the technological trajectory of the textiles and clothing firms but is consistent with evolutionary postulations that firms, industries, and embedding organizations and policy instruments evolve over time (Nelson, 2008; Rasiah, 2011).

The updating of the taxonomy by trajectory of technological, and organizational and management capability levels in the textiles and clothing industry followed the evolutionary tradition of looking at industry-specific developments by location and timing of the evaluation, which helped us identify nine levels of technological capabilities, and six levels of organizational and management capabilities. The exploration into the 'forest' of textile and clothing firms to examine the 'trees' produced an interesting account of the 'nuts and bolts' of the industry in Pakistan (Chapter 5). Although some firms have reached technological capability level 7 in the trajectory of the industry, the bulk of the large and medium firms are still at technological capability levels from 1 to 5. This explains why the industry's exports from Pakistan have largely stagnated in low value-added activities despite enjoying strong natural resource endowments and a long period of export experience.

Yet, despite the concentration of firms in relatively low technological levels, the progress of some national firms to levels 6 and 7 (despite lacking institutional support from the critical pillars of basic infrastructure, STI infrastructure, global integration, and network cohesion), suggest that the potential is there for a broader upward mobility of firms to levels 8 and 9. A profound evaluation of the experience of Everest Textiles, TAL, and Toray in reaching level 9 technological capability shows that these firms can offer Pakistan's national firms the direction to upgrade, albeit the future, capturing random events, also requires recalibrations to absorb the new developments.

Drivers of Firm Performance

Chapter 6 focused on the impact of technology transfer and technological capabilities on firm performance through the mediating effect of organizational and management capabilities. The findings show that technology transfer and technological capabilities are strongly correlated with firm performance, but the latter had a higher impact than technology transfer on firm performance. The coefficients show that the HR dimension had the highest impact, while process technologies showed the lowest impact among the technological capabilities' components.

The evidence also shows that organizational and management capabilities have played a significant mediating role on the relationship between technological capabilities and technology transfer, and firm performance (see Chapter 6). Although organizational and management capabilities do not capture tacit knowledge exhaustively, being the closest to approximate embodied competence levels as it is strongly influenced by strategies and conduct, to some extent it does demonstrate the significance of these practices in stimulating technology transfer and technological capabilities to drive firm performance. These results are consistent with the findings of Helfat and Peteraf (2003, p. 1004), that organizational and management capabilities depend on the ability of managers to work in sync with firms' objectives targeted at technological upgrading. Similarly, the results also support the findings of Rasiah (2003, 2004a) that technological capabilities have a positive and significant impact on firm performance. Pakistan's textiles and clothing industry is no exception in this regard although firms in this country are located in an infrastructure significantly weaker than the firms studied by most others.

Embedding Ecosystem

Drawing on arguably the most novel approaches to examine the embedding ecosystem that is critical to offer the institutional support essential for stimulating technological upgrading in firms, Chapter 7 used the Saaty (1990), Simon (1997), and Rasiah (2019) approaches to assess the factors that influence successful industrial upgrading in the textile and clothing industry in Pakistan. For the reasons explained in Chapter 7, Rasiah's (2007, 2019) systemic pillars were preferred over Porter's (1990) diamond model and Best's (2018) productivity triad to develop the industrial upgrading index (IUI). Following a pilot with eight industry experts endowed with extensive experiential and tacit knowledge to identify the critical embedding ecosystem that influence firm-level upgrading, detailed interviews were carried out with 50 experts from industry professionals, academicians, and government officials with the dimensions and sub-dimensions drawn from the four systemic pillars (dimensions) that constitute the systemic quad. The eight experts unanimously concurred with the relevance of the four dimensions but added more sub-criterion factors than those Rasiah (2019) had used (see Chapter 7).

The overall mean IUI of 2.26 is low compared to the high (3.00–3.99) and very high (4.00–5.00) levels. Hence, given that 31 of the 503 firms studied were operating at technological level 7 in 2018, albeit the embedding ecosystem supporting these firms is weak, the evidence suggests that improvements to the IUI will potentially stimulate the movement of several textile and clothing firms in Pakistan to technological capability levels 8 and 9 (see Chapter 7).

Among the dimensions, the systemic pillar of global integration got the highest priority weightage of 0.308, denoting the importance of integration with global factor and final markets. The sub-dimension results show management strategies to enjoy the highest priority weightage at 0.097 followed by global production networks at 0.068, and producer–user relationships at 0.066 (see Chapter 7).

These findings are consistent with the assessments made by Rasiah (2009a), Rasiah and Amin (2010), Kumar et al. (2015). However, because the factors influencing successful technological transfer varies from country to country owing to the specificities associated with the systemic pillars, any attempt to generalize must be done carefully as the active instruments in the ecosystems vary with location and timing. Hence, the IUI obtained for Pakistan's textiles and clothing industry should apply well for the federal government and local governments of the country to focus on strengthening them to stimulate technological upgrading. Similar IUIs should be constructed for different locations, industries, and times for it to be a useful guide for strengthening the ecosystem to promote industrial upgrading.

In addition, it is important to note that these firms have been operating in locations with poor political stability, and several shortcomings in the basic and STI infrastructure, which needs correction to stimulate such a progression among the national firms (see Chapters 6 and 7). Without political stability it is difficult to imagine why innovating firms would invest in risky and uncertain frontier innovation activities, while frequent power shortages and poor communication connections have only added undue transaction costs that continue to hold back the competitiveness of national firms.

Contribution to Methodology and Theory

The technological, and organizational and management capability framework offered an incisive path to locate firms in Pakistan on the world's technology trajectory of the textiles and clothing industry. The taxonomy by trajectories that was prepared for the book is arguably the most contemporaneous, and one that was developed through a profound study of the different activities that constitute the layout, processes, and structure of textiles and clothing manufacturing firms. It took on earlier frameworks developed through assessing others works (e.g., Lall, 1992; Figueiredo, 2003; Rasiah, 2003). The Figuiredo (2014) and Rasiah (2005) taxonomies by trajectories were extended, refined, and finalized with advancements to nine levels of technological capabilities and six levels of organizational and management capabilities, including the industry's world's frontier firms located abroad. The latter captures instruments of firms' conduct and strategies, inter-firm linkages, marketing strategies, collaboration with cluster suppliers, R&D labs, and fashion houses, as well as frontier firms' practices, such as management's focus on digitalization and digitization, and sustainable development. Consequently, the taxonomy by trajectories developed has not only become an update from 2014 to 2018, but also one that uses organizational and management capabilities to capture the evolution of firm-level strategies vertically. The taxonomy by trajectories developed took on a profound study of the world's leading textiles and clothing manufacturing firms, including Toray and TAL, and Everest Textiles.

While the taxonomy by trajectories developed for the book is a major upgrade from previous ones on the textiles and clothing industry, it is expected to evolve further with time that will vary with location and industry type. Nevertheless, it offers a clear and contemporaneous trajectory by nine technological capability levels, and six levels of organizational and management capabilities to locate firms now (see Chapters 5 and 6).

In addition to the specificity of the different levels of technologies used in textiles and clothing manufacturing, the findings reveal four major developments, viz., firstly, that process, machinery, and production technologies have evolved to allow technology-intensive operations in both developed and developing countries; secondly, robots are increasingly entering production with precision and control that is helping advanced firms with latest technologies to enjoy competitiveness over low-technology firms specialized in labour-intensive operations; thirdly, the increased use of robotics is transforming the industry from being 'dirty, dangerous, and demeaning' to harmonize with the pursuit of carbon neutrality; and fourthly, the progression of textiles and clothing firms to the technological frontier is propelled by an equal progression of the embedding ecosystem (see Chapters 5, 6, and 7). Robots and central coordination systems are not only displacing humans but are also reducing wastage and enabling supply–demand coordination more effectively than those only using automated cellular manufacturing systems.

Furthermore, the evolution of textiles and clothing manufacturing firms does not suggest that it is a natural step that frontier manufacturing firms in the industry will dislodge and leapfrog brandholders. The nature of final markets where competitive sales pricing and volumes can be determined, is structured in such a way that it will take a wider set of strategies that combine high leverage with a wide capital and product base for fashion houses associated with conglomerates to integrate different product and customer markets to appropriate monopsony rents *à la* Blue Ocean strategy that continues to keep the barriers to entry high for new entrants (see Kim & Marbourgne, 2005; Rasiah, 2022).

The findings also show a strong statistical relationship between technological capabilities and technology transfer on firm performance, including with mediating role of organizational and management capabilities in that relationship (see Chapter 6). The statistical evidence on the role of technology transfer from abroad is highly significant, but the relationship between technological capabilities and firm performance is stronger still. This is to be expected as successful technology transfer adds to firm-level technological capabilities and successive flows of technologies strengthen strongly technological capabilities of firms besides making the firms more capable of absorbing foreign technologies, as well as developing their own technologies.

In addition, the evolutionary emphasis of firm strategies, captured using organizational and management capabilities, also show a positive and significant mediating role in the relationship between technological capabilities and technology transfer, and firm performance. In short, technological capabilities, technology transfer, and organizational and management capabilities drive firm performance, which is consistent with the arguments of Prahalad (2012). Although organizational and management practices do not specifically measure tacit knowledge, it nevertheless offers a reasonable association of the likelihood of capturing tacit knowledge through deliberate strategies to stimulate industrial upgrading.

The ecosystem framework used enabled the estimation of the IUI that absorbed the key evolutionary conditions of industry specificity, locational specificity, and timing of the assessment to identify and estimate the relative significance of all the key factors (dimensions and sub-dimensions) and their relative statistical influence on governing the upgrading of firms over the technology trajectory. In doing so, the book breaks ground from typical assessments of the competitiveness of firms that rely on Porter's (1990) diamond. As explained in Chapters 4 and 7, the systemic quad examines the four critical pillars that firms rely on from institutions and meso-organizations that support their operations, including industrial upgrading in a comprehensive way. Best's (2018) productivity triad offers a superior understanding of clusters and the drivers of competitive advantage than that of Porter's (1990) diamond. However, it neither offers a path towards understanding how firms move up the technological trajectory through the different and yet always evolving stages nor provides a profound articulation of the organizational and management strategies that support industrial upgrading. Finally, by focusing on an inductive framework determined by industrial specificity, location, and timing, the systemic quad is equipped for adaptation to meet new developments and specificities.

Three important contributions were critical for the construction of the methodology for estimation the IUI, viz., at the theoretical level, the systemic quad, and at the methodological level the decision-making process approach by Simon (1977) and the Analytical Hierarchical Procedure (AHP) by Saaty (1990) for estimating and analysing the responses. In doing so, the approaches deployed in the book to evaluate the importance of the embedding instruments essential for stimulating upgrading in firms used experts drawn from industry, university, and related organizations. Consequently, it avoided relying on purely firm's assessments as their representatives may not have a profound understanding of the different stages and the differentiating technological, organizational, and management capabilities in the technology trajectory of the industry (see Chapter 7).

While the IUI estimated in the book is specific to Pakistan, the framework can be adapted and deployed to estimate similar IUIs for other countries. Also, as the taxonomy developed in Chapter 5 is specific to the textiles and clothing industry, any attempt to promote other industries will require a revision of the technological trajectory levels to fit the dynamics that define the other industries. In doing so, attempts can be made to establish a timeline or a roadmap for firms to catch up, which includes foresight scenario building to anticipate the potential paths particular industries may take, but with constant updating and recalibration to absorb new random developments.

While the GVC framework went beyond neoclassical approaches to address governance issues in the value chain by focusing on power relations and control, its emphasis on the role of the embedding ecosystem (especially intermediary organizations and institutions) remains a problem as host-site systemic pillars play a critical role in stimulating firm-level industrial upgrading. To understand deeply in what way latecomer firms map their business models to develop standards for their potential customers and to upgrade their position in GVCs across distinct stages, this book offers room for upgrading the resource acquisition strategies identified earlier (i.e., linkage, leverage, learning and imitability, technological catch-up, and transferability) (Mathews, 2006). In doing so, the proposed framework with its dimensions in this study allows the crafting of effective catch-up paths for latecomers. Moreover, the framework used in this study also enriches the knowhow of industrial dynamics and specificities that compliment technological innovation and learning, which is crucial for formulating industrial policies directed at catching up when integrating in GVCs (see Chapter 7).

In doing so, the empirical evidence analysed in this book calls for a major revision on how ODM manufacturing firms relate to the OBMs engaged in clothing fashion and sales. While brandholders (such as Levis, Adidas, Nike, GAP, Louis Vuitton, JC Penney, H&M, Stella McCartney, Zara, Ralph Lauren, ASOS, and Quicksilver) have increasingly conditioned their main suppliers to absorb sustainable technologies that include fabric production that reduces GHG emissions and energy use, the leading manufacturers operate at technology capability level 9 and organizational and management capability level 6, such as TAL, Toray, Everest Textiles, Kanebo, Teijin, Toyobo, Mitsubishi, and Tai Yuen, which are at the globe's technology frontier and are supported by cutting-edge R&D in the manufacture of fibres, textiles, and clothing. Many lead firms in manufacturing also operate as OBMs either regionally or in their own countries, which include TAL and Everest Textiles. Even Pakistan's firms, such as Sapphire Textiles and Nishat Chunian manufacture clothing for the national market using their own brandname (see Chapter 5).

In addition, the leading textiles and clothing firms in Japan, Hong Kong, China, Taiwan, and South Korea are also either directly driving or through collaboration with other firms engaged in the upgrading of state-of-the-art machinery and equipment, which strongly use digitization and digitalization to coordinate production and distribution, and logistics to enjoy strong power and control to dominate governance jointly with brandholders in value chains. While Toray and Everest Textiles own some of these robotics' firms, TAL collaborates with machine tool firms to upgrade its machinery and equipment. Hence, like the TSMC in logic chips, which also fabricate chips for Intel and draws ODM support from other firms (Rasiah & Yap, 2019), the lead manufacturing firms share control of the textiles and clothing global value chains.

Whereas Hamilton (1791), Young (1928), Gerchenkron (1952), and List (1856) initiated policy focus to stimulate industrial policy, Amsden (1989), Wade (1990), and Chang (2003) used national examples to capture industrial policies for spearheading catch-up nationally. While Nelson and Winter (1982) emphasized the importance of institutional change and the evolutionary nature of industrial change, Mazzucato (2013, 2018) went on to focus on the entrepreneurial role of mission-oriented states. These broad-based approaches have offered considerable insights to refine the instruments of industrial policy. Especially the works of Mazzucato (2013), Kattel and Mazzucato (2018), and Foray (2018) have focused succinctly on the general and the specific aspects of industrial policy. However, effective industrial policies need rooting in specific but constantly evolving industries, which require technological roadmaps and governance that are specific to industries, location, and timing. Hence, several scholars worked on the construction of technological capabilities (e.g., Dahlman et al., 1987; Lall, 1992; Bell & Pavitt, 1995; Figueiredo, 2003; Rasiah, 2003; Dutrénit, 2004).

This book went beyond the above advances to map in detail the technological, and organizational and management capabilities critical to locate textiles and clothing firms in a nine-stage technological capability trajectory and a six-stage organizational and management capability trajectory that can be used as a roadmap for firms and policy-makers to plan industrial upgrading in the industry (see Chapters 5, 6, and 7). The analysis not only thoroughly travelled through the specific industry of textiles and clothing in the global trajectory of technological, and organizational and management capabilities, it also screened the embedding ecosystem to capture institutional influences on industrial upgrading. In doing so, the book strengthened the role of industrial policy to be an effective approach to stimulate industrial upgrading by constructing an industrial upgrading index using the systemic pillars (dimensions and sub-dimensions) as the underlying embedding ecosystem to promote industrialization.

Policy Lessons

Any attempt for governments to strategize technological upgrading must be cognizant of the stark reality that poor countries are often gripped with, such as frequent balance of payments deficits and external debt service problems, and hence, lack the financial capital to invest in the upgrading of basic and STI infrastructure. Pakistan is one of those countries that faces serious balance of payments deficits and external debt service problems. Nevertheless, there should be some effort to address the severe power supply problems, and to consider the development of designated export manufacturing zones proximate to the sea that are equipped with good transport and telecommunications networks and security and stability *à la* Malaysia and Vietnam. Such a development should strengthen the basic infrastructure while reducing downtimes and lead times. Indeed, the government's announcement of Rs7 billion (US$31.4 million) over and above the Rs12 billion (US$53.8 Million) claims by the exporters in 2019 to promote the fashion industry by encouraging the training of fashion designers through fashion schools and training institutes has yet to attract interest owing to political instability and frequent changes in government decisions (MTC, 2020). The Textiles and Apparel Policy report outlined a roadmap for the upgrading of the industry over the period 2020–2025. In doing so, the Ministry of Commerce in association with the Ministry of Federal Education and Professional Training (MoFEPT) agreed to support craft institutes to strengthen collaboration between them and the textiles and clothing industry. Under such a collaborative initiative, institutes, such as the Pakistan institute of fashion and designing (PIFD) are expected to be promoted to share latest fashion trends and market intelligence with the industry (MTC, 2020). In this regard, infrastructure development through China–Pakistan Economic Cooperation (CPEC) that connects China through Western Pakistan to the port of Gowdar promises to open strong transport links to reduce lead times, though it will require massive investment in basic infrastructure to attract relocation of both firms and the workers.

The carrots and stick approach that was advanced by Sen (1983) and was so successfully implemented in Japan (Johnson, 1982), South Korea (Amsden, 1989), and Taiwan (Wade, 1990) should be adopted by governments to stimulate industrial upgrading in the textiles and clothing industry. Incentives and grants should be considered with stringent performance standards to stimulate industrial upgrading, including in support of R&D activities. In doing so, stringent performance standards should not only be introduced, they should also be enforced to minimize rent dissipation, and to prevent its abuse. Its application should include direct support for training and R&D, adoption of cutting-edge technologies (e.g., development of frontier materials, diffusion of industrial revolution 4.0 technologies, such as robots in the supporting infrastructure, such as Big Data analytics, cloud computing, Internet of Things, and cybersecurity controls), and fashion design upgrades. Such support instruments have become strong in Hong Kong, Japan, and Taiwan where Toray and TAL, and Everest Textiles operate (see Chapter 7).

Formal institutions alone are not sufficient to stimulate productive connections and coordination between firms and intermediary organizations (see Zhang and Rasiah, 2015). Pakistan has since the 1970s and 1980s launched most of the equivalent organizations that support frontier firms in Hong Kong, Japan, and Taiwan. However, political instability and the lack of passionate efforts to build productive inter-firm relations and to draw up and implement roadmaps for intermediary organizations (including the Textile Ministry, Textile training institutes, machine tool industry, and universities) and firms enjoying incentives have resulted in little socioeconomic synergy to strengthen knowledge networks in the country. In fact, the machine tool industry that was established in 1978 to manufacture heavy mechanical parts for ring frames locally closed in 2000 because of a lack of links between textiles and clothing firms and the industry (see Chapter 2). Nevertheless, the government of Pakistan has approved the handing over of Pakistan Machine Tools Factory (PMTF) to the Strategic Plans Division of the state to revive the suffering state-owned machine tools manufacturing unit. PMTF, a unit of the State Engineering Corporation, started operation in the year 1972. Its capabilities include manufacturing of traditional machines, parts for automotive vehicles, and a range of defence-related equipments.

Also, the 503 firms in the survey reported a lack of collaboration between the firms and the R&D centres, including the Pakistan Council for Science and Technology (PCST), which is the country's central body supporting R&D activity. While no two successful governance networks are the same, it will help to review the successful cluster networks that have evolved in Hong Kong, Japan, and Taiwan, (which embed the frontier textile and clothing manufacturing firms of TAL, Toray, and Everest Textiles) to strengthen such networks in Pakistan.

There is a need to restart efforts to develop the machine tool industry, which should be viewed as the producer goods industry that will be paramount to building competitiveness in the consumer goods industries, such as the textiles and clothing industry. However, unlike the typical heavy industry approach of the twentieth century, it should be focused on light (for control) and heavy technologies (for the hardware required) to enable the appropriation of digitalization and digitization in manufacturing and logistics coordination. The complimentary but dissimilar machine tool industry that evolved in Hong Kong, Japan, and Taiwan have played a key role in supporting TAL, Toray, and Everest Textiles to reach the technology frontier in the textiles and clothing manufacturing. Instead of internalizing the fabrication of robots, independent machine tool firms (including those with equity ownership by textile and clothing firms) should be promoted with incentives in the formative years. The development of the machine tool industries in Japan and Taiwan should serve as lessons for not just Pakistan, but also India, Bangladesh, Malaysia, the Philippines, Vietnam, and Indonesia.

Technological capability level 7 and organizational and management capability level 4 firms in Pakistan, such as Sapphire Textiles and Nishat Chunian enjoy strong international links and exports to Western markets. However, such support facilities should be made available to all textiles and clothing firms in Pakistan through the initiatives of the Ministry of Textiles and Clothing and the Finance Ministry, which sought to promote through the third textiles and apparel policy (2020–2025 through incentives for exports, and initiatives to connect and coordinate with the importing organizations at major markets, and where specialized R&D on textiles and clothing, and leading fashion houses exist, including with machinery and material development firms. This is critical to strengthen network cohesion and further integration into global factor and final markets. The national brands, such as Diners, Khaadi, Sana Safinaz, and Sapphie can be promoted in regional markets as the starting points before they are considered for other markets.

Footsteps into the Future

This book focused on mapping technological, organizational, and management capabilities of textiles and clothing firms in Pakistan against lead firms in the world using firm-level data targeted at the formulation of industrial upgrading strategies. Future research should investigate in further detail the interface between learning dynamics and industrial upgrading, including the sources of synergy towards sustaining industrial upgrading to quicken their reach to the technology frontier in the industry. Given that industries evolve over time, and vary with industry-type, and location, new taxonomies of trajectories must be developed through the mapping of each of the industries, which should then be updated over time to capture the new developments.

Given its evolutionary focus, rather than forecasting the future of the industry through quantitative modelling, the evidence gathered should offer likely paths into the governance of textiles and clothing value chains in the future. A combination of the 2006–2007 global financial crisis and the COVID-19 pandemic that crippled several brandholders, the next few decades since shall see the sharing of control in the textiles and clothing value chain. Several major apparel firms that faced cashflow crisis, such as Gadzooks, Linens' n Thing, and Ascena Retail Group filed for bankruptcy by 2020 while an ailing JCPenny was taken over by Simon Property Group and Browfield Asset Management in 2020 (Reuters, 2023).

Meanwhile, the emergence of technologically sophisticated manufacturers in the newly industrialized countries that enjoyed a rapid rise in incomes, such as Japan, Korea, Taiwan, and China have created major shifts in clothing demand as the locus of fashion is increasingly losing its Western monopoly. These developments suggest the sharing of control over drivers of apparel value chains over the next decades with lead firms in Japan, China, South Korea, and Taiwan. The lead textiles and clothing firms in Bangladesh, India, Pakistan, Malaysia, Thailand, and Vietnam have undergone considerable automation and digitalization (ILO, 2016; WFX, 2023). However, for lead firms in Pakistan (India, Bangladesh, Malaysia, Thailand, and Vietnam) to be able to share leadership of global apparel value chains the embedding ecosystem (systemic quad) of firms in the country needs strong upgrading, which should be the industrial policy focus of these countries. Pakistan is the most disadvantaged among these countries owing to the macroeconomic problems it has faced in 2020–24. Pakistan already has its own famous brand names that sell strongly in the country, such as Khaadi, Sana Safinaz, Limelight, Sapphire, and Diners. Similar expansion into apparel manufacturing has also taken place in Bangladesh and India. For example, Ha-meem Group (2024) from Bangladesh manufactures global brands, such as Gap, Abercrombie, and JC Penney, and its own brands Lycra, Thermolite, and Coolmax, while Arvind Limited (2024) from India manufactures for Arrow, US POLO ASSN, and Calvein Klein, and its own brands of Colt, Ruggers, and Excalibur.

Finally, international organizations, such as UNIDO and UNCTAD, should consider adopting the industrial upgrading approach specified in evolutionary terms by industry-type that should be reviewed and improved every five years to locate firms in the international industrial trajectory rather than the current practice of classifying exporting firms on the basis of low, medium, and high technology. The IUI could serve policy-makers and researchers as a critical guide to locate countries in the industrial capability trajectory.

Bibliography

Abramovitz, M. (1956). *Resource and output trends in the United States since 1870. American Economic Review, 46*(1), 5–23.

Agarwal, R., & Karahanna, E. (2000). Time flies when you're having fun: Cognitive absorption and beliefs about information technology usage. *MIS Quarterly, 24*(4), 665–694.

Ahmed, Y. (2008). *Textile industry of Pakistan*. Horizon Securities SMC, Pvt. Ltd, 2.

Alam, M. S., & Natsuda, K. (2016). The competitive factors of the Bangladeshi garment industry in the post-MFA era. *Canadian Journal of Development Studies/Revue canadienne d'études du développement, 37*(3), 316–336.

Al-Mabrouk, K., & Soar, J. (2009). Identification of key issues for successful technology transfer in the Arab countries: A Delphi study. *International Journal of Technology Transfer and Commercialisation, 8*(1), 22–50.

Al-Obaidi, Z. (1993). *International technology transfer mode selection: A case study of Valmet's experience in developing countries*, Helsinki: Helsingin kauppakorkeakoulu.

Amjad, R., & Burki, S. J. (Eds) (2015). *Pakistan: Moving the economy*, Delhi: Cambridge University Press.

Amsden, A. H. (1985). The division of labour is limited by the rate of growth of the market: The Taiwan machine tool industry in the 1970s. *Cambridge Journal of Economics, 9*(3), 271–284.

Amsden, A. H. (1989). *Asia's next giant: South Korea and late industrialization*. New York: Oxford University Press.

Amsden, A. H. (1991). Diffusion of development: The late-industrializing model and greater East Asia. *The American Economic Review, 81*(2), 282–286.

Amsden, A. H., & Tschang, F. T. (2003). A new approach to assessing the technological complexity of different categories of R&D (with examples from Singapore). *Research Policy, 32*(4), 553–572.

Anderson, P. (1999). Perspective: Complexity theory and organization science. *Organization science, 10*(3), 216–232.

Ando, M., & Kimura, F. (2007). *The formation of international production and distribution networks in East Asia*, NBER Working Paper No. 10167.

APTMA (2014). *Textile industry's economic contribution 2011–12*. All Pakistan Textile Mills Association. Retrieved from http://www.aptma.org.pk/Pak_Textile_Statistics/tec.ASP.

APTMA (2019). *Industry: Power sector*. 20 November 2019. Available at https://aptma.org.pk/power-sector/.

Arbuckle, J. L. (1996). Full information estimation in the presence of incomplete data. *Advanced Structural Equation Modeling: Issues and Techniques, 243*, 277.

Argote, L. (1999). *Organizational learning: Creating, retaining, and transferring knowledge*. Boston (MA): Academic Publishers.

Argote, L., & Ingram, P. (2000). Knowledge transfer: A basis for competitive advantage in firms. *Organizational Behavior and Human Decision Processes, 82*(1), 150–169.

Arkebe, O., Cramer, C., Chang, H. J., & Kozul-Wright, R. (Eds) (2020). *Oxford handbook of industrial policy*. Oxford: Oxford University Press.

Armstrong, J. S. (1982). The value of formal planning for strategic decisions: Review of empirical research. *Strategic Management Journal*, *3*(3), 197–211.
Arnold, D. (2006). Free trade agreements and Southeast Asia. *Journal of Contemporary Asia*, *36*(2), 195–216.
Arnold, E., & Thuriaux, B. (1997). Developing firms' technological capabilities. *Technopolis Group Report.*
Arrow, K. J. (1962). The economic implications of learning by doing. *The Review of Economic Studies*, *29*(3), 155–173.
Arvind Limited (2024). Powering fashion in India, downloaded on 6 June 2024 from https://www.arvindfashions.com/.
Attewell, P. (1992). Technology diffusion and organizational learning: The case of business computing. *Organization Science*, *3*(1), 1–19.
Audretsch, D. B., Lehmann, E. E., & Wright, M. (2014). Technology transfer in a global economy. *Journal of Technology Transfer*, *39*(3), 301–312.
Azadeh, A., Nazari-Shirkouhi, S., Hatami-Shirkouhi, L., & Ansarinejad, A. (2011). A unique fuzzy multi-criteria decision making: Computer simulation approach for productive operators' assignment in cellular manufacturing systems with uncertainty and vagueness. *International Journal of Advanced Manufacturing Technology*, *56*(1–4), 329–343.
Banerjee, S., & Soberman, D. A. (2013). Product development capability and marketing strategy for new durable products. *International Journal of Research in Marketing*, *30*(3), 276–291.
Baranson, J., & Roark, R. (1985). *Trends in North–South transfer of hightechnology*. In N. Rosenberg, & C. Frischtak (Eds), *International technology transfer: Concepts, measures and comparisons* (pp. 24–42). New York: Praeger Press.
Barney, J. (1991). Firm resources and sustained competitive advantage. *Journal of Management*, *17*(1), 99–120.
Bartlett, C. A., & Ghoshal, S. (1993). Beyond the M-form: Toward a managerial theory of the firm. *Strategic Management Journal*, *14*(S2), 23–46.
Bassioni, H. A., Price, A. D., & Hassan, T. M. (2004). Performance measurement in construction. *Journal of Management in Engineering*, *20*(2), 42–50.
Battistella, C., Biotto, G., & De Toni, A. F. (2012). From design driven innovation to meaning strategy. *Management Decision*, *50*(4), 718–743.
Beattie, R. S. (2006). Line managers and workplace learning: Learning from the voluntary sector. *Human Resource Development International*, *9*(1), 99–119.
Bell, M. (1987). *The acquisition of imported technology for industrial de¨elopment: Problems of strategies and management in Arab region* (pp. 13–29). Baghdad: ESCWA, UN.
Bell, M. (2006). Time and technological learning in industrialising countries: How long does it take? How fast is it moving (if at all)? *International Journal of Technology Management*, *36*(1–3), 25–39.
Bell, M., & Pavitt, K. (1995). The development of technological capabilities. *Trade, Technology and International Competitiveness*, *22*(4831), 69–101.
Bernstein, J. F., & Wernstein, D. E. (2002). Do endowments predict the location of production? Evidence from national and international data, *Journal of International Economics*, 56: 55–76.
Best, M. (2001). *The new competitive advantage: The renewal of American industry.* OUP Catalogue.
Best, M. (2018). *How growth really takes place: The making of economic miracles through production, governance, and skills.* Princeton: Princeton University Press.
Best, M. H., & Rasiah, R. (2003). *Malaysian electronics: At the crossroads.* Geneva: UNIDO, Programme Development and Technical Cooperation Division.

Bettis, R. A., & Hitt, M. A. (1995). The new competitive landscape. *Strategic Management Journal, 16*(S1), 7–19.

Bhagat, R. S., Kedia, B. L., Harveston, P. D., & Triandis, H. C. (2002). Cultural variations in the cross-border transfer of organizational knowledge: An integrative framework. *Academy of Management Review, 27*(2), 204–221.

Bhagwati, J. N. (1979). International factor movements and national advantage, *Indian Economic Review, 14*(2), 73–100.

Biggs, T., Shah, M., & Srivastava, P. (1988). *Technological capabilities and learning in African enterprises.* World Bank technical paper, No. 289, African Teaching Department Series.

Bin, G. (2008). Technology acquisition channels and industry performance: An industry-level analysis of Chinese large-and medium-size manufacturing enterprises. *Research Policy, 37*(2), 194–209.

Bloom, N., & Van Reenen, J. (2007). Measuring and explaining management practices across firms and countries. *The Quarterly Journal of Economics, 122*(4), 1351–1408.

Bloom, N., Schankerman, M., & Van Reenen, J. (2013). Identifying technology spillovers and product market rivalry. *Econometrica, 81*(4), 1347–1393.

Bollen, K. A. (1989). A new incremental fit index for general structural equation models. *Sociological Methods & Research, 17*(3), 303–316.

Boxall, P., & Purcell, J. (2011). *Strategy and human resource management.* Basingstoke: Palgrave Macmillan.

Bozeman, B. (2000). Technology transfer and public policy: A review of research and theory. *Research Policy, 29*(4–5), 627–655.

Brady, M. K., & Robertson, C. J. (2001). Searching for a consensus on the antecedent role of service quality and satisfaction: an exploratory cross-national study. *Journal of Business Research, 51*(1), 53–60.

Bruhn, M., Georgi, D., & Hadwich, K. (2008). Customer equity management as formative second-order construct. *Journal of Business Research, 61*(12), 1292–1301.

Burgelman, R. A. (1996). A process model of strategic business exit: Implications for an evolutionary perspective on strategy. *Strategic Management Journal, 17*(S1), 193–214.

Carlile, P. R., & Rebentisch, E. S. (2003). Into the black box: The knowledge transformation cycle, *Management Science, 49*(9), 1180–1195.

Carpenter, M. A., Geletkanycz, M. A., & Sanders, W. G. (2004). Upper echelons research revisited: Antecedents, elements, and consequences of top management team composition. *Journal of Management, 30*(6), 749–778.

Carrillo, J. E., & Gaimon, C. (2004). Managing knowledge-based resource capabilities under uncertainty. *Management Science, 50*(11), 1504–1518.

Cassel, C. M., Hackl, P., & Westlund, A. H. (2000). On measurement of intangible assets: A study of robustness of partial least squares. *Total Quality Management, 11*(7), 897–907.

Cassiman, B., & Veugelers, R. (2002). R&D cooperation and spillovers: Some empirical evidence from Belgium. *American Economic Review, 92*(4), 1169–1184.

Chand, M. H. E., & Lee, L. W. (2022). The future of sustainable clothing industry: Reimagine, regenerate and close the loop. In *2022 academy of international business Asia Pacific Regional Conference:" Resilience in International Business"* (p. MS0113). The Hang Seng University of Hong Kong.

Chandler Jr, A. D. (1977). *The visible hand: The managerial revolution in American business.* Cambridge, MA: Belknap Press.

Chang, D. Y. (1996). Applications of the extent analysis method on fuzzy AHP. *European Journal of Operational Research, 95*(3), 649–655.

Chang, H. J. (2003). *Kicking away the ladder.* London: Chanthem Press.

Chaudhry, S. A., & Hamid, J. (1988). Foreign trade barriers to exports: Pakistan. In *Foreign trade barriers to export growth* (pp. 182–236). Manila: Asian Development Bank.

Chaudhry, T. T., & Faran, M. (2016). Same jeans, same stitch? A comparison of Denim production across three factories in Punjab, Pakistan. Lahore Journal of Economics, *21*(SE), 211–236.

Chen, L. (2017). Globalisation and trade liberalisation in supporting GVCs upgrade: The case of the Republic of Korea. *Journal of Korea Trade, 21*(2), 161–170.

Chen Chiu, L. I. (2009). Industrial policy and structural change in Taiwan's textile and garment industry. *Journal of contemporary Asia, 39*(4), 512–529.

Chesbrough, H. (2003). The logic of open innovation: Managing intellectual property. *California Management Review, 45*(3), 33–58.

Child, J. (1972). Organizational structure, environment, and performance: The role of strategic choice. *Sociology,* 6(1), 1–22.

Chin, W. W. (1998). The partial least squares approach to structural equation modeling. *Modern Methods for Business Research, 295*(2), 295–336.

Chin, W. W., & Newsted, P. R. (1999). Structural equation modeling analysis with small samples using partial least squares. In Hoyle, R. H. (Ed.), *Statistical strategies for small sample research* (1st ed., pp. 307–341). Thousand Oaks (CA): SAGE.

Chin, W. W. (2010). How to write up and report PLS analyses. In V. Esposito Vinzi, W. W. Chin, J. Henseler, & H. Wang (Eds), *Handbook of partial least squares: Concepts, methods and applications* (pp. 655–690). London: Springer.

Christensen, E., & Fjermestad, J. (1997). Challenging group support systems research: The case for strategic decision making. *Group Decision and Negotiation,* 6(4), 351–372.

Coase, R. H. (1937). The nature of the firm. *Economica, 4*(16), 386–405.

Cohen, J. (2013). *Statistical power analysis for the behavioral sciences.* London: Routledge.

Cohen, W. M., & Levinthal, D. A. (1990). *Absorptive capacity: A new perspective on learning and innovation. Administrative Science Quarterly, 35*(1), 128–152.

Cole-Gomolski, B. (1999). Knowledge 'czars' fall from grace. *Computerworld,* 33(1), 1–13.

College of Fashion and Textiles (2022). *A leading edge fashion school,* accessed on 23 August from https://www.ft.fju.edu.tw/en/157-2/.

Comtrade (2020). Trade data, Accessed on 18 May 2020 from https://comtradeplus.un.org/TradeFlow?Frequency=A&Flows=X&CommodityCodes=TOTAL&Partners=251&Reporter.

Cooke-Davies, T. (2002). The 'real' success factors on projects. *International Journal of Project Management, 20*(3), 185–190.

Cooper, R. G. (1986). *Winning at new products* (Vol. 26). Reading, MA: Addison-Wesley.

Cororaton, C. B., & Orden, D. (2008). *Pakistan's cotton and textile economy: Intersectoral linkages and effects on rural and urban poverty* (Vol. 158). Intl Food Policy Res Inst.

Creighton, J. W., Jolly, J. A., & Buckles, T. A. (1985). The manager's role in technology transfer. *Journal of Technology Transfer, 10*(1), 65–81.

Crema, M., Verbano, C., & Venturini, K. (2014). Linking strategy with open innovation and performance in SMEs. *Measuring Business Excellence, 18*(2), 14–27.

Cricelli, L., & Grimaldi, M. (2010). Knowledge-based inter-organizational collaborations. *Journal of Knowledge Management, 14*(3), 348–358.

Cronbach, L. J. (1951). Coefficient alpha and the internal structure of tests. *Psychometrika, 16*(3), 297–334.

Cummings, J. L., & Teng, B. S. (2003). Transferring R&D knowledge: The key factors affecting knowledge transfer success. *Journal of Engineering and Technology Management, 20*(1–2), 39–68.

Cusumano, M. A., & Elenkov, D. (1994). Linking international technology transfer with strategy and management: A literature commentary. *Research Policy, 23*(2), 195–215.

Dahlman, C. J., Ross-Larson, B., & Westphal, L. E. (1987). Managing technological development: Lessons from the newly industrializing countries. *World Development*, *15*(6), 759–775.

Davenport, S., Davies, J., & Grimes, C. (1998). Collaborative research programmes: Building trust from difference. *Technovation*, *19*(1), 31–40.

Day, G. S. (2011). Closing the marketing capabilities gap. *Journal of Marketing*, *75*(4), 183–195.

Dibiaggio, L., & Nasiriyar, M. (2009). Knowledge integration and vertical specialization in the semiconductor industry. *European Management Review*, *6*(4), 265–276

Denison, D. R., & Mishra, A. K. (1995). Toward a theory of organizational culture and effectiveness. *Organization Science*, *6*(2), 204–223.

Desai, A. V. (1984). India's technological capability: An analysis of its achievements and limits. *Research Policy*, *13*(5), 303–310.

Dess, G. G., & Robinson Jr, R. B. (1984). Measuring organizational performance in the absence of objective measures: The case of the privately-held firm and conglomerate business unit. *Strategic Management Journal*, *5*(3), 265–273.

De Toni, A. F., Nonino, F., & Pivetta, M. (2011). A model for assessing the coherence of companies' knowledge strategy. *Knowledge Management Research & Practice*, *9*(4), 327–341.

De Toni, A. F., Biotto, G., & Battistella, C. (2012). Organizational design drivers to enable emergent creativity in web-based communities. *The Learning Organization*, *19*(4), 335–349.

Device Plus (2018) *SewBot revolutionizing the clothing manufacturing industry*, accessed on 4 November 2021 from https://www.deviceplus.com/trending/sewbot-in-the-clothing-manufacturing-industry/.

Diamantopoulos, A., & Riefler, P. (2011). Using formative measures in international marketing models: a cautionary tale using consumer animosity as an example. In M. Sarstedt, M. Schwaiger, & C. R. Taylor (Eds.), *Measurement and research methods in international marketing* (pp. 11–30). Leeds: Emerald Group Publishing Limited.

Diamantopoulos, A., & Siguaw, J. A. (2006). Formative versus reflective indicators in organizational measure development: A comparison and empirical illustration. *British Journal of Management*, *17*(4), 263–282.

Dosi, G. (1995). Hierarchies, markets and power: Some foundational issues on the nature of contemporary economic organizations. *Industrial and Corporate Change*, *4*(1), 1–19.

Dosi, G., Nelson, R., & Winter, S. (Eds). (2001). *The nature and dynamics of organizational capabilities*. Oxford: Oxford University Press.

Dunning, J. H. (2001). The eclectic (OLI) paradigm of international production: Past, present and future. *International Journal of the Economics of Business*, *8*(2), 173–190.

Dussauge, P., Garrette, B., & Mitchell, W. (2004). Asymmetric performance: the market share impact of scale and link alliances in the global auto industry. *Strategic Management Journal*, *25*(7), 701–711.

Dutrénit, G. (2004). Building technological capabilities in latecomer firms: A review essay. *Science, Technology and Society*, *9*(2), 209–241.

Dutrénit, G. (2006). Instability of the technology strategy and building of the first strategic capabilities in a large Mexican firm. *International Journal of Technology Management*, *36*(1–3), 43–61.

Dutrénit, G. (2007). The transition from building-up innovative technological capabilities to leadership by latecomer firms. *Asian Journal of Technology Innovation*, *15*(2), 125–149.

Dyer, J. H., & Hatch, N. W. (2006). Relation-specific capabilities and barriers to knowledge transfers: Creating advantage through network relationships. *Strategic Management Journal*, *27*(8), 701–719.

Dyer, J. H., & Singh, H. (1998). The relational view: Cooperative strategy and sources of interorganizational competitive advantage. *Academy of Management Review*, *23*(4), 660–679.

Dyer, R. F., & Forman, E. H. (1992). Group decision support with the analytic hierarchy process. *Decision Support Systems*, *8*(2), 99–124.

Edquist, C., & Jacobssen, S. (1987). The integrated circuit industries in India and South Korea in an international techno-economic context. *Industry and Development*, *21*, 1–62.

Efron, B., & Tibshirani, R. J. (1994). *An introduction to the bootstrap*. London: CRC Press.

Eisenhardt, K. M., & Martin, J. A. (2000). Dynamic capabilities: What are they? *Strategic Management Journal*, *21*(10–11), 1105–1121.

Ellinger, A. D., Ellinger, A. E., & Keller, S. B. (2003). Supervisory coaching behavior, employee satisfaction, and warehouse employee performance: A dyadic perspective in the distribution industry. *Human Resource Development Quarterly*, *14*(4), 435–458.

Enders, C. K. (2006). Analyzing structural equation models with missing data. In G. R. Hancock, & R. O. Mueller (Eds.), *Structural equation modeling: A second course* (pp. 313–342. Greenwich, CT: Information Age Publishing.

EPA (2004). National priority chemicals trends report, Washington DC: United States Environmental Protection Agency, downloaded on 18 June 2025 from https://nepis.epa.gov/Exe/ZyNET.exe/

Ethiraj, S. K., Kale, P., Krishnan, M. S., & Singh, J. V. (2005). Where do capabilities come from and how do they matter? A study in the software services industry. *Strategic Management Journal*, *26*(1), 25 45.

Etzkowitz, H. (2003). Innovation in innovation: The triple helix of university-industry-government relations. *Social Science Information*, *42*(3), 293–337.

Etzkowitz, H., & Leydesdorff, L. (2000). The dynamics of innovation: From national systems and 'Mode 2' to a triple helix of university–industry–government relations. *Research Policy*, *29*(2), 109–123.

Feldman, D. C. (2001). Career coaching: What HR professionals and managers need to know. *People and Strategy*, *24*(2), 26.

Felin, T., & Hesterly, W. S. (2007). The knowledge-based view, nested heterogeneity, and new value creation: Philosophical considerations on the locus of knowledge. *Academy of Management Review*, *32*(1), 195–218.

Ferdows, K. (2006). POM forum: Transfer of changing production know-how. *Production and Operations Management*, *15*(1), 1–9.

Figueiredo, P. N. (2003). Learning, capability accumulation and firms differences: Evidence from latecomer steel. *Industrial and Corporate Change*, *12*(3), 607–643.

Figueiredo, P. N. (2014). Beyond technological catch-up: An empirical investigation of further innovative capability accumulation outcomes in latecomer firms with evidence from Brazil. *Journal of Engineering and Technology Management*, *31*, 73–102.

Figueiredo, P. N., & Cohen, M. (2019). Explaining early entry into path-creation technological catch-up in the forestry and pulp industry: Evidence from Brazil. *Research Policy*, *48*(7), 1694–1713.

Fibre2Fashion (2019). 3D smart vision sensors into garment production in Taiwan, downloaded on 18 June 2025 from https://www.fibre2fashion.com/news/apparel-news/3d-smart-vision-sensors-into-garment-production-in-taiwan-253633-newsdetails.htm

Foray, D. (2018). Smart specialization strategies as a mission-oriented policy—a case study on the emergence of policy practices. *Industrial and Corporate Change*, *27*(5), 817–832.

Fornell, C., & Larcker, D. F. (1981). Structural equation models with unobservable variables and measurement error: Algebra and statistics. *Journal of Marketing Research*, *18*(3), 382–388.

Fornell, C., & Cha, J. (1994). Partial least squares. In R. P. Bagozzi (Ed.), *Advanced methods of marketing research* (pp. 52–78). Oxford: Basil Blackwell.

Fornell, C., & Cha, J. (1994). Partial least squares. *Advanced Methods of Marketing Research, 407*(3), 52–78.

Fransman, M. (1986). International competitiveness, technical change and the state: The machine tool industry in Taiwan and Japan. *World Development, 14*(12), 1375–1396.

Freeman, C. (1995). The 'national system of innovation'in historical perspective. *Cambridge Journal of Economics, 19*(1), 5–24.

Fu, X. (2011). Processing trade, FDI and the exports of indigenous firms: Firm-level evidence from technology-intensive industries in China. *Oxford Bulletin of Economics and Statistics, 73*(6), 792–817.

Fu, X., & Gong, Y. (2011). Indigenous and foreign innovation efforts and drivers of technological upgrading: evidence from China. *World Development, 39*(7), 1213–1225.

Fu, X., Pietrobelli, C., & Soete, L. (2011). The role of foreign technology and indigenous innovation in the emerging economies: Technological change and catching-up. *World Development, 39*(7), 1204–1212.

Gefen, D., & Straub, D. (2005). A practical guide to factorial validity using PLS-Graph: Tutorial and annotated example. *Communications of the Association for Information Systems, 16*(1), 5.

Geisser, S. (1974). A predictive approach to the random effect model. *Biometrika, 61*(1), 101–107.

Gereffi, G. (1999). International trade and industrial upgrading in the apparel commodity chain. *Journal of International Economics, 48*(1), 37–70.

Gereffi, G., Humphrey, J., & Sturgeon, T. (2005). The governance of global value chains. *Review of International Political Economy, 12*(1), 78–104.

Gerschenkron, A. (1952a). Backwardness in historical perspective. In B. Hoselitz (Ed.), *Progress of underdeveloped countries* (pp. 3–29). Chicago: Chicago University Press.

Giuliani, E. (2005). Cluster absorptive capacity: Why do some clusters forge ahead and others lag behind? *European Urban and Regional Studies, 12*(3), 269–288.

Goh, S. C. (2002). Managing effective knowledge transfer: An integrative framework and some practice implications. *Journal of Knowledge Management, 6*(1), 23–30.

Gold, A. H., Malhotra, A., & Segars, A. H. (2001). Knowledge management: An organizational capabilities perspective. *Journal of Management Information Systems, 18*(1), 185–214.

Government of Pakistan. (2018). *Economic Survey of Pakistan 2017–18*. Islamabad: Finance Division, Economic Adviser's Wing.

Government of Pakistan, Finance Division (2020). *Economic survey of Pakistan 2019–20*. Chapter 3. Available at https://www.finance.gov.pk/survey/chapter_20/03_Manufacturing_and_Mining.pdf.

Government of Pakistan, Finance Division (2021). *Economic survey of Pakistan 2020–21*. Chapter 3. Available at https://www.finance.gov.pk/survey/chapters_21/PES_2020_21.pdf

Grant, R. M. (1996). Toward a knowledge-based theory of the firm. *Strategic Management Journal, 17*(S2), 109–122.

Gray, P. H., & Meister, D. B. (2004). Knowledge sourcing effectiveness. *Management Science, 50*(6), 821–834.

Gray, P., & Durcikova, A. (2006). The role of knowledge repositories in technical support environments: Speed versus learning in user performance. *Journal of Management Information Systems, 22*(3), 159–190.

Grossman, G. M., & Helpman, E. (1994). Endogenous innovation in the theory of growth. *Journal of Economic Perspectives, 8*(1), 23–44.

Guan, J. C., Yam, R. C., Mok, C. K., & Ma, N. (2006). A study of the relationship between competitiveness and technological innovation capability based on DEA models. *European Journal of Operational Research, 170*(3), 971–986.

Guarte, J. M., & Barrios, E. B. (2006). Estimation under purposive sampling. *Communications in Statistics-Simulation and Computation, 35*(2), 277–284.

Guilfoos, S. J. (1989). Bashing the technology insertion barriers. *Air Force Journal of Logistics, 13*(1), 27–32.

Gujarati, D. N. (2003). *Basic econometrics.* New York: McGraw-Hill.

Gupta, A. K., & Govindarajan, V. (2000). Knowledge flows within multinational corporations. *Strategic Management Journal, 21*(4), 473–496.

Gupta, B. S. (2007). Manufactured textile fibers. In *Kent and Riegel's handbook of industrial chemistry and biotechnology* (pp. 431–498). Boston, MA: Springer US.

Hair, J. F., Sarstedt, M., Hopkins, L., & Kuppelwieser, V. G. (2014). Partial least squares structural equation modeling (PLS-SEM): An emerging tool in business research. *European Business Review, 26*(2), 106–121.

Hair, J. F., & Anderson, R. E. (1995). *Multivariate data analysis.* Upper Saddle River: Prentice-Hall.

Hamdani, K. (2014). Foreign direct investment and technological capabilities: The relevance of the East Asian experience for Pakistan. *Lahore Journal of Economics, 19*, 267.

Ha-meem Group (2024). *Ha-Meem textiles*, downloaded on 6 June 2024 from https://hameemtextiles.com/#.

Hamel, G., & Prahalad, C. K. (1993). Strategy as stretch and leverage. *Harvard Business Review, 71*(2), 75–84.

Hamilton, A. (1791) *Report on the structure of manufactures*, accessed on 2 October 2022 from https://founders.archives.gov/documents/Hamilton/01-10-02-0001-0007.

Hamid, N., Nabi, I., & Zafar, R. (2014). The textiles and garments sector: Moving up the value chain. *The Lahore Journal of Economics, 19*(special Edition), 283–306.

Hamid, N., & Khan, M. (2015). Pakistan: A case of premature deindustrialization? *Lahore Journal of Economics, 20*(SI), 107–141.

Hamna, A. (2009). Capital flows and real exchange rate overvaluation—a chronic ailment: Evidence from Pakistan, *Lahore Journal of Economics, 14*(SE), 51–86.

Haour, G., & Zedtwitz, Mv. (2016). *Created in China: How China is becoming a global innovator.* London: Bloomsbury.

Hatch, N. W., & Dyer, J. H. (2004). Human capital and learning as a source of sustainable competitive advantage. *Strategic Management Journal, 25*(12), 1155–1178.

Hayami, Y., & Ruttan, V. W. (1971). Induced innovation and agricultural development. Retrieved from the University Digital Conservancy, on 26 June from https://hdl.handle.net/11299/54243.

Helfat, C. E., & Peteraf, M. A. (2003). The dynamic resource-based view: Capability lifecycles. *Strategic Management Journal, 24*(10), 997–1010.

Hendersen, J. (1989). *Globalisation of high technology production.* London: Routledge.

Henseler, J. (2010). On the convergence of the partial least squares path modeling algorithm. *Computational Statistics, 25* (1), 107–120.

Henseler, J., & Fassott, G. (2010). Testing moderating effects in PLS path models: An illustration of available procedures. In V. Esposito Vinzi, W. Chin, J. Henseler, & H. Wang (Eds.), *Handbook of partial least squares* (pp. 713–735). Berlin: Springer.

Hill, C. W. (1990). Cooperation, opportunism, and the invisible hand: Implications for transaction cost theory. *Academy of Management Review, 15*(3), 500–513.

Hirschleifer, J. (1971). *Liquidity, uncertainty, and the accumulation of information.* Western Management Science Institute, University of California.

Hirschman, A. O. (1958). *The strategy of economic development*, New Haven: Yale University Press

Hirschman, A. O. (1970). *Exit, voice, and loyalty: Responses to decline in firms, organizations, and states*. Cambridge, MA: Harvard University Press.

Ho, R. (2006). *Handbook of univariate and multivariate data analysis and interpretation with SPSS*. Chapman & Hall/CRC.

Hobday, M., & Rush, H. (2007). Upgrading the technological capabilities of foreign transnational subsidiaries in developing countries: The case of electronics in Thailand. *Research policy*, *36*(9), 1335–1356.

Hoekman, B. M., Maskus, K. E., & Saggi, K. (2005). Transfer of technology to developing countries: Unilateral and multilateral policy options. *World Development*, *33*(10), 1587–1602.

Hotek, D. R. (2002). Skills for the 21st century supervisor: What factory personnel think. *Performance Improvement Quarterly*, *15*(2), 61–83.

Huang, B., Zhao, J., Geng, Y., Tian, Y., & Jiang, P. (2017). Energy-related GHG emissions of the textile industry in China. *Resources, Conservation and Recycling*, *119*, 69–77.

Humphrey, J., & Schmitz, H. (2000). *Governance and upgrading: Linking cluster and global value chain research*. IDS Working Paper 120, downloaded on 14 February 2025 from https://www.ids.ac.uk/download.php?file=files/Wp120.pdf.

Hussain, D., Figueiredo, M., & Ferreira, F. (2009). SWOT analysis of Pakistan textile supply chain. In *Proceedings of IX. Congreso Galego de Estatística e Investigación de Operacións* (pp. 12–14). https://www.researchgate.net/publication/228447616_SWOT_Analysis_of_Pakistan_Textile_Supply_Chain

Iguchi, C., & Cantwell, J. (2005). Multinationals and their relationships with local suppliers: Effects on local suppliers' development path in the Malaysian electrical and electronics industry. In A. Giroud, D. Yang, & A.Mohr (Eds), *Multinationals and Asia: Organizational and institutional relationships* (pp. 54–71). London: Routledge.

ILO (2016). ASEAN in transformation: The future of jobs at risk of automation, July, Bangkok: International Labour Organization, downloaded on 18 June from https://www.ilo.org/sites/default/files/wcmsp5/groups/public/@ed_dialogue/@act_emp/documents/publication/wcms_579554.pdf.

ILO (2020). *Employment, wages, and productivity trends in the Asian garment sector: data and policy for the future of work*. Geneva: International Labour Organization.

Itoh, T., & Krueger, A. O. (Eds) (1995). *Growth theories in light of the East Asian experience*. Chicago: Chicago University Press.

Japan (2019). Japan's International Cooperation: Building a future for connecting the world, Tokyo: Ministry of Foreign Affairs. Downloaded from https://www.mofa.go.jp/mofaj/gaiko/oda/files/100161448.pdf

Jennings, N. R. (2000). On agent-based software engineering. *Artificial intelligence*, *117*(2), 277–296.

Johnson, C. (1982). *MITI and the Japanese miracle: The growth of industrial policy 1925–1975*. Stanford: Stanford University Press.

Jones, M. L. (2001). Sustainable organizational capacity building: Is organizational learning a key? *The International Journal of Human Resource Management*, *12*(1), 91–98.

Jung, M., Lee, Y. B., & Lee, H. (2015). Classifying and prioritizing the success and failure factors of technology commercialization of public R&D in South Korea: Using classification tree analysis. *Journal of Technology Transfer*, *40*(5), 877–898.

Jyoti, Banwet, D. K., & Deshmukh, S. G. (2010). Modelling the success factors for national R&D organizations: A case of India. *Journal of Modelling in Management*, *5*(2), 158–175.

Kale, P., Singh, H., & Perlmutter, H. (2000). Learning and protection of proprietary assets in strategic alliances: Building relational capital. *Strategic Management Journal, 21*(3): 217–237.

Kangis, P., Gordon, D., & Williams, S. (2000). Organisational climate and corporate performance: An empirical investigation. *Management Decision, 38*(8), 531–540.

Kattel, R., & Mazzucato, M. (2018). Mission-oriented innovation policy and dynamic capabilities in the public sector. *Industrial and Corporate Change, 27*(5), 787–801.

Katz, J. M. (2001). Structural reforms and technological behaviour: The sources and nature of technological change in Latin America in the 1990s, *Research Policy, 30*(1), 1–19.

Kazmi, S. A. Z., & Takala, J. (2014). An overview of Pakistan's textile sector from operational competitive perspective—a suggestive analysis! *World Journal of Engineering and Technology, 2*(2), 124.

Khan, J. A. (2011). *Research methodology*. New Delhi: APH Publishing Corporation.

Khan, N. Z. (1998). Textiles sector of Pakistan: The challenge beyond 2004 [with Comments]. *The Pakistan Development Review 37*(4), 595–619.

Khan, M., & Afzal, U. (2016). The diversification and sophistication of Pakistan's exports: The need for structural transformation. *The Lahore Journal of Economics, 21*(special edition), 99–127.

Khan, M. A., Qayyum, A., Sheikh, S. A., & Siddique, O. (2005). Financial development and economic growth: The case of Pakistan. *Pakistan Development Review, 44*(4), 819–837.

Kim, L. (1997). The dynamics of Samsung's technological learning in semiconductors. *California Management Review, 39*(3), 86–100.

Kim, L. (1998). Crisis construction and organizational learning: Capability building in catching-up at Hyundai Motor. *Organization Science, 9*(4), 506–521.

Kim, L. (1999). Building technological capability for industrialization: Analytical frameworks and Korea's experience. *Industrial and Corporate Change, 8*(1), 111–136.

Kim, L. (2000). The dynamics of technological learning in industrialisation, UNU-INTECH Discussion Paper Series 2000–07, United Nations University–INTECH.

Kim, L., & Lee, H. (1987). Patterns of technological change in a rapidly developing country: A synthesis. *Technovation, 6*(4), 261–276.

Kim, W. C., & Marbourgne, R. (2005). Blue ocean strategy: From theory to practice. *Califronia Management Review, 47*(3), 105–121.

Knott, A. M. (2003). The organizational routines factor market paradox. *Strategic Management Journal, 24*(10), 929–943.

Kotabe, M., Dunlap-Hinkler, D., Parente, R., & Mishra, H. A. (2007). Determinants of cross-national knowledge transfer and its effect on firm innovation. *Journal of International Business Studies, 38*(2), 259–282.

Krasnikov, A., & Jayachandran, S. (2008). The relative impact of marketing, research-and-development, and operations capabilities on firm performance. *Journal of Marketing, 72*(4), 1–11.

Krejcie, R. V., & Morgan, D. W. (1970). Determining sample size for research activities. *Educational and Psychological Measurement, 30*(3), 607–610.

Krueger, A. (1995). East Asian experience and endogenous growth theory. In T. Itoh & A. Krueger (Eds), *Growth theories in light of the East Asian experience* (pp. 9–36). Chicago: Chicago University Press.

Kumar, S., Luthra, S., & Haleem, A. (2015). Benchmarking supply chains by analyzing technology transfer critical barriers using AHP approach. *Benchmarking: An International Journal, 22*(4), 538–558.

Kumar, S., Luthra, S., Haleem, A., Mangla, S. K., & Garg, D. (2015). Identification and evaluation of critical factors to technology transfer using AHP approach. *International Strategic Management Review, 3*(1–2), 24–42.

Lall, S. (1987). *Learning to industrialize: The acquisition of technological capability by India.* New York: Springer.
Lall, S. (1992). Technological capabilities and industrialization. *World Development, 20*(2), 165–186.
Lall, S. (1998). Exports of manufactures by developing countries: Emerging patterns of trade and location. *Oxford Review of Economic Policy, 14*(2), 54–73.
Lall, S. (2000). The technological structure and performance of developing country manufactured exports, 1985–98. *Oxford Development Studies, 28*(3), 337–369.
Lall, S., & Narula, R. (2004). Foreign direct investment and its role in economic development: Do you need a new agenda? *European Journal of Development Research, 16*(3), 447–464.
Lang, D., & Wittig-Berman, U. (2000). Managing work-related learning for employee and organizational growth. *SAM Advanced Management Journal, 65*(4), 37.
Latan, H., & Ghozali, I. (2014). Partial least squares: Concepts, techniques and applications using program WarpPLS 4.0. Semarang: Diponegoro University Press.
Laursen, K., & Foss, N. J. (2003). New human resource management practices, complementarities and the impact on innovation performance. *Cambridge Journal of Economics, 27*(2), 243–263.
Lee, J., Bae, Z. T., & Choi, D.K. (2007). Technology development processes: A model for a developing country with a global perspective, *R&D Management, 18*(3), 235–250.
Lee, S., Kim, W., Kim, Y. M., & Oh, K. J. (2012). Using AHP to determine intangible priority factors for technology transfer adoption. *Expert Systems with Applications, 39*(7), 6388–6395.
Leischnig, A., Geigenmueller, A., & Lohmann, S. (2014). On the role of alliance management capability, organizational compatibility, and interaction quality in interorganizational technology transfer. *Journal of Business Research, 67*(6), 1049–1057.
Levitt, B., & March, J. G. (1988). Organizational learning. *Annual Review of Sociology, 14*(1), 319–338.
Lin, C., Pervan, G., & McDermid, D. (2007). Issues and recommendations in evaluating and managing the benefits of public sector IS/IT outsourcing. *Information Technology & People, 20*(2), 161–183.
List, F. (1856). *National system of political economy.* Philadelphia: J.B. Lippincott & Company.
List, F. (1885). *The national system of political economy,* Translated by Sampson S. llyod, London: Longman, Green and Company.
Ljungquist, U. (2007). How do core competencies discriminate? Identification of influencing similarities and differences. *Knowledge and Process Management, 14*(4), 237–247.
Lohmöller, J. B. (1989). Latent variable path modeling with partial least squares. New York: Springer.
Lucas Jr, R. E. (1988). On the mechanics of economic development. *Journal of Monetary Economics, 22*(1), 3–42.
Lundvall, B. Å. (Ed.) (2010). *National systems of innovation: Toward a theory of innovation and interactive learning.* London: Anthem Press.
Macneil, C. (2001). The supervisor as a facilitator of informal learning in work teams. *Journal of Workplace Learning, 13*(6), 246–253.
Mahmood, T. (2014). *Assessment of German–Pakistani relations in trade, investment and strategic cooperation* (No. P 2014-004). WZB Discussion Paper.
Maister, D. H. (2001). What drives profits in consulting firms? *Consulting to Management, 12*(2), 45.
Malik, A. (2000). *Demand for textile and clothing exports of Pakistan.* PIDE-Working Papers, No. 180.
Malik, K. (2002). Aiding the technology manager: A conceptual model for intra-firm technology transfer. *Technovation, 22*(7), 427–436.

Malik, K., & Hattasingh, T. (2013). International technology transfer human resource issues for the technology recipient. In *ISPIM Conference Proceedings* (p. 1). The International Society for Professional Innovation Management (ISPIM).

Malmberg, A., & Maskell, P. (2006). Localized learning revisited. *Growth and Change, 37*(1), 1–18.

Mansfield, E. (1975). International technology transfer: forms, resource requirements, and policies. *American Economic Review, 65*(2), 372–376.

March, J. G. (1991). Exploration and exploitation in organizational learning. *Organization Science, 2*(1), 71–87.

Marinova, D. (2004). Actualizing innovation effort: the impact of market knowledge diffusion in a dynamic system of competition. *Journal of Marketing, 68*(3), 1–20.

Marshall, A., (1920). *The economics of industry*. London: Macmillan.

Martin, X., & Salomon, R. (2003). Knowledge transfer capacity and its implications for the theory of the multinational corporation. *Journal of International Business Studies, 34*(4), 356–373.

Marx, K. (1867). Capital Volume One: The process of production of capital. In German, Translated version, translated in 1887 by Samuel Moore and Edward Aveling, Edited by Frederick Engels, Moscow: Progress Publishers.

Marx, K. (1954). *Das Kapital*. Volumes I and III, Moscow: Progress Publishers.

Mathews, J. (2006). Catch-up strategies and the latecomer effect in industrial development, *New Political Economy, 11*(3), 313–335.

Mayer, S., & Blaas, W. (2002). Technology transfer: an opportunity for small open economies. *The Journal of Technology Transfer, 27*(3), 275–289.

McClelland, D. C. (1961). *The achieving society*. New York: D. Van Nostrand Company.

McKelvie, A., & Davidsson, P. (2009). From resource base to dynamic capabilities: An investigation of new firms. *British Journal of Management, 20*(s1), S63–S80.

McMullan, W., & Melnyk, K. (1988). University innovation centres and academic venture formation. *R&D Management, 18*(1), 5–12.

Mazzucato, M. (2013). *The entrepreneurial state: Debunking public vs. private sector myths*, London: Anthem Press.

Mazzucato, M. (2018). Mission-oriented innovation policies: challenges and opportunities, *Industrial and Corporate Change, 27*(5), 805–815.

Memon, N. A. (2010). Pakistan as major Asian market for textile machinery manufacturing nations. *Pakistan Textile Journal, 60*(8), August 31.

Merrilees, B., Rundle-Thiele, S., & Lye, A. (2011). Marketing capabilities: Antecedents and implications for B2B SME performance. *Industrial Marketing Management, 40*(3), 368–375.

Miller, D., Eisenstat, R., & Foote, N. (2002). Strategy from the inside out: Building capability-creating organizations. *California Management Review, 44*(3), 37–54

Miller, R. G. (1974). The jackknife—a review. *Biometrika, 61*(1), 1–15.

MTC (2020). *Textiles and apparel policy 2020–25, Karachi: Ministry of Textiles and Clothing*, downloaded on 16 December 2022 from https://www.commerce.gov.pk/wp-content/uploads/2022/02/Textiles-and-Apparel-Policy-2020-25.pdf.

Mizik, N., & Jacobson, R. (2003). Trading off between value creation and value appropriation: The financial implications of shifts in strategic emphasis. *Journal of Marketing, 67*(1), 63–76.

Mohamed, A. S., Sapuan, S. M., Ahmad, M. M., Hamouda, A. M. S., & Baharudin, B. H. T. B. (2012). Modeling the technology transfer process in the petroleum industry: Evidence from Libya. *Mathematical and Computer Modelling, 55*(3–4), 451–470.

Moore, J. I. (2001). *Writers on strategy and strategic management: Theory and practice at enterprise, corporate, business and functional levels*. Harmondsworth: Penguin.

Morrison, A., Pietrobelli, C., & Rabellotti, R. (2008). Global value chains and technological capabilities: A framework to study learning and innovation in developing countries. *Oxford Development Studies*, *36*(1), 39–58.

Morrissey, M. T., & Almonacid, S. (2005). Rethinking technology transfer. *Journal of Food Engineering*, *67*(1–2), 135–145.

Mowery, D. C., Oxley, J. E., & Silverman, B. S. (1996). Strategic alliances and interfirm knowledge transfer. *Strategic Management Journal*, *17*(S2), 77–91.

Mytelka, L. K. (2002). Mergers, acquisitions and inter-firm technology agreements in the global learning economy. In D. Archibugi & B.-Å. Lundval (Eds), *The globalising learning economy* (pp. 127–144). Oxford: Oxford University Press.

Mubarik, M. S., Chandran, V. G. R., & Devadason, E. S. (2018). Measuring human capital in small and medium manufacturing enterprises: What matters? *Social Indicators Research*, *137*, 605–623.

Nabi, I., & Hamid, N. (2013). *Garments as a driver of economic growth: Insights from Pakistan case studies*. Lahore: International Growth Center, Pakistan.

Nadvi, K., & Sayyed, A. (2004). *Drivers of change—Pakistan: Industrial capital and pro-poor change*. Institute for Development Studies, Sussex. Mimeo.

Nahapiet, J., & Ghoshal, S. (1998). Social capital, intellectual capital, and the organizational advantage. *Academy of Management Review*, *23*(2), 242–266.

Nahar, N., Lyytinen, K., Huda, N., & Muravyov, S. V. (2006). Success factors for information technology supported international technology transfer: Finding expert consensus. *Information & Management*, *43*(5), 663–677.

Nalcaci, G., & Yagci, M. I. (2014). The effects of marketing capabilities on export performance using resource-based view: assessment on manufacturing companies. *Procedia-Social and Behavioral Sciences*, *148*, 671–679.

Nasiriyar, M., Nesta, L., & Dibiaggio, L. (2010). Technological assets as platforms for business diversification. *DRUD Summer conference* (pp. 16–18), London.

Nazeer, N., & Rasiah, R. (2016). Explaining Pakistan's premature deindustrialization, *Lahore Journal of Economics*, *21*(SE), 351–368.

Nazeer, N. (2018). *Technology transfer and technological capability building* [Doctoral thesis] approved by Universiti Malaya, Kuala Lumpur.

Nelson, R. R. (2008). Economic development from the perspective of evolutionary economic theory. *Oxford Development Studies*, *36*(1), 9–21.

Nelson, R. R. (ed.). (1993). *National innovation systems: A comparative analysis*. Oxford: Oxford University Press.

Nelson, R. R., & Winter, S. G. (1982). *An evolutionary theory of economic change*. Cambridge, MA: Belknap Press.

Newman, C., Rand, J., Talbot, T., & Tarp, F. (2015). Technology transfers, foreign investment and productivity spillovers. *European Economic Review*, *76*, 168–187.

Ngai, E. W., & Chan, E. W. C. (2005). Evaluation of knowledge management tools using AHP. *Expert Systems with Applications*, *29*(4), 889–899.

Nonaka, I., & Von Krogh, G. (2009). Perspective—tacit knowledge and knowledge conversion: Controversy and advancement in organizational knowledge creation theory. *Organization Science*, *20*(3), 635–652.

Nordas, H. (2004). *The global textile and clothing industry post the agreement on textiles and clothing*. WTO Discussion Paper No. 5.

North, D. (1993). Economic performance through time: The limits to knowledge. *American Economic Review*, *84*(3), 359–368.

Nunnally, J. C., & Bernstein, I. H. (1994). *Psychometric theory (McGraw-Hill Series in Psychology)* (Vol. 3). New York: McGraw-Hill.

O'Cass, A., & Grace, D. (2003). An exploratory perspective of service brand associations. *Journal of Services Marketing, 17*(5), 452–475.

Ocasio, W., & Joseph, J. (2008). Rise and fall—or transformation?: The evolution of strategic planning at the General Electric Company, 1940–2006. *Long Range Planning, 41*(3), 248–272.

O'Cass, A., & Grace, D. (2008). Understanding the role of retail store service in light of self-image—store image congruence. *Psychology & Marketing, 25*(6), 521–537.

Odom, R. Y., & Boxx, W. R. (1988). Environment, planning processes, and organizational performance of churches. *Strategic Management Journal, 9*(2), 197–205.

Otto Scharmer, C. (2001). Self-transcending knowledge: Sensing and organizing around emerging opportunities. *Journal of Knowledge Management, 5*(2), 137–151.

Page, J., & Tarp, F. (Eds) (2017). *The practice of industrial policy: Government–business coordination in Africa and East Asia.* Oxford: Oxford University Press.

Pakistan (2007). *Year book 2007–2008.* Ministry of Textile Industry Islamabad, Islamabad: Government of Pakistan.

Pakistan (2002). *Year book 2002–2007.* Ministry of Textile Industry Islamabad, Islamabad: Government of Pakistan.

Pakistan (2014). *Textile policy 2014–2019.* Islamabad: Ministry of Textile Industry.

Pakistan (2015). *An overview of FPCCI.* Federation of Pakistan Chambers of Commerce and Industry, downloaded on 15 January 2020 from www.fpcci.com.pk/.

Pakistan (2021). *Yearbook 2020–21*, Ministry of Commerce, Islamabad: Government of Pakistan.

Pavitt, K. (1984). Sectoral patterns of technical change: Towards a taxonomy and a theory. *Research Policy, 13*(6), 343–373.

Penrose, E. T. (1959). *The theory of the growth of the firm.* New York: Sharpe.

Peppard, J., Lambert, R., & Edwards, C. (2000). Whose job is it anyway? Organizational information competencies for value creation. *Information Systems Journal, 10*(4), 291–322.

Phene, A., Fladmoe-Lindquist, K., & Marsh, L. (2006). Breakthrough innovations in the US biotechnology industry: The effects of technological space and geographic origin. *Strategic Management Journal, 27*(4), 369–388.

Pietrobelli, C., & Rabellotti, R. (2006). *Upgrading to compete.* Global Value Chains, Clusters, and SMEs in Latin America. Washington, DC: Inter-American Development Bank.

Poister, T. H. (2010). The future of strategic planning in the public sector: Linking strategic management and performance. *Public Administration Review, 70*(1), 246–254.

Polanyi, M. (1966). The logic of tacit inference. *Philosophy, 41*(155), 1–18.

Polanyi, M. (1967). The growth of science in society. *Minerva, 5*(4), 533–545.

Polidano, C. (2001). Don't discard state autonomy: Revisiting the East Asian experience of development. *Political Studies, 49*(3), 513–527.

Porter, M. E. (1980). *Competitive Strategy: Techniques for Analyzing Industries and Competitors.* New York: Free Press.

Porter, M. E. (1990). The competitive advantage of nations. *Harvard Business Review,* 73, 91.

Powell, W. W. (1998). Learning from collaboration: Knowledge and networks in the biotechnology and pharmaceutical industries. *California Management Review, 40*(3), 228–240.

Prahalad, C. K., & Hamel, G. (1990). The core competencies of the corporation. *Harvard Business Review, 68*(3), 79–91.

Prahalad, C. K. (2012). Bottom of the pyramid as a source of breakthrough innovations. *Journal of Product Innovation Management, 29*(1), 6–12.

Pryor, M. G., Anderson, D., Toombs, L. A., & Humphreys, J. H. (2007). Strategic implementation as a core competency: The 5P's model. *Journal of Management Research, 7*(1), 3.

Radosevich, R., & Smith, G. S. (1997). A model for entrepreneurship infrastructure development in the creation of technopolis. In J. B. Sedaitis (Ed.), *Commercializing high technology: East and west* (pp. 95–118). London: Rowman & Littlefield.

Rana, P. I. (2017, 1 April). *Karachi port users lament congestion surcharge.* Dawn. https://www.dawn.com/news/1324085

Ranft, A. L., & Lord, M. D. (2002). Acquiring new technologies and capabilities: A grounded model of acquisition implementation. *Organization Science, 13*(4), 420–441.

Rasiah, R. (1988). The semiconductor industry in Penang: Implications for the new international division of labour theories. *Journal of Contemporary Asia, 18*(1), 24–46.

Rasiah, R. (1994). Flexible production systems and local machine tool subcontracting: Electronics component transnationals in Malaysia. *Cambridge Journal of Economics, 18*(3), 279–298.

Rasiah, R. (1995). *Foreign capital and industrialization in Malaysia.* New York: Springer.

Rasiah, R. (2003). Foreign ownership, technology and elecronics exports from Malaysia and Thailand. *Journal of Asian Economics, 14*(5), 785–811.

Rasiah, R. (2004a). Foreign firms, exports and technological capabilities: A Study of Electronics Firms in Indonesia, Malaysia, Philippines and Thailand. *European Journal of Development Research, 16*(3), 141–177.

Rasiah, R. (2004b). Technological intensities in East and Southeast Asian electronics firms: Does network strength matter? *Oxford Development Studies, 32*(3), 433–455. https://doi.org/10.1080/1360081042000260610

Rasiah, R. (2007). Export-orientation and technological intensities in auto parts firms in East and Southeast Asia: Does ownership matter? *Asian Economic Papers, 6*(2), 55–76.

Rasiah, R. (2008). Ownerships, institutions and technological intensities: Automotive and electronics firms in East and SoutheastAsia. In J. Eatwell, & P. Arestis (Eds), *Issues in Finance and Industry* (pp. 137–166). London: Macmillan.

Rasiah, R. (2009). Garment manufacturing in Cambodia and Laos. *Journal of the Asia Pacific Economy, 14*(2), 150–161.

Rasiah, R. (2010). Are electronics firms in Malaysia catching up in the technology ladder? *Journal of the Asia Pacific Economy, 15*(3), 301–319.

Rasiah, R. (2011). The role of institutions and linkages in learning and innovation. *Institutions and Economies, 3*(2), 165–172.

Rasiah, R. (2012). Beyond the multi-fibre agreement: how are workers in east Asia Faring? *Institutions and Economies, 4*(3), 1–20.

Rasiah, R. (2017). The role of institutions and linkages in learning and innovation. *Institutions and Economies, 3*(2), 165–172.

Rasiah, R. (2019). Building networks to harness innovation synergies: Towards an open systems approach to sustainable development. *Journal of Open Innovation: Technology, Market, and Complexity, 5*(3), 70.

Rasiah, R. (2020). Industrial policy and industrialization in South East Asia. In O. Arkebe, C. Cramer, H. J. Chang, & R. Kozul-Wright (Eds), *The Oxford handbook of industrial policy* (pp. 681–715). Oxford: Oxford University Press.

Rasiah, R. (2022). Manufacturing transformation. In R. Rasiah, K. Salih, & C. K. Cheong (Eds), *Malaysia's leap into the future: The building blocks towards balanced development* (pp. 141–164). Singapore: Springer.

Rasiah, R., & Amin, A. S. (2010). Ownership and technological capabilities in Indonesia's automotive parts firms. *Journal of the Asia-Pacific Economy, 15*(3), 288–300.

Rasiah, R., & Gachino, G. (2005). Are foreign firms more productive and export- and technology-intensive than local firms in Kenyan manufacturing? *Oxford Development Studies, 33*(2), 211–227.

Rasiah, R., & Lin, Y. (2005). Learning and innovation: The role of market, government and trust in the information hardware industry in Taiwan. *International Journal of Technology and Globalisation, 1*(3–4), 400–432.

Rasiah, R., & Mint, M. M. (2013). Ownership, technological capabilities and exports of garment firms in Myanmar. *Technological and Economic Development of Economy, 19*(1), S22–S42. https://doi.org/10.3846/20294913.2013.869513.

Rasiah, R., & Nazeer, N. (2015). The state of manufacturing in Pakistan. *Lahore Journal of Economics, 20*(SE), 205–224.

Rasiah, R., & Nazeer, N. (2016). Comparing industrialization in Pakistan and the East Asian economies. *Lahore Journal of Economics, 21*(SI), 167–192.

Rasiah, R., & Wong, S. H. (2021). Industrial upgrading in the semiconductor industry in East Asia.*Innovation and Development, 11*(2–3), 413–440.

Rasiah, R., & Yap, X. S. (2019). How much of Raymond Vernon's product cycle thesis is still relevant today: Evidence from the integrated circuits industry. *International Journal of Technological Learning, Innovation and Development, 11*(1), 56–77.

Rasiah, R., & Zhang, M. (2024). Economics of catching up and leapfrogging: How have Malaysia and Thailand fared against South Korea and Taiwan in the electronics industry. *Journal of the Asia Pacific Economy*, 1–24. https://doi.org/10.1080/13547860.2024.2398828.

Rasiah, R., Singh, A., & Ernst, D. (2015a). Alice Hoffenberg Amsden: A consummate dirigiste on latecomer economic catch-up. *Institutions and Economies, 7*(1), 1–8.

Rasiah, R., Yap, X. S., & Yap, S. F. (2015b). Sticky spots on slippery slopes: The development of the integrated circuits industry in emerging East Asia. *Institutions and Economies, 7*(1), 52–79.

Rasiah, R., Zhang, M., & Kong, X. X. (2013). Can China's miraculous growth continue? *Journal of Contemporary Asia, 43*(2), 295–313.

Raj-Reichert, G (2015). Exercising power over labour governance in the electronics industry. *Geoforum, 67*, 89–92.

Ray, G., Barney, J. B., & Muhanna, W. A. (2004). Capabilities, business processes, and competitive advantage: Choosing the dependent variable in empirical tests of the resource-based view. *Strategic Management Journal, 25*(1), 23–37.

Reddy, N. M., & Zhao, L. (1990). International technology transfer: A review. *Research policy, 19*(4), 285–307.

Reed, R., & DeFillippi, R. J. (1990). Causal ambiguity, barriers to imitation, and sustainable competitive advantage. *Academy of Management Review, 15*(1), 88–102.

Reinert, E. S. (2007). *How rich countries got rich and why poor countries stay poor*. London: Anthem Press.

Reisman, A. (2005). Transfer of technologies: A cross-disciplinary taxonomy. *Omega, 33*(3), 189–202.

Reuters (2023). The 10 biggest U.S. retail bankruptcies in 5 years, January 9, downloaded on 18 June 2025 from https://www.reuters.com/business/retail-consumer/10-biggest-us-retail-bankruptcies-5-years-2023-01-09/

Riege, A. (2005). Three-dozen knowledge-sharing barriers managers must consider. *Journal of Knowledge Management, 9*(3), 18–35.

Ripolles, M., Blesa, A., & Monferrer, D. (2011). Role of international precocity in born global firms. *International Journal of Technology Transfer and Commercialisation, 10*(3–4), 247–267.

Robinson, R. B., & Pearce, J. A. (1988). Planned patterns of strategic behavior and their relationship to business-unit performance. *Strategic Management Journal*, *9*(1), 43–60.

Robock, S. H., & Calkins, R. D. (1980). *The international technology transfer process*. National Academies.

Rodríguez, J. L., & Rodríguez, R. M. G. (2005). Technology and export behaviour: A resource-based view approach. *International Business Review*, *14*(5), 539–557.

Romer, P. M. (1986). Increasing returns and long-run growth. *Journal of Political Economy*, *94*(5), 1002–1037.

Romer, P. M. (1994). The origins of endogenous growth. *Journal of Economic Perspectives*, *8*(1), 3–22.

Roper-Lowe, G. C., & Sharp, J. A. (1990). The analytic hierarchy process and its application to an information technology decision. *Journal of the Operational Research Society*, *41*(1), 49–59.

Rosenberg, N. (1976). *Perspectives on technology*, Cambridge: Cambridge University Press.

Rosenberg, N. (1982). *Inside the black box: Technology and economics*. Cambridge University Press.

Rossiter, J. R. (2002). The C-OAR-SE procedure for scale development in marketing. *International Journal of Research in Marketing*, *19*(4), 305–335.

Rothaermel, F. T., & Deeds, D. L. (2004). Exploration and exploitation alliances in biotechnology: A system of new product development. *Strategic Management Journal*, *25*(3), 201–221.

Rust, R. T., Lemon, K. N., & Zeithaml, V. A. (2004). Return on marketing: Using customer equity to focus marketing strategy. *Journal of Marketing*, *68*(1), 109–127.

Saaty, T. L. (1990). How to make a decision: The analytic hierarchy process. *European Journal of Operational Research*, *48*(1), 9–26.

Saaty, T. L. (1994). How to make a decision: The analytic hierarchy process. *Interfaces*, *24*(6), 19–43.

Saaty, T. L. (2001). Fundamentals of the Analytic Hierarchy Process. In D. L. Schmoldt, J. Kangas, G. A. Mendoza, & M. Pesonen (Eds), *The Analytic Hierarchy Process in Natural Resource and Environmental Decision Making. Managing Forest Ecosystems*, (Vol 3., pp. 15–35), Dordrecht: Springer.

Saaty, T. L., & Vargas, L. G. (2001). *Models, methods, concepts & applications of the analytic hierarchy process*. New York (NY): Springer.

Sammarra, A., & Biggiero, L. (2008). Heterogeneity and specificity of inter-firm knowledge flows in innovation networks. *Journal of Management Studies*, *45*(4), 800–829.

Saxenian, A. L. (1994). *The regional advantage: Culture and competition in Silicon Valley and route 128*. Cambridge, MA: Harvard University Press.

Saxenian, A. (2006). *The new Argonauts: Regional advantage in global perspective*. Cambridge: Harvard University Press.

Scarbrough, H. (1998). Path (ological) dependency? Core competencies from an organizational perspective. *British Journal of Management*, *9*(3), 219–232.

Scherer, F. M. (1980). *Industrial market structure and economic performance*. Boston: Houghton Mifflin.

Schot, J., & Steinmueller, W. E. (2018). Three frames for innovation policy: R&D, systems of innovation and transformative change, *Research Policy*, *47*(9), 1554–1567.

Schumacher, E. F. (1973). *Small is beautiful: A study of ecomonics as if people mattered*. Vintage.

Schumpeter, J. A. (1912). *Theory of economic development*. London: Routledge.

Schumpeter, J. A. (1934). *The theory of economic development: An inquiry into profits, capital, credit, interest, and the business cycle*. Cambridge, MA: Harvard University Press.

Schumpeter, J. A. (1939). *Business cycles*. New York: McGraw-Hill.

Schumpeter, J. A. (1942). *Capitalism, socialism and democracy*. New York: Harvard University Press.

Sen, A. (1983). Carrots, sticks and economics: Perception problems in incentives. *Indian Economic Review, 18*(1), 1–16.

Seth, A. (1990). Value creation in acquisitions: A re-examination of performance issues. *Strategic Management Journal, 11*(2), 99–115.

Shafiq, M. (2012). Implementation of quality management systems and business excellence frameworks in Pakistani textile companies. *Journal of Quality and Technology Management, 7*(2), 11–23.

Shujaat, M., Devadason, E. S., & Chandran, V. G. R. (2016). Theoretical framework to analyze human capital–Performance relationship. *International Journal of Economic Perspectives, 10*(4), 157–165.

Siegmann, K. A. (2005). The agreement on textiles and clothing: Potential effects on gendered employment in Pakistan. *International Labour Review, 144*(4), 401–421.

Simon, H. A. (1977). *The logic of heuristic decision making and other topics in the methods of science*. Boston: Reidel.

Simon, H. A. (1991). Bounded rationality and organizational learning. *Organization Science, 2*(1), 125–134.

Simon, H. A. (1997). *Models of bounded rationality: Empirically grounded economic reason* (Vol. 3). Cambridge, MA: MIT Press.

Simonin, B. L. (2004). An empirical investigation of the process of knowledge transfer in international strategic alliances. *Journal of International Business Studies, 35*(5), 407–427.

Singh, K., Ang, S. H., & Leong, S. M. (2003). Increasing replication for knowledge accumulation in strategy research. *Journal of Management, 29*(4), 533–549.

SMEDA (2015). *Enterprises development*. Small and Medium Enterprises Development Authority (SMEDA), available at: www.smeda.org/.

SMEDA (2016). *Enterprises development*. Small and Medium Enterprises Development Authority (SMEDA), available at: www.smeda.org/.

Smith, A. (1776). *An inquiry into the nature and causes of the wealth of nations*. London: W. Strahan & T. Cadell.

Solow, R. M. (1957). Technical change and the aggregate production function. *Review of Economics and Statistics, 39*(3), 312–320.

Song, M., Di Benedetto, C. A., & Nason, R. W. (2007). Capabilities and financial performance: The moderating effect of strategic type. *Journal of the Academy of Marketing Science, 35*(1), 18–34.

Song, M., Droge, C., Hanvanich, S., & Calantone, R. (2005). Marketing and technology resource complementarity: An analysis of their interaction effect in two environmental contexts. *Strategic Management Journal, 26*(3), 259–276.

Song, M., Nason, R. W., & Di Benedetto, C. A. (2008). Distinctive marketing and information technology capabilities and strategic types: A cross-national investigation. *Journal of International Marketing, 16*(1), 4–38.

Spanos, Y. E., & Lioukas, S. (2001). An examination into the causal logic of rent generation: Contrasting Porter's competitive strategy framework and the resource-based perspective. *Strategic Management Journal, 22*(10), 907–934.

Spanos, Y. E., & Prastacos, G. (2004). Understanding organizational capabilities: Towards a conceptual framework. *Journal of Knowledge Management, 8*(3), 31–43.

Spender, J. C. (1996). Making knowledge the basis of a dynamic theory of the firm. *Strategic Management Journal, 17*(S2), 45–62.

Spinanger, D. (1995). Prosperity for all? Reflecting on the MFA complex after Marrakech. *The World Economy, 18*(5), 665–680.

Stiglitz, J. E. (2002). Information and the change in the Paradigm in economics. *American Economic Review, 92*(3), 460–501.
Stock, G. N., & Tatikonda, M. V. (2000). A typology of project-level technology transfer processes. *Journal of Operations Management, 18*(6), 719–737.
Stock, G. N., Greis, N. P., & Fischer, W. A. (2001). Absorptive capacity and new product development. *The Journal of High Technology Management Research, 12*(1), 77–91.
Sturgeon, T. (2002). Modular production networks: A new American model of industrial organization. *Industrial and Corporate Change, 11*(3), 451–496.
Sung, T. K., & Gibson, D. V. (2005). Critical success factors in electronic commerce: Korean experiences. *Journal of Organizational Computing and Electronic Commerce, 15*(1), 19–34.
Sydow, J., Schreyögg, G., & Koch, J. (2009). Organizational path dependence: Opening the black box. *Academy of Management Review, 34*(4), 689–709.
Szulanski, G. (1996). Exploring internal stickiness: Impediments to the transfer of best practice within the firm. *Strategic Management Journal, 17*(S2), 27–43.
Szulanski, G., Cappetta, R., & Jensen, R. J. (2004). When and how trustworthiness matters: Knowledge transfer and the moderating effect of causal ambiguity. *Organization Science, 15*(5), 600–613.
Tabachnick, B. G., & Fidell, L. S. (1996). *Using multivariate statistics.* Northridge (CA): HarperCollins.
Tallman, S., Jenkins, M., Henry, N., & Pinch, S. (2004). Knowledge, clusters, and competitive advantage. *Academy of Management Review, 29*(2), 258–271.
Tanriverdi, H., & Iacono, C. S. (1999). Diffusion of telemedicine: A knowledge barrier perspective. *Telemedicine Journal, 5*(3), 223–244.
Teece, D. J. (2007). Explicating dynamic capabilities: the nature and microfoundations of (sustainable) enterprise performance. *Strategic Management Journal, 28*(13), 1319–1350.
Teece, D. J. (2009). *Dynamic capabilities and strategic management: Organizing for innovation and growth.* Oxford: Oxford University Press.
Teece, D., Pisano, G., & Shuen, A. (1997). Dynamic capabilities and strategic management, *Strategic Management Journal, 18*(7), 509–533.
Tenenhaus, M., Vinzi, V. E., Chatelin, Y. M., & Lauro, C. (2005). PLS path modeling. *Computational Statistics & Data Analysis, 48*(1), 159–205.
Tether, B. S. (2002). Who co-operates for innovation, and why: An empirical analysis. *Research Policy, 31*(6), 947–967.
Textile Policy, Ministry of Textile Industry, Government of Pakistan 2014–2019. Available at: https://www.rdacell.com/Documents/Textile%20Policy%202014-19.pdf.
Thornhill, A., & Saunders, M. N. (1998). What if line managers don't realize they're responsible for HR?. *Personnel Review, 27*(6), 460–476.
Tikoria, J., Banwet, D. K., & Deshmukh, S. G. (2010). Ranking national R&D organisations: A data envelopment analysis. *International Journal of Society Systems Science, 2*(2), 176–193.
Todorova, G., & Durisin, B. (2007). Absorptive capacity: Valuing a reconceptualization. *Academy of Management Review, 32*(3), 774–786.
Tomer, J. F. (1987). *Organizational capital: The path to higher productivity and well-being.* Westport, CT: Praeger Publishers.
Toor, S. U. R., & Ogunlana, S. O. (2008). Problems causing delays in major construction projects in Thailand. *Construction Management and Economics, 26*(4), 395–408.
Torres, A., & Jasso, J. (2017). Entrepreneurial capabilities and innovation in firms from late industrialising countries: A case study of a Mexican firm. *International Journal of Work Innovation, 2*(1), 101–120.
Tsai, T., & Cheng, B. (2006). *The silicon dragon: High-tech industry in Taiwan.* Cheltenham: Edward Elgar Publishing.

Tsai, H. T., & Eisingerich, A. B. (2010). Internationalization strategies of emerging markets firms. *California Management Review, 53*(1), 114–135.
Tsai, W. (2000). Social capital, strategic relatedness and the formation of intraorganizational linkages. *Strategic Management Journal, 21*(9), 925–939.
Tsai, W. (2001). Knowledge transfer in intraorganizational networks: Effects of network position and absorptive capacity on business unit innovation and performance. *Academy of Management Journal, 44*(5), 996–1004.
Tsang, E. W., Nguyen, D. T., & Erramilli, M. K. (2004). Knowledge acquisition and performance of international joint ventures in the transition economy of Vietnam. *Journal of International Marketing, 12*(2), 82–103.
Turovets, J. (2021). Intangible assets and the efficiency of manufacturing firms. *Engineering Management in Production and Services, 13*(1), 7–26.
Tushman, M. L., & Anderson, P. (1986). Technological discontinuities and organizational environments. *Administrative Science Quarterly, 31*, 439–465.
UNCTAD (2002). *World investment report.* Geneva: United Nations Conference for Trade and Development (UNCTAD).
UNCTAD (2014). *Transfer of technology and knowledge sharing for development countries.* Technology and innovation report N8 2014: Geneva: United Nations Conference for Trade and Development.
UNIDO (2004). *Inserting local industries into global value chains and global production networks: Opportunities and challenges for upgrading.* UNIDO Working paper, United Nations Industrial Development Organisation, Vienna.
UNIDO (2002). *Industrial Development Report 2002–2003: Competing through innovation and learning,* Geneva: United Nations Industrial Development Report.
UNIDO (2013). *Sustaining employment growth: The role of manufacturing and structural change.* Industrial Development Report: United Nations Industrial Development Organization (UNIDO ID/446).
UNComtrade (2021) *Pakistan, imports and exports, 2009–2020,* accessed from ttps://comtrade.un.org/ on 16 April 2021.
US International Trade Commission (2004). *Textiles and apparel: Assessment of the competitiveness of certain foreign suppliers to the US market. Volume I, Investigation* (pp. 332–448).
Ustundag, A., Uğurlu, S., & Serdar Kilinc, M. (2011). Evaluating the performance of technology transfer offices. *Journal of Enterprise Information Management, 24*(4), 322–337.
Utterback, J. M., & Kim, L. (1985). Invasion of a stable business by radical innovation. In P. R. Kleindorfer (Eds), *The management of productivity and technology in manufacturing* (pp. 113–151). Springer, Boston, MA.
Van de Ven, A. H., & Johnson, P. E. (2006). Knowledge for theory and practice. *Academy of Management Review, 31*(4), 802–821.
Vanhaverbeke, W., & Peeters, N. (2005). Embracing innovation as strategy: Corporate venturing, competence building and corporate strategy making. *Creativity and Innovation Management, 14*(3), 246–257.
Veblen, T. (1915), *Imperial Germany and industrial revolution.* London: Macmillan.
Venkatesh, V., Speier, C., & Morris, M. G. (2002). User acceptance enablers in individual decision making about technology: Toward an integrated model. *Decision Sciences, 33*(2), 297–316.
Vernon, R. (1966). International investment and international trade in the product cycle. *Quarterly Journal of Economics, 80*(2), 190–207.
Vorhies, D. W., & Morgan, N. A. (2005). Benchmarking marketing capabilities for sustainable competitive advantage. *Journal of Marketing, 69*(1), 80–94.

Wade, R. (1990). *Governing the market: Economic theory and the role of government in East Asian industrialization.* Princeton: Princeton University Press.

Wadho, W., & Chaudhry, A. (2016). Innovation in the textiles sector: A firm-level analysis of technological and non-technological innovation. *Lahore Journal of Economics, 21*, 129.

Wajid, J., & Memon, A. (2002). *Adding value: Building value—addition alliances, backward linkages in the textile and clothing sector of Pakistan.* In Executive Forum on National Export Strategies.

Weerawardena, J., & O'Cass, A. (2009). Examining the role of international entrepreneurship, innovation and international market performance in SME internationalization. *European Journal of Marketing, 43*(11/12), 1325–1348.

Wei, L. (1995). International technology transfer and development of technological capabilities: A theoretical framework. *Technology in Society, 17*(1), 103–120.

Weick, K. E. (1979). Cognitive processes in organizations. *Research in Organizational Behavior, 1*(1), 41–74.

Westphal, L. E., Kim, L. S., & Dahlman, C. (1999). Reflections on the Republic of Korea's acquisition of technological capability. In L. S. Kim (Ed), *Learning and innovation in economic development* (pp. 38–92). Cambridge: Cambridge University Press.

Williamson, O. (1988). *The Economic institutions of capitalism: Firms, markets,relations, contracting.* New York: The Free Press.

Wilson, B. (2010). *Using PLS to investigate interaction effects between higher order branding constructs.* In V. Esposito Vinzi, W. Chin, J. Henseler, & H. Wang, (Eds) *Handbook of partial least squares* (pp. 621–652). Springer, Berlin, Heidelberg.

WIPO, P. (2014). US2004/025763. *International Search Report, Aug., 5*, 3. pp. 6–8.

WITS (2024). *World Integrated Trade System*, downloaded on 12 March 2024 from https://wits.worldbank.org/CountryProfile/en/Country/PAK/Year/2021/TradeFlow/Export/Partner/all/Product/50-63_TextCloth#.

Wold, H. (1985). Systems analysis by partial least squares. In P. Nijkamp, H. Leitner, & N. Wrigley (Eds), Measuring the unmeasurable (pp. 221–252). Dordrecht: MartinusNijhoff.

World Bank (2023). *World Development Indicators*, Washington, DC: World Bank Institute.

WFX (2023). *Rising star: Overview of Vietnam's growing textile and garment industry*, 13 October, World Fashion Exchange (WFX), downloaded on 14 February from https://www.worldfashionexchange.com/blog/vietnam-growing-textile-and-garment-industry/.

Yli-Renko, H., Autio, E., & Sapienza, H. J. (2001). Social capital, knowledge acquisition, and knowledge exploitation in young technology-based firms. *Strategic Management Journal, 22*(6-7), 587–613.

Young, A. (1928). Increasing returns and economic progress, *Economic Journal*, 38(152), 527–542.

Young, A. (1994). Lessons from the East Asian NICs: A contrarian view. *European Economic Review, 38*(3–4), 964–973.

Yusof, S., & Evenett, S. J. (2002) *Can East Asia compete? Innovation for global markets.* Washington DC: World Bank & Oxford University Press.

Zahra, S. A. (2005). A theory of international new ventures: A decade of research. *Journal of International Business Studies, 36*(1), 20–28.

Zahra, S. A., & George, G. (2002). Absorptive capacity: A review, reconceptualization, and extension. *Academy of Management Review, 27*(2), 185–203.

Zhang, M., & Rasiah, R. (2015) *Institutionalization of state policy: Evolving urban housing reforms in China.* Singapore: Springer.

Zhou, K. Z., & Wu, F. (2010). Technological capability, strategic flexibility, and product innovation. *Strategic Management Journal, 31*(5), 547–561.

Zikmund, W. G. (2003). Sample designs and sampling procedures. *Business Research Methods, 7*(2), 368–400.

Appendices

Appendix A Cross Loadings

	Organizational capability	AC	AS	COMP	EXP	HR	INNO	KI	PR	PROC	PRYD	RD
KM	**0.781**	0.254	0.151	0.375	0.232	0.29	0.384	0.086	0.202	0.092	0.369	0.14
Strt.P	**0.759**	0.243	0.165	0.446	0.211	0.27	0.352	0.095	0.151	0.098	0.363	0.208
LBD	**0.797**	0.237	0.196	0.368	0.254	0.262	0.386	0.097	0.213	0.147	0.366	0.262
MK.C	**0.785**	0.246	0.27	0.412	0.32	0.267	0.37	0.071	0.192	0.077	0.307	0.247
AC1	0.154	**0.746**	0.294	0.198	0.12	0.065	0.134	0.147	0.06	0.125	0.048	0.051
AC2	0.244	**0.764**	0.172	0.263	0.125	0.178	0.139	0.198	0.047	0.057	0.083	0.007
AC3	0.328	**0.891**	0.242	0.355	0.184	0.207	0.222	0.196	0.093	0.078	0.124	0.095
AC4	0.211	**0.769**	0.225	0.235	0.011	0.165	0.119	0.189	0.02	0.042	0.032	0.04
AS1	0.215	0.247	**0.831**	0.171	0.11	0.108	0.172	0.209	0.005	0.07	0.054	0.073
AS2	0.165	0.17	**0.83**	0.1	0.128	0.063	0.105	0.091	0.054	0.094	0.092	0.136
AS3	0.198	0.286	**0.855**	0.183	0.06	0.035	0.134	0.146	0.023	0.064	0.074	0.067
AS4	0.237	0.272	**0.852**	0.161	0.093	0.053	0.126	0.152	0.032	0.066	0.137	0.067

Continued

Appendix A *Continued*

	Organizational capability	AC	AS	COMP	EXP	HR	INNO	KI	PR	PROC	PRYD	RD
COMP1	0.434	0.23	0.127	**0.807**	0.1	0.299	0.292	0.085	0.104	0.108	0.14	0.164
COMP3	0.393	0.234	0.178	**0.804**	0.155	0.236	0.242	0.058	0.14	0.097	0.17	0.117
COMP4	0.458	0.286	0.147	**0.861**	0.202	0.305	0.294	0.072	0.149	0.152	0.161	0.127
COMP7	0.307	0.302	0.121	**0.6**	0.137	0.259	0.251	0.119	0.096	0.093	0.136	0.057
EXP1	0.188	0.087	0.063	0.1	**0.735**	0.004	0.299	0.091	0.208	0.06	0.194	0.169
EXP2	0.306	0.098	0.114	0.183	**0.778**	0.078	0.32	0.052	0.291	0.026	0.286	0.189
EXP3	0.216	0.092	0.095	0.08	**0.772**	0.057	0.367	0.029	0.238	0.044	0.249	0.212
EXP4	0.234	0.084	0.039	0.089	**0.725**	0.076	0.251	0.021	0.206	0.06	0.162	0.194
EXP5	0.285	0.115	0.096	0.174	**0.813**	0.067	0.275	0.065	0.245	0.004	0.187	0.206
EXP6	0.235	0.158	0.094	0.223	**0.64**	0.175	0.318	0.05	0.172	0.077	0.165	0.073
HR2	0.19	0.06	0.023	0.165	0.009	**0.524**	0.04	0.047	0.014	0.042	0.065	0.047
HR3	0.267	0.167	0.077	0.264	0.122	**0.784**	0.243	0.066	0.109	0.077	0.124	0.099
HR4	0.305	0.188	0.064	0.303	0.085	**0.735**	0.215	0.032	0.089	0.045	0.18	0.049
HR5	0.311	0.139	0.071	0.293	0.118	**0.765**	0.206	0.062	0.101	0.009	0.136	0.061
HR6	0.241	0.105	0.027	0.24	0.058	**0.777**	0.194	−0.005	0.044	0.023	0.098	0.027
HR7	0.244	0.181	0.043	0.274	0.043	**0.771**	0.235	0.092	0.116	0.036	0.139	0.075
HR8	0.221	0.146	0.083	0.267	0.066	**0.768**	0.266	0.076	0.042	0.038	0.078	0.057
Inno7	0.392	0.168	0.107	0.262	0.33	0.227	**0.832**	0.019	0.214	0.071	0.281	0.135
Inno8	0.383	0.147	0.108	0.269	0.324	0.209	**0.864**	0.061	0.255	0.105	0.349	0.142
Inno9	0.393	0.139	0.158	0.29	0.383	0.24	**0.823**	−0.044	0.264	0.09	0.26	0.183
Innov10	0.382	0.182	0.131	0.275	0.37	0.234	**0.869**	0.056	0.292	0.105	0.3	0.203
KI1	0.057	0.221	0.133	0.097	0.061	0.041	−0.005	**0.821**	−0.004	0.005	0.042	−0.029
KI3	0.148	0.17	0.16	0.084	0.089	0.061	0.113	**0.837**	0.009	0.025	0.076	0.052
KI4	0.099	0.197	0.166	0.086	0.028	0.082	−0.014	**0.893**	−0.066	−0.009	0.016	−0.001
PR1	0.18	0.077	0.016	0.12	0.191	0.05	0.193	−0.007	**0.788**	0.066	0.226	0.186

PR2	0.199	0.066	−0.011	0.133	0.269	0.108	0.25	−0.003	**0.881**	0.084	0.274	0.181
PR3	0.248	0.085	0.063	0.143	0.303	0.125	0.262	−0.05	**0.893**	0.09	0.307	0.213
PR4	0.248	0.015	0.039	0.145	0.275	0.069	0.3	−0.02	**0.843**	0.052	0.335	0.229
PROC1	0.1	0.075	0.068	0.122	0.082	0.012	0.104	−0.036	0.099	**0.829**	0.096	0.122
PROC2	0.121	0.085	0.101	0.15	0.055	0.067	0.1	0.03	0.081	**0.905**	0.089	0.165
PROC3	0.078	0.075	0.038	0.088	0.003	0.051	0.053	0.025	0.03	**0.754**	−0.003	0.102
PRYD1	0.366	0.084	0.083	0.14	0.245	0.137	0.316	0.023	0.323	0.069	**0.898**	0.202
PRYD2	0.443	0.099	0.118	0.201	0.248	0.148	0.329	0.036	0.264	0.082	**0.881**	0.201
PRYD4	0.368	0.061	0.075	0.172	0.247	0.142	0.283	0.079	0.3	0.052	**0.848**	0.211
RD1	0.179	0.025	0.055	0.083	0.202	0.019	0.13	−0.002	0.196	0.166	0.188	**0.751**
RD3	0.233	0.042	0.09	0.097	0.186	0.037	0.136	−0.039	0.16	0.179	0.14	**0.819**
RD4	0.217	0.097	0.076	0.164	0.156	0.129	0.172	0.051	0.21	0.046	0.18	**0.766**
RD5	0.253	0.038	0.092	0.144	0.203	0.073	0.196	0.019	0.192	0.118	0.234	**0.846**

Appendix B Correlation Matrix for the Constructs (Fornell-Larcker Criterion)

	OC	AS	ABC	COMP	EXP	HR	INNO	KI	PR	PROC	PRYD	RD
OC	**0.795**											
AS	0.293	**0.842**										
ABC	0.3	0.244	**0.785**									
COMP	0.335	0.185	0.519	**0.774**								
EXP	0.142	0.115	0.33	0.193	**0.746**							
HR	0.197	0.077	0.348	0.354	0.102	**0.737**						
INNO	0.196	0.161	0.474	0.349	0.411	0.28	**0.832**					
KI	0.23	0.18	0.12	0.104	0.069	0.072	0.037	**0.851**				
PR	0.071	0.033	0.258	0.159	0.307	0.105	0.296	−0.025	**0.853**			
PROC	0.094	0.086	0.121	0.147	0.059	0.053	0.105	0.008	0.086	**0.831**		
PRYD	0.093	0.106	0.449	0.196	0.282	0.163	0.354	0.052	0.337	0.077	**0.876**	
RD	0.064	0.099	0.278	0.154	0.234	0.082	0.2	0.009	0.238	0.159	0.234	**0.797**

Appendix C Heterotrait-Monotrait Ratio of Correlations (HTMT)

	OC	AS	ABS	COMP	EXP	HR	INNO	KI	PR	PROC	PRYD	RD
OC												
AS	0.349											
ABS	0.359	0.284										
COMP	0.43	0.225	0.641									
EXP	0.176	0.134	0.39	0.237								
HR	0.235	0.093	0.408	0.436	0.126							
INNO	0.229	0.183	0.549	0.425	0.475	0.315						
KI	0.287	0.212	0.144	0.138	0.087	0.092	0.086					
PR	0.09	0.05	0.298	0.193	0.353	0.122	0.334	0.054				
PROC	0.121	0.103	0.148	0.136	0.088	0.066	0.124	0.046	0.11			
PRYD	0.109	0.123	0.529	0.243	0.33	0.187	0.407	0.073	0.39	0.094		
RD	0.082	0.121	0.336	0.19	0.284	0.108	0.235	0.059	0.283	0.204	0.282	

Index

For the benefit of digital users, indexed terms that span two pages (e.g., 52–53) may, on occasion, appear on only one of those pages.

Note: Tables and figures are indicated by an italic *t* and *f* following the page number.